THE TODDLER IN CHIEF

THE

Toddler in Chief

WHAT
DONALD TRUMP
TEACHES US ABOUT
THE MODERN PRESIDENCY

Daniel W. Drezner

THE UNIVERSITY OF CHICAGO PRESS
CHICAGO AND LONDON

The University of Chicago Press, Chicago 60637
The University of Chicago Press, Ltd., London
© 2020 by The University of Chicago
Published 2020
Printed in the United States of America

29 28 27 26 25 24 23 22 21 20   1 2 3 4 5

ISBN-13: 978-0-226-66791-1 (cloth)
ISBN-13: 978-0-226-71425-7 (paper)
ISBN-13: 978-0-226-71439-4 (e-book)
DOI: https://doi.org/10.7208/chicago/9780226714394.001.0001

Library of Congress Cataloging-in-Publication Data
Names: Drezner, Daniel W., author.
Title: The toddler in chief : what Donald Trump teaches us about the modern
    presidency / Daniel W. Drezner.
Description: Chicago : University of Chicago Press, 2020. | Includes
    bibliographical references and index.
Identifiers: LCCN 2019057950 | ISBN 9780226667911 (cloth) |
    ISBN 9780226714257 (paperback) | ISBN 9780226714394 (ebook)
Subjects: LCSH: Trump, Donald, 1946– —Psychology. | Presidents—United
    States—Psychology. | United States—Politics and government—2017–
Classification: LCC E913.3 .D74 2020 | DDC 973.933092—dc23
LC record available at https://lccn.loc.gov/2019057950

♾ This paper meets the requirements of ANSI/NISO Z39.48-1992
(Permanence of Paper).

I'm so young, I can't believe it. I'm the youngest person.

PRESIDENT DONALD J. TRUMP, APRIL 26, 2019

CONTENTS

INTRODUCTION

Once upon a Time, a Toddler Was Elected President . . .

At age two, children view the world almost exclusively through their own needs and desires. Because they can't yet understand how others might feel in the same situation, they assume that everyone thinks and feels exactly as they do. And on those occasions when they realize they're out of line, they may not be able to control themselves.

AMERICAN ACADEMY OF PEDIATRICS,
CARING FOR YOUR BABY AND YOUNG CHILD

In this book I make two arguments, one simple and one not so simple. The simple argument is that Donald Trump behaves more like the Toddler in Chief than the Commander in Chief. Many of Trump's critics have argued this, but that is not the primary source of my evidence supporting this claim. In more than a thousand instances since his inauguration, Trump's own supporters and subordinates have made this comparison as well. The staffers who work for Trump in the White House, the cabinet and subcabinet officers who serve in his administration, the kitchen cabinet of friends and confidants who talk to him on the phone, Republican members of Congress attempting to enact his agenda, and longstanding treaty allies of the United States trying to ingratiate themselves to this President have all characterized Donald Trump as possessing the maturity of a petulant child rather than a man in his seventies.

The less simple argument is that having a President who behaves like a toddler is a more serious problem today than it would have been, say, fifty years ago. Formal and informal checks on the presidency have eroded badly in recent decades, and Trump assumed the office at the zenith of its power. For a half-century, Trump's predecessors have expanded the powers of the presidency at the expense of countervailing institutions, including Congress and the Supreme Court. Presidents as ideologically diverse as Ronald Reagan, Bill Clinton, George W. Bush, and Barack Obama all took steps to enhance executive power. To be sure, Trump has attempted massive executive-branch power grabs as well. This is problematic, but the underlying trends—all of which predate Trump's inauguration—make the existence of a Toddler in Chief far more worrisome now than even during the heightened tensions of the Cold War.

Consider navigating the ship of state as analogous to driving a car on a twisty mountain road. The risk of driving off the side of a mountain is real. Two things can prevent a catastrophe: the driver's good sense and guardrails separating the road from the precipice. The guardrails were badly damaged before 2016, but a skilled driver could still navigate the road. In that year, however, the country elected the most immature candidate in American history to drive the car. The result has been a reckless President operating the executive branch like a bumper car, without any sense of peril. The car has not careened completely off the road yet, but that is due more to luck than skill. The possibility for a fatal crash remains ever-present. Even more disturbing, the driver is not getting any better at his job. He is just getting more confident that there is no risk to what he is doing.

Far too much of Donald Trump's behavior is comparable to that of a bratty toddler. Let me be as precise as possible about what this means. I am not saying that Trump *is* a toddler. Multiple physicians—some of admittedly dubious provenance—have confirmed that Donald Trump is a borderline-obese white male over the age of 70. Furthermore, even casual observation reveals that this is not a Benjamin Button situation in which Trump is aging into a small child. Biologically, the 45th President of the United States is a fully grown man—just like the 43 men who preceded him.[1] I am arguing that unlike his predecessors, Trump's psychological makeup approximates that of a toddler. He is not a small child, but he sure as heck acts like one.

Furthermore, I am not indicting the behavior of toddlers by comparing Trump to them. The 45th President shares a lot of behavioral traits with small children. The difference, however, is that toddlers have a valid justification for their behavior. Many of the unsavory traits associated with toddlers reflect their effort to make sense of the world given their limited capabilities. At the toddler stage of cognitive and emotional development, children throw tantrums and act impulsively because they have no other means to cope with their environment. Over time, of course, toddlers grow out of these behaviors. Donald Trump shows no such signs of maturation. He offers the greatest example of pervasive developmental delay in American political history.

These are strong statements to make, and readers should approach such provocative claims with skepticism. This is particularly true for those Americans who voted for and continue to support the 45th President. Donald Trump is a polarizing figure in polarized times. The incentive to ridicule the

President is strong among those who resist Trump's agenda. Since Trump's election, Democrats have frequently characterized the President as possessing the maturity of a boy who has yet to master his toilet training. Numerous party leaders have deployed this analogy. In December 2018, Senate Minority Leader Chuck Schumer accused Trump of throwing a "temper tantrum" when a bipartisan appropriations bill contained no funding for a wall along the US-Mexico border. In January 2019, former Deputy Attorney General Sally Yates tweeted that Trump was behaving "like a spoiled two year old holding his breath." Speaker of the House Nancy Pelosi blasted Trump for his obduracy during the 2018/19 government shutdown, telling reporters, "I'm the mother of five, grandmother of nine. I know a temper tantrum when I see one."[2] A few months later, Pelosi told the *New York Times* that Trump has a short attention span as well as a "lack of knowledge of the subjects at hand."[3] 2020 Democratic candidates for President have also compared Trump to a preschooler.[4]

Nor is it difficult to find examples of commentators characterizing Trump as a toddler. Indeed, these analogies predated his inauguration day. In June 2016, *Politico*'s Jack Shafer wrote, "This is the first time we've seen a candidate assume the psychological and reactive profile of a small child. Trump seethed like an irritable 2-year-old instead of exhibiting the kind of restraint and comity we usually associate with a finalist in the presidential sweepstakes."[5] One textual analysis from the 2016 campaign concluded that Trump's speeches had the emotional maturity of a toddler.[6] A few weeks after his election victory, *The Daily Show*'s Trevor Noah made the comparison more explicit: "We've come to realize that there's a good chance that President-elect Trump might have the mind of a toddler, and if you think about it, it makes sense. He loves the same things that toddlers do. They like building things. They love attention . . . always grabbing things they're not supposed to."[7]

Trump's inauguration did not slow the use of the toddler analogy—if anything, its frequency increased. On television, commentators ranging from Don Lemon to P. J. O'Rourke have characterized the President as a two-year-old brat. Protestors and editorial cartoonists depict Trump as a giant man-baby. Within the first few months of his presidency, even conservative columnists such as David Brooks and Ross Douthat were explicitly comparing Trump to a child.[8] In the fall of 2017, the *Atlantic*'s David Graham wrote, "How does the presidency work when the President's aides treat him like a child? The immediate answer is, not very well."[9]

By 2019 the analogy's use had proliferated even further. The *Washington Post*'s Dana Milbank penned a column predicated on the idea of Trump's immaturity as President: "Though we often hear the mantra 'this is not normal,' what the President is doing actually is normal. For a 2-year-old. If you want to understand this White House, turn off Wolf Blitzer and pick up Benjamin Spock."[10] The *Atlantic*'s Adam Serwer leaned on the analogy during the January 2019 government shutdown, going so far as to describe the new Democrat-controlled House of Representatives as a parent trying to introduce discipline into a young boy's upbringing: "The inauguration of a new Congress means that for Trump, the days of easily getting his way are over. And like a child facing his first taste of discipline, he is chafing at the restrictions. But that's what makes maintaining them so important. . . . As any parent knows, rewarding misbehavior only invites more of it."[11]

Clearly, there is no shortage of claims by Democrats and pundits that the President of the United States acts like a toddler. For defenders of the President, these examples merely confirm their suspicion that the charge is politically motivated. Donald Trump has repeatedly labeled the mainstream media to be "fake news" and therefore "the enemy of the American people." His defenders would argue, correctly, that previous Presidents have also been caricatured by their political opponents. Consider the opposition narratives of Trump's most recent predecessors. Republicans depicted Barack Obama as an aloof, out-of-touch intellectual. Democrats characterized George W. Bush as an incurious simpleton, the puppet of craftier politicians. Both depictions possessed some small grains of truth but were exaggerated so badly that partisans dismissed them out of hand. It is easy for Trump's defenders to do the same with the toddler analogy. *Of course* Democrats would paint him in unflattering terms; as the opposition party, they are invested in belittling a GOP President. *Surely* a mainstream media under constant attack by President Trump would respond with brickbats and petty insults. And #NeverTrump conservatives? To use the argot of #MAGA, butthurt media whores don't count.

This Trumpist refutation of the Toddler-in-Chief analogy suffers from flaws, however. First, political polarization fails to explain why the caricature of Trump involves a comparison to tots. It would be a curious move for Democratic partisans to make if the charge is without foundation. Donald Trump is the oldest person ever to be elected President. Trump's personal scandals include serial adultery, casual bigotry and misogyny, sexual assault, multiple bankruptcies, and tax fraud, all accompanied by copious amounts of profanity. Trump's political scandals include campaign finance violations, acceptance of foreign emoluments, obstruction of justice, and abuse of power. One does not associate any of these activities with small children. Toddlers evoke innocence, and that is the last word anyone would use to describe the 45th President. Why, then, do Trump's critics compare him to a toddler so frequently?

Second, the 45th President appears to be uniquely sensitive to accusations that he is immature. Trump has been the target of rhetorical slings and arrows for most of his adult life, but he usually revels in negative publicity. He contacted Tony Schwartz about ghostwriting *The Art of the Deal* after reading the critical profile of Trump that Schwartz wrote for *New York* magazine. As Schwartz explained in 2016, "He was obsessed with publicity, and he didn't care what you wrote."[12] In *The Art of the Deal* itself, Schwartz and Trump wrote, "From a bottom-line perspective, bad publicity is sometimes better than no publicity at all. Controversy, in short, sells."[13] Despite being inured to bad press, however, Trump has been acutely sensitive to being infantilized in the press. During his time in politics Trump has taken pains to deny being a baby. In August 2016, Trump reacted badly to a *New York Times* story that detailed the degree of dysfunction within his presidential campaign and the tendency of his subordinates to go on television to capture Trump's attention.[14] The day after the story dropped, Trump exploded at his campaign chairman Paul Manafort, saying, "You treat me like a baby! Am I like a baby to you? I sit there like a little baby and watch TV and you talk to me?"[15] Indeed, Trump views this as the worst of insults. He disparaged former New York mayor Rudy Giuliani's cable TV defense of Trump after the *Access Hollywood* tape was released by saying, "Rudy, you're a baby! They took your diaper off right there. You're like a little baby that needs to be changed."[16] In his October 2018 *60 Minutes* interview with Leslie Stahl, Trump defended himself by saying—twice—"I'm not a baby."[17] Multiple press reports indicate the media narrative that incenses the 45th President the most is that "The is sometimes in need of adult daycare," as CNN's Jim Acosta has put it.[18] If a toddler trait is to define themselves by loudly denying that they are a baby, then Donald Trump has at least one thing in common with toddlers.

Third, President Trump, his family, and his biographers have all made it clear that the 45th President is not the most mature of individuals. Trump himself told biographer Michael D'Antonio, "When I look at myself in the first grade and I look at myself now, I'm basically the same. The temperament is not that different."[19] He wrote in *The Art of the Deal* that "even early on I had a tendency to stand up and make my opinions known in a very forceful way."[20] Trump's sister Maryanne told the *Washington Post* during the 2016 campaign that her brother was "still a simple boy from Queens."[21] Admittedly, a first-grader is older than a toddler, but the fact remains that Trump and his family agree that his psychological makeup has remained unchanged from when he was a very small boy. Most of the biographers and biographies of Trump make a similar point: Trump has experienced little emotional or psychological development since he was a toddler. Tim O'Brien, the author of *TrumpNation: The Art of Being the Donald*, warned *Politico* after Trump's election that "we now have somebody who's going to sit in the Oval Office who is lacking in a lot of adult restraints and in mature emotions."[22]

The last and most powerful argument supporting the Toddler-in-Chief thesis, however, is laid out in the rest of this book. It is not only Trump's political opponents who frequently liken him to an immature child. His closest political allies and subordinates draw the same comparison. This is the strongest rebuttal to the claim that those comparing Trump to a toddler are simply partisan hacks. Individuals with a vested interest in the success of Donald Trump's presidency nonetheless describe him as small boy in desperate need of a time-out. They have done so repeatedly and persistently since his inauguration.

I should know. Somewhat by accident, I began collecting data on this phenomenon in early 2017, soon after Trump was inaugurated. At the time, it seemed like a lark; it did not occur to me that this trope would define Trump's style of political leadership.

I was naive.

This project started innocently enough. Back in early 2017, some mainstream media commentators pushed the narrative that Donald Trump, a man with no governing experience whatsoever, was growing into the presidency. After Trump's first address to a joint session of Congress, CNN's Van Jones said on camera, "He became President of the United States in that moment, period."[23] A month later, after Trump addressed the nation to explain why he launched Tomahawk cruise missiles at Syria, CNN's Fareed Zakaria told his viewers, "I think Donald Trump became President of the United States last night."[24]

Perhaps these approbations arose from an understandable psychological yearning for normalcy. But they were unpersuasive. Too many stories of Trump acting like a small child and his staff acting like exasperated caregivers were floating in the ether. This became clear to me after reading a *Washington Post* story by Ashley Parker and Robert Costa describing Trump's obsession with watching television. This part stood out:

> Trump turns on the television almost as soon as he wakes, then checks in periodically throughout the day in the small dining room off the Oval Office, and continues late into the evening when he's back in his private residence. *"Once he goes upstairs, there's no managing him,"* said one adviser.[25]

There are two noteworthy aspects to this story. The first is the way that Trump is characterized as someone who needed to be managed like a toddler. The second is that the person describing Trump like an unruly child is *someone with a stake in seeing Donald Trump succeed as President of the United States.*

In response to that story, I tweeted out, "I'll believe that Trump is growing into the presidency when his staff stops talking about him like a toddler."[26]

A few days later, another story appeared in *Politico* in which the White House staff used a similar characterization.[27] I tweeted that out as well, threading it below the initial tweet. Soon I noticed something: Trump's staff and surrogates routinely and repeatedly characterized him as a toddler to the press. And so I decided to collect every example I could find of a Trump ally describing him as such.

That was three years and more than one thousand tweets ago.

As it turns out, a *lot* of people with a rooting interest in Donald Trump's agenda have described him as a very immature boy. One person described NATO's preparations for Trump's first attendance at a meeting of the alliance as "preparing to deal with a child—someone with a short attention span and mood who has no knowledge of NATO, no interest in in-depth policy issues, nothing."[28] A Trump White House staffer characterized one dubious White House press release as an action designed solely to appease the President, "the equivalent of giving a sick, screaming baby whiskey instead of taking them to the doctor and actually solving the problem."[29] In 2017 Trump's Deputy Chief of Staff Katie Walsh described trying to identify Trump's goals as "trying to figure out what a child wants."[30] In 2018, a senior GOP member of Congress told Trump supporter Erick Erickson, "I don't know what the f*** he wants and in talking to him I'm pretty sure he doesn't know what the f*** he wants. He just wants, like a kid who's

Daniel W. Drezner ✓
@dandrezner

I'll believe that Trump is growing into the presidency when his staff stops talking about him like a toddler.
washingtonpost.com/politics/every...

> Trump turns on the television almost as soon as he wakes, then checks in periodically throughout the day in the small dining room off the Oval Office, and continues late into the evening when he's back in his private residence. "Once he goes upstairs, there's no managing him," said one adviser.

10:23 AM · 4/25/17 · Twitter for iPhone

ıllı View Tweet activity

6,652 Retweets **14.8K** Likes

so hungry nothing sounds good anymore and he's just pissed off."[31] In 2019, a person close to Trump's legal team explained the perils of advising him: "There's just no getting through to him, and you can kiss your plans for the day goodbye because you're basically stuck looking after a 4-year-old now." A US official described cajoling Trump to keep troops in Syria as "like feeding a baby its medicine in yogurt or applesauce."[32]

Both Secretary of Defense James Mattis and White House Chief of Staff John Kelly told officials that they viewed their job as being "babysitter" to the President.[33] Indeed, during Trump's first year in office Kelly and Mattis reportedly made a pact that at least one of them would stay in the country when Trump was in Washington, just in case he did something crazy.[34] Press accounts are riddled with anonymous staff quotes like "He just seemed to go crazy today" or "He doesn't really know any boundaries" or "Sometimes he wants to blow everything up."[35] There are so many examples of Trump's staffers characterizing him as a toddler that even the most hardcore MAGA supporter must acknowledge that the President occasionally needs a time-out.[36]

Perhaps the most notorious example of a Trump official comparing him to a toddler is an anonymous September 5, 2018 *New York Times* op-ed penned by a senior official in the Trump administration. The author does not explicitly say that the President is a toddler, but the inference is clear. That op-ed describes Trump's leadership style as "impetuous, adversarial, petty and ineffective" and notes that "it may be cold comfort in this chaotic era, but Americans should know that there are adults in the room. We fully recognize what is happening. And we are trying to do what's right even when Donald Trump won't."[37] Variations of this message from anonymous insiders have recurred throughout the Trump presidency. In the summer of 2019, a senior national security official told CNN's Jake Tapper, "Everyone at this point ignores what the president says and just does their job. The American people should take some measure of confidence in that."[38]

Some of the individuals named above have denied the quotes attributed to them. Most of the quotes that appear in this book are attributed to anonymous sources. Trump has berated the mainstream media numerous times for relying on such tactics: for example, "When you see 'anonymous source,' stop reading the story, it is fiction!" or "The fact is that many anonymous sources don't even exist."[39]

What makes Trump staffers, allies, and advisors stand out compared to previous administrations, however, is not their desire for anonymity. Every administration has its anonymous sources. Even Corey Lewandowski, Trump's first campaign manager and one of his most loyal acolytes, acknowledged to the *New York Times* that "some of these people do exist."[40] What makes Trump surrogates stand out is the number of times they compare him to a toddler. And there are plenty of on-the-record statements from prominent Trump supporters and allies that make him sound like a rambunctious two-year-old:

Speaker of the House Newt Gingrich: "There are parts of Trump that are almost impossible to manage."[41]

Trump White House Chief Strategist Steve Bannon: "I'm sick of being a wet nurse for a 71 year old."[42]

US Senator Bob Corker: "It's a shame the White House has become an adult day care center."[43]

GOP campaign consultant Karl Rove: "Increasingly it appears Mr. Trump lacks the focus or self-discipline to do the basic work required of a President. His chronic impulsiveness is apparently unstoppable and clearly self-defeating."[44]

Newsmax CEO and longtime Trump friend Christopher Ruddy: "This is Donald Trump's personality. He just has to respond. He's been so emotional. . . . It takes a toll on him, and the way he deals with it is to lash out."[45]

Fox News commentator Tucker Carlson: "I've come to believe that Trump's role is not as a conventional President who promises to get certain things achieved to the Congress and then does. I don't think he's capable. I don't think he's capable of sustained focus. I don't think he understands the system."[46]

Secretary of State Rex Tillerson: "What was challenging

for me coming from the disciplined, highly process-
oriented ExxonMobil corporation [was] to go to work
for a man who is pretty undisciplined, doesn't like to
read, doesn't read briefing reports, doesn't like to get
into the details of a lot of things, but rather just kind of
says, 'This is what I believe.'"[47]

US Representative Ryan Costello: "The notion that a shutdown creates more pressure on Dems is toddler logic."[48]

US Senator Lindsey Graham: "The president's been—he
can be a handful—that's just the way it is."[49]

US Representative Adam Kinzinger: "This is so beneath the
office you hold. It's childish, and yet it's getting really
old."[50]

Speaker of the House Paul Ryan: "I'm telling you he didn't
know *anything* about government. . . . I wanted to scold
him all the time."[51]

Governor Chris Christie: "He acts and speaks on impulse.
He doesn't always grasp the inner workings of government."[52]

Trump surrogates do not make these statements only to
reporters; they make them under oath as well. The Mueller
report confirms that when Trump aides have testified under
penalty of perjury, they frequently characterize the President
as possessing the emotional and intellectual maturity of a
small boy. White House Chief of Staff Reince Priebus told
Mueller's investigators that when Trump was angry at his
National Security Advisor Michael Flynn he would pretend
that Flynn was not in the room.[53] Chris Christie, Steve Bannon, and White House Counsel Don McGahn all testified that
Trump made requests that were "nonsensical," "ridiculous,"
or "silly."[54] Bannon, McGahn, National Security Administration head Mike Rogers, and White House Communications

Director Hope Hicks all described the President having temper tantrums when informed of bad news.[55] Multiple officials described similar toddler-like behavior during the House impeachment inquiry.[56]

Classified diplomatic cables from the British ambassador to the United States leaked to a British tabloid paint a similar picture. Sir Kim Darroch characterized Trump as "inept" and "incompetent" to the Foreign Ministry. He advised his superiors that in speaking to the 45th President, "you need to start praising him for something that he's done recently" and that "you need to make your points simple, even blunt." He further warned, "There is no filter."[57] All these assessments were based on Darroch's frequent interactions with Trump's coterie of advisors. Other diplomats based in Washington soon confirmed that Darroch's assessments matched cables they had dispatched to their home countries.[58] In response, Trump insulted Darroch repeatedly and then declared him *persona non grata* via Twitter, thereby confirming the ambassador's assessment of him.[59]

These examples are merely a small portion of a long list. It would be one thing if these kinds of comments emerged once a quarter. Every President misbehaves on occasion. Ambitious subordinates have an intermittent incentive to leak unflattering stories about their Commander in Chief. If this trope appeared only a few times since Trump's inauguration, that would warrant a media trend story and nothing more.

But between April 2017 and December 2019, I have recorded well over one thousand instances in which an ally or subordinate of Donald Trump has described the President as if he were a toddler.[60] The rate is greater than one toddler depiction per day. That seems like a lot.

To be fair, there are elements of Trump's toddler-like behavior that could be categorized in multiple ways. It is undeniably true that some of the behaviors described herein are not unique to small children. Teenagers can be moody and undisciplined. Adolescents, senior citizens, and overstressed parents can lose their temper. Lazy people can refuse to do productive tasks and demand to watch television instead. As will be discussed more fully in the concluding chapter, however, too many examples have surfaced during my curation of the #ToddlerinChief thread that simply do not fit any other category. Consider this anecdote from a May 2017 *Time* magazine profile of Trump's after-hours life in the White House:

> The waiters know well Trump's personal preferences. As he settles down, they bring him a Diet Coke, while the rest of us are served water, with the Vice President sitting at one end of the table. With the salad course, Trump is served what appears to be Thousand Island dressing instead of the creamy vinaigrette for his guests. When the chicken arrives, he is the only one given an extra dish of sauce. At the dessert course, he gets two scoops of vanilla ice cream with his chocolate cream pie, instead of the single scoop for everyone else.[61]

Or this lead from an August 2019 *Washington Post* story:

> President Trump on Tuesday abruptly called off a trip to Denmark, announcing in a tweet that he was postponing the visit because the country's leader was not interested in selling him Greenland.
>
> The move comes two days after Trump told reporters that owning Greenland, a self-governing country that is part of the kingdom of Denmark, "would be nice" for the United States from a strategic perspective.[62]

Demanding extra ice cream with one's dessert might be the best "know it when you see it" definition of unsupervised toddlerhood imaginable. And canceling a trip because a piece of territory is not for sale sounds like a story that belongs in a children's animated cartoon instead of the *Washington Post*.

None of this is to say that Trump is not capable of acting like a mature adult. There have been moments during his presidency—his first address to a joint session of Congress, his comportment at George H. W. Bush's funeral, his 2019 D-Day commemoration speech—when he has acted "presidential." But those moments have been few and far between. As the subsequent chapters in this book demonstrate, the toddler-like behavior has been unrelenting. Indeed, a count of additions to the #ToddlerinChief thread by quarter shows that Trump's immature behavior is increasing, not decreas-

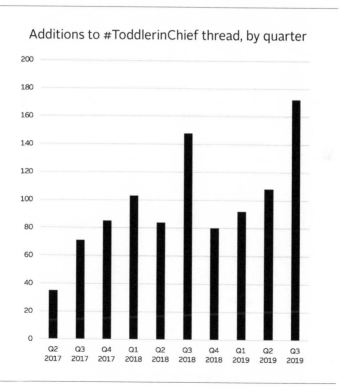

Additions to #ToddlerinChief thread, by quarter

ing. This matches the accounts of the Trump administration written by critical observers and staffers (such as Bob Woodward and Omarosa Maningault Newman) as well as more sympathetic portrayals by Fox News hosts and staffers (such as Howard Kurtz and Cliff Sims).[63] There are simply too many of these characterizations collected by too many outlets to dismiss these reports as "fake news."

The bulk of this book will be devoted to proving that President Trump's behavior closely matches that of a small, bratty child. This raises an important question, however: even if Trump acts like a toddler, does it really matter? Hasn't the system successfully contained him?

🗣

As the President of the United States, Donald J. Trump is the most powerful man in the free world. Like any modern President, however, he is also cosseted by an array of constraints. A welter of formal institutions, informal institutions, laws, and social norms have accumulated to function as a straitjacket on any individual President. These constraints started with the country's founding. The American Revolution colored how the Founding Fathers approached the office of the presidency. The bulk of the Declaration of Independence was a list of grievances about the dangers of unchecked executive authority. The Articles of Confederation were purposefully designed with a weak executive. The Constitution established a stronger executive as one of three coequal branches of government, but the presidency is not even first among equals; Article I addresses the legislative branch, not the executive. The Constitution explicitly gives the President very few unilateral powers and endows the congressional and judicial branches with considerable abilities to check presidential overreach.[64] The framers made sure that the power to tax, spend, declare war, and ratify treaties all reside with Congress. They were equally explicit in their intention for the Constitution to prevent an unconstrained presidency. James Madison noted in Federalist no. 51, "In republican government the legislative authority, necessarily, dominates."[65] Even Alexander Hamilton, who advocated for a strong presidency, stressed the importance of ensuring that the President's powers were weaker than those of a Monarch.[66]

The constitutional checks on the presidency are the oldest and most revered. Beginning in the 19th century, however, an array of statutes was enacted to limit the powers of the President even as the executive branch grew. American political development scholars stress the erosion of patronage power and the rise of civil service protections as additional checks on presidential caprice.[67] As voters demanded that the federal government provide more public goods, the bureaucracy expanded and professionalized itself to be able to consume and produce policy expertise. In domestic affairs, the Progressive Era, the New Deal, and the Great Society programs increased the size and scope of the federal bureaucracy. The Second World War, the Cold War, and the Global War on Terror concomitantly expanded the foreign policy bureaucracy. It could be argued that the creation of new regulatory agencies and cabinet departments empowers the President vis-à-vis the legislative branch. Even if housed in the executive branch, however, Congress authorized them with statutes that strictly demarcated the limits of direct presidential influence. The ability of presidents to order these agencies to execute their every whim is further constrained by laws like the Administrative Procedures Act. Statutes prevent President Trump from firing his Federal Reserve Chairman—even though he has repeatedly expressed his desire to do so.[68] Furthermore, each new bureaucracy has developed its own norms, procedures, and cultures. These make it difficult for Presidents to order executive agencies to take actions that contravene these practices. Jimmy Carter, hardly an advocate of enhanced presidential powers, lamented to the *New York Times* in 1977 that "I underestimated the inertia or the momentum of the federal bureaucracy. . . . It is difficult to change."[69]

Beyond abiding by black-letter constitutional law and statutory restrictions, Presidents have long been expected to behave in accordance with unspoken norms and customs. Some political scientists describe these practices as "informal institutions": unwritten but socially shared rules that are created, communicated, and enforced outside of laws or official channels.[70] Julia Azari and Jennifer Smith have explored how these informal institutions play vital roles in supplementing gaps in formal rules or ameliorating possible contradictions in rules. They note that even if these norms are not codified, "political actors in the United States do, in fact, alter their behavior in accordance with unwritten rules."[71] The growing role of professional expertise in governing also acted as an additional guardrail. The presence of acknowledged experts in the government can constrain the President. Defying an expert consensus on an issue in which expertise is valued would traditionally be viewed as politically costly.[72] The combination of statutory restrictions, bureaucratic autonomy, and informal institutions explain why Barack Obama said immediately after the 2016 election, "One of the things you discover about being President is that there are all these rules and norms and laws and you've got to pay attention to them. And the people who work for you are also subject to those rules and norms."[73]

The accumulation of all these constraints is why so many presidential scholars have argued that the presidency is a fundamentally weak institution. Richard Neustadt remains the most widely cited scholar on the presidency. In his magnum opus, *Presidential Power*, he argues that the President's chief power is the ability to persuade other actors—members of Congress, members of the executive branch, and the American people—to act in accordance with presidential preferences. Without the ability to persuade, Neustadt suggests, the President's powers are feeble: "In form all Presidents are leaders nowadays. In fact this guarantees no more than that they will be clerks."[74] Successive generations of scholars have echoed this point. Terry Moe and Will Howell, for example, argued as recently as 2016 that the Constitution has excessively hampered the ability of the President to solve problems. They advocate for a stronger presidency because, in their words, "The Constitution sees to it—purposely, by design—that [Presidents] are significantly limited in the formal powers they wield and heavily constrained by the checks and balances formally imposed by the other branches."[75]

Donald Trump posed an excellent test of these theories of institutional constraint. In 2016 many people were saying that he was unfit to occupy the office of President of the United States. His behavior during the campaign ranged from petulant to racist. His behavior during the transition period ran the gamut from petty to unethical. Trump's inauguration address—which was, in retrospect, one of his more coherent speeches—was so far outside the norms of the presidency that even George W. Bush described it as "some weird shit."[76] Nonetheless, many commentators believed that Congress, the courts, and the bureaucracy would tie him down like Gulliver.[77]

As it turns out, most of these arguments have not held up. Unfortunately, someone with the emotional maturity of a small child was elected to an office that, over time, had been designed for the last adult in Washington, DC.

●

Why has Donald Trump tested the guardrails of the American political system in ways that his predecessors did not? Even a cursory review of past Presidents reveals a few great men, some good men, and a mélange of liars, cheats, fools, drunks, depressives, and racists. Every President prior to Trump has been accused of some scandal or act of malfeasance.[78] The modern American presidency has seen philanderers (Kennedy, Clinton), bullies (LBJ), bumblers (Ford, George W. Bush), eggheads (Carter, Obama), and paranoids (Nixon) occupy the office. Despite this rogues' gallery, the Republic has survived and thrived. Is Trump really so different?

Most of this book will argue yes, Trump really is different. Equally important, however, is that the times are different. The checks and balances constraining the presidency have worn thin.

Growing dysfunction in other spheres of political life has shifted greater power to the executive branch. Each time efforts have been made to curb the power of the presidency—immediately after the Civil War, in response to the Progressive Era, after Watergate—the presidency has struck back. Historian Arthur Schlesinger wrote about this phenomenon in *The Imperial Presidency*: "Confronted by presidential initiatives in foreign affairs, Congress and the courts, along with the press and the citizenry, often lack confidence in their own information and judgement and are likely to be intimidated by executive authority."[79] This growing power of the presidency predates Trump by several decades; many observers are only now grasping the problem.

Consider the formal checks and balances. While some might argue that the Constitution imposes significant checks on the executive branch, history offers a different guide. The presidency has, for the past century plus, amassed an increasing array of formal and informal powers. As the head of the executive branch, the President now possesses several ways to act without consulting the other branches of government. These include executive orders, executive agreements, presidential proclamations, presidential memoranda, signing statements, declarations of states of emergency, and national security directives.[80] As American history has unfolded, Presidents have availed themselves of these forms of direct action at an accelerating rate. Political scientist William Howell concludes, "The president's powers of unilateral action exert just as much influence over public policy, and in some cases more, than the formal powers that presidency scholars have examined so carefully."[81] Presidential scholar Julia Azari concurs:

> Congress has the power of the purse and to declare war, as well as a role in the foreign policy duties of the president (like the requirement for the Senate to ratify treaties). Yet the structure of the government puts the president in a position to both make decisions and articulate them in a way that Congress rarely can. . . .
>
> The government structure created by the Constitution allows the president a great deal of power and flexibility. The text does very little to describe the nature of this power or its limits, leaving presidents free to do what they can get away with politically much of the time.[82]

Another reason constitutional checks and balances have eroded is that the other branches of government have voluntarily ceded some of their authority to the executive branch. This has been most evident in foreign relations, which was the wellspring of Schlesinger's concerns about an imperial presidency.[83] Congress has not formally declared war since 1942, but that has not stopped the President from using military force hundreds of times, including in Korea, Vietnam, Panama, and Afghanistan, and twice in Iraq.[84] Presidents have relied on the 2001 Authorization for Use of Military Force passed in the wake of the September 11 attacks to justify the use of force in Somalia, Syria, and Yemen. Congress has demonstrated neither the will nor the capacity to claw back those powers.[85] The vast system of alliances has further empowered the President to deploy military forces without consulting Congress.[86] Similarly, after passing the disastrous Smoot-Hawley Tariff Act in 1930, Congress decided it could not responsibly execute its constitutional responsibilities on trade.[87] Over the ensuing decades, it delegated many of those powers to the President, marking the beginning of a sustained decline in congressional influence over foreign economic policy.

On questions of oversight, congressional power has eroded badly. The number of hearings on foreign policy issues has declined precipitously.[88] Members of Congress simply lack the electoral incentive to devote time and energy into national security and foreign policy concerns.[89] After Newt Gingrich's Contract with America, Congress handicapped itself further by reducing its own staff and resources. This has weakened its ability to rely on expertise independent of the executive branch. Again and again, Congress has eschewed responsibility and delegated authority to the President. As William Howell concludes, "The notion that a watchful Congress will rise up and snub any President who dares challenge it could hardly be further from the truth."[90]

Political polarization has further debilitated Congress, encouraging the expansion of presidential powers.[91] Over the past 50 years, Democrats in Congress have shifted to the left, and Republicans have shifted way, way to the right.[92] As partisanship has paralyzed Congress, the legislature has become less able to pass significant legislation beyond funding the government. Over time, Presidents have simply seized more power in response to a dysfunctional legislative branch. They have done so secure in the knowledge that the very polarization that stymies Congress also prevents it from responding effectively to presidential power grabs. Presidents, even unpopular ones, can count on party loyalists in Congress to block measures that would constrain or reverse presidential overreach. Unsurprisingly, political scientists have found that Presidents are both more likely and more able to act unilaterally when the legislative branch is paralyzed by polarization. Andrew Rudalevige concluded in *The New Imperial Presidency* that increased partisan polarization "enhanced the incentives for the President, whoever the incumbent, to claim unilateral authority and make it stick."[93]

This phenomenon has been particularly salient during the 21st century, as polarization within Congress has skyrocketed to new highs. Both the Bush and Obama administrations stretched the boundaries of executive power before Donald Trump was sworn into office. The Bush administration expanded the federal government's powers to monitor communication and financial transactions, as well as indefinitely detain enemy combatants. The Obama administration used executive orders to enable the Environmental Protection Agency to regulate greenhouse gas emissions and grant work permits to illegal immigrants. President Obama negotiated international agreements on climate change and the Iranian nuclear deal using executive authority alone. Ironically, before he was President, Trump criticized Obama repeatedly for executive overreach. This changed quickly after January 20, 2017. Trump soon bragged that he had issued more executive orders than Obama in his first hundred days.[94] In 21st-century America, presidential ambition does not just check congressional ambition, it checkmates it.

As for the judicial branch, the courts demonstrated considerable deference to the executive branch long before Trump came on the political scene. Part of this reflects a sense of self-preservation. Judges have no enforcement power and are therefore understandably reluctant to referee disputes between the congressional and executive branches. They have developed legal rationales, such as the political questions doctrine, to avoid hearing challenges to the President. Analyses of judicial rulings on questions of executive branch overreach reveal that the courts have largely refrained from directly confronting the President. When they do rule on challenges to presidential power, they side with the President more than 80 percent of the time.[95] Furthermore, even when federal courts have ruled against the President, they have done so in as narrow a manner as possible. The result has been that the President has amassed significant levers of power with fewer checks and balances than Americans commonly realize.

A similar story can be told with respect to the executive branch's constraints on the presidency. A web of bureaucratic units ranging from the Office of Management and Budget to the US Trade Representative to the National Security Council staff are housed within the Executive Office of the President. Each of these organizations has grown much more quickly than the relevant cabinet agencies. The autonomy of cabinet officers has also shrunk over the last half-century. Beginning with the Reagan administration, Presidents have exerted greater control over subcabinet appointments across the federal government. The White House has taken care to oversee political cabinet appointments at the Deputy Secretary, Undersecretary, and Assistant Secretary level.[96] The political loyalties of these appointees lie with the President rather than their cabinet Secretary.

The autonomy of the federal bureaucracy was under

assault well before the Toddler in Chief was inaugurated. Beginning with the Nixon administration, successive Presidents learned how to shape the permanent bureaucracy in accordance with their policy preferences.[97] The expansion of political appointments and executive orders have made it easier for the President to dictate to executive agencies. More recently, elected officials have starved the bureaucracy of manpower. Post-2008 hiring freezes within the federal government ensured that the median age of a federal bureaucrat was higher than that of the private-sector workforce.[98] Still, the Trump administration has accelerated this phenomenon by taking actions to weaken the autonomous power of the civil service. During the interregnum between Obama and Trump, the latter's transition teams walled themselves off from high-ranking career professionals in numerous cabinet agencies (when they bothered to show up at all).[99] One month into the Trump administration, White House Advisor Steve Bannon proclaimed a daily war aimed at the "deconstruction of the administrative state."[100] President Trump has gone further than his predecessors to intrude into the areas of the executive branch—military justice, the intelligence community, the Justice Department—that are supposed to be insulated from White House interference.

The breakdown of these formal guardrails extends to the more informal ones, such as deference to the opinions of experts. For this to matter, expertise must be held in high esteem. Well before Trump, however, there had been a steady decline of trust in authority and expertise.[101] Over the past half-century there has been an erosion of public trust in almost every major public institution. The public opinion data showing rising levels of pessimism toward major institutions and professions is incontrovertible. Whether one looks at polling data from Gallup, Pew, the General Social

Survey, or other sources, faith in the federal government has plummeted. Gallup also polls Americans about their belief in other institutions: local police, unions, public schools, organized religion, business, and the health care system. The results for all are the same: a secular trend of rising distrust. Similarly, trust in major sources of information—including television news and newspapers—is also at an all-time low.[102] Trust in professional journalists also declined over the past decade, falling well below that for chiropractors.[103] The General Social Survey data show a similar loss of confidence in expert communities such as scientists and educators.[104] In essence, suspicion of every institution in the United States has risen in this century, with the exception of the military. Unfortunately, the ability of experts to kill harebrained ideas ain't what it used to be. Indeed, this very distrust contributed to the political rise of Donald Trump in the first place.

The informal norms designed to regulate political behavior have also faded. Even before Trump, rising levels of partisanship had permitted politicians on both sides to escalate the level of vitriol toward the opposing party. Conspiracy theories bled into mainstream political discourse. Without foundation, Hillary Clinton was suspected of orchestrating the murder of a White House staffer. George W. Bush was accused without any evidence of being responsible for the September 11 terrorist attacks. Politicians hit by scandals learned that if they could tough out the initial wave of shock and disgust, they could often retain their office. Trump's very election eviscerated many of the norms of political behavior. He shot to prominence in far-right Republican circles by questioning whether Barack Obama was born in the United States. While running for office, Trump denigrated ethnic minorities and Gold Star families. The *Access Hollywood* tape revealed his demeaning attitude toward women. In one presidential debate he told Hillary Clinton that she would face prosecution if he was elected. Despite all these norm breaches, Trump won the 2016 presidential election. As President, he has been unconstrained by the traditional norms of the presidency.

Each of these guardrails checking presidential power had begun to fail before Trump was elected President. During his tenure, they have almost completely broken down. As I discuss further in the concluding chapter, the Toddler in Chief is like most other toddlers—bad at building structures but fantastic at making a complete mess of existing ones.

Institutionalists have been warning about the breakdown of democratic guardrails for quite some time. An optimist might have fretted about these trends but noted that everything would be okay so long as the President acted like, you know, a grown-up—someone who recognized that with great power comes great responsibility. Unfortunately, Donald Trump really does think and act like a toddler. He has done so for most of his life.

Beyond the checks and constraints studied by political scientists, pundits gravitated toward two additional "guardrail narratives" in the early months of the Trump administration. The first was that he would grow into the office of the presidency. Trump himself promised this during the 2016 campaign, stating repeatedly that he would be "so presidential you will be so bored."[105] At key junctures in Trump's first months as President, if he demonstrated even a hint of maturity, commentators would describe it as the moment when Trump truly became the President.

Republicans relied on a variation of this line of argument during Trump's first year in office. When news broke of Trump violating a norm or possibly a law, fellow Republicans often explained it away as "the actions of a political newcomer unfamiliar with what is appropriate presidential conduct."[106] The implication, of course, was that as Trump moved down the learning curve as President, he would engage in this kind of transgressive behavior less frequently and comport himself in a more presidential manner.

The other guardrail narrative was that even if Trump behaved erratically, he had surrounded himself with advisors and cabinet members who would function as an "Axis of Adults" to constrain the Commander in Chief.[107] While many Americans questioned Trump's maturity, no one viewed Gary Cohn, John Kelly, James Mattis, H. R. McMaster, or Rex Tillerson as immature. Political scientists put great stock in the power of advisors to shape and mold a President's thinking on vital issues.[108] Sure, Trump might rant and rave, the thinking went, but "the Generals" would rein him in. The core thesis of the anonymous *New York Times* op-ed by a senior Trump official was that there would be adults in the room to constrain Trump.

These narratives sounded savvy and knowing in 2017. They were designed to allay the fears of Americans anxious about President Trump. In retrospect, however, they were naive. Trump has not crashed the economy or started a nuclear war. However, as this book will take pains to demonstrate, there is simply no getting around the point that President Donald Trump has acted an awful lot like a badly behaved toddler, and there is little his staff has done to contain his outbursts.

The Toddler in Chief has failed to mature even in areas that ostensibly cater to his professed base. Trump has proclaimed that he is the biggest booster of the military and that the uniformed services support him. Yet he has done nothing to better understand his role as the Commander in Chief of the

Armed Forces. The 45th President has restricted his encounters with the families of those killed in action because he finds the experience to be too intense.[109] Despite repeatedly calling the top brass at the Pentagon "my generals," the Chairman of the Joint Chiefs of Staff upbraided him for unproductive interventions in national security meetings.[110] Colonel David Lapan, a retired Marine who served as the spokesperson for the Department of Homeland Security during the first year of the Trump administration, told the *New York Times*, "There was the belief that over time, he would better understand, but I don't know that that's the case. I don't think that he understands the proper use and role of the military and what we can, and can't, do."[111] Trump's former Secretary of the Navy acknowledged that "the President has very little understanding of what it means to be in the military, to fight ethically or to be governed by a uniform set of rules and practices."[112] Military officers have expressed increasing discomfort with Trump's use of the uniformed services as a partisan prop.[113]

Furthermore, Trump's Axis of Adults proved unable to rein in his toddler-like behavior. In the fall of 2017, Senator Bob Corker talked to reporters about "the tremendous amount of work that it takes by people around [Trump] to keep him in the middle of the road." Referencing White House Chief of Staff John Kelly, National Security Advisor H. R. McMaster, Secretary of State Rex Tillerson, and Secretary of Defense James Mattis, Corker concluded that "as long as there are people like that around him who are able to talk him down when he gets spun up, you know, calm him down and continue to work with him before a decision gets made, I think we'll be fine."[114] All of these people saw their authority denuded by the Toddler in Chief.[115] Indeed, like burned-out nannies, most of them have resigned. Many others have been fired. By the start of Trump's third year in office, all of them

had left government service, along with Corker. As former
Trump White House staffer Cliff Sims told *Politico*, "What
we are seeing is the erosion of the presidency to where what
is left is just the president."[116]

One can hardly blame the staff for the high burn rate. Normal parents shepherd their children through the terrible twos
for only a short spell. Trump's advisors are required to deal
with a Commander in Chief who will never really grow up.
Furthermore, the standard means of exercising authority in a
childcare setting are unavailable to the White House staff. He
is the President of the United States; in the end his staff must
obey Trump's dictates, resign in protest, or wait to be fired.

It does not matter whether Trump has been at the job for
two years, or four, or six; he will never grow into the presidency. He is who he is, which happens to be the essence of a
petulant child. In the first year of Trump's presidency, one diplomat in Washington told the *Washington Post*, "The idea that
he would inform himself, and things would change, that is no
longer operative."[117] Two years later, a G-7 diplomat described
coping with Trump's behavior: "You just try to get through the
summit without any damage. . . . Every one of these, you just
hope that it ends without any problem. It just gets harder and
harder."[118] Even Trump's closest advisors acknowledge that he
has not matured into the office. Chapter 8 will demonstrate
that they have instead seen a devolution in his behavior.[119]
As one April 2019 *Politico* story surmised, "Even some former administration officials who admire the president and
his policies acknowledge that he does not pay attention to
traditional rules of the government and often does not know
the legal boundaries of his job since he's only two years into
his term. . . . They perceive that Trump's impatience with the
obstacles standing in his way has only increased in recent
months as he's grown more comfortable in the office."[120] If

anything, Trump's toddler traits have become more visible over time.

Trump's enablers now justify his transgressive behavior by extoling him as an "untraditional" President. When it was revealed that 60 percent of Trump's daily schedule was unstructured "Executive Time," White House Press Secretary Sarah Huckabee Sanders responded, "President Trump has a different leadership style than his predecessors and the results speak for themselves."[121]

This book is divided into eight chapters. The first seven examine different dimensions of Trump's toddler-like traits. This includes behavior ranging from Trump's temper tantrums to his poor impulse control to his short attention span to a potpourri of childlike habits. Chapter 8 takes a closer look at how Trump's aides, subordinates, and supporters have coped with staffing the Toddler in Chief. Spoiler alert: the answer is, not well. The conclusion considers what it means for the country to have a Toddler in Chief and what can be done to prevent worst-case scenarios—including future Toddlers in Chief.

CHAPTER ONE

Temper Tantrums

*When he oversteps a limit and is pulled back, he often reacts with
anger and frustration, possibly with a temper tantrum or sud-
den rage. . . . At this age, he just doesn't have much control over
his emotional impulses, so his anger and frustration tend to erupt
suddenly. . . . It's his only way of dealing with the difficult realities of
life. He may even act out in ways that unintentionally harm himself
or others. It's all part of being two.*

AMERICAN ACADEMY OF PEDIATRICS,
CARING FOR YOUR BABY AND YOUNG CHILD

He had grown enraged by the Russia investigation, two advisers
said, frustrated by his inability to control the mushrooming narrative
around Russia. He repeatedly asked aides why the Russia investigation
wouldn't disappear and demanded they speak out for him. He would
sometimes scream at television clips about the probe, one adviser said.

**Josh Dawsey, "Behind Comey's Firing: An Enraged Trump, Fuming about
Russia,"** *Politico,* **May 10, 2017**

Everyone gets angry. Political leaders are hardly exempt from
this emotion. Presidents ranging from Andrew Jackson to
Harry Truman to Bill Clinton were known to blow a gasket
from time to time. Still, an important distinction between
an adult and a toddler is the causality, frequency, and sever-

ity of those outbursts. Mature adults possess the capacity to regulate their emotions. Mature leaders are expected to cope with setbacks without losing emotional control, particularly in front of people who might tattle to others about bad behavior. Political leaders are presumed to possess the necessary metacognition to know not to make key decisions when filled with rage.

Donald Trump is not one of those leaders.

Trump's grievances and moods often bleed into one another. Frustration with the investigation stews inside him until it bubbles up in the form of rants to aides about unfair cable television commentary or as slights aimed at Attorney General Jeff Sessions and his deputy, Rod J. Rosenstein.

Ashley Parker and Philip Rucker, "Trump Is Struggling to Stay Calm on Russia, One Morning Call at a Time," *Washington Post*, **June 23, 2017**

Multiple Trump administration officials detailed to The Daily Beast how senior staffers have a long-standing practice of assuring Trump of the quantity of his major accomplishments (of which he has barely any legislative and some administrative) and of placating him by flagging positive media coverage, typically from right-wing outlets. This is, in part, *a means to avoid further upsetting a president who is already prone to irrationally taking out his anger and professional frustrations on senior staff and who also has a penchant for yelling at the TV.*

Sam Stein, Lachlan Markay, and Asawin Suebsaeng, "Trump Keeps Failing to Destroy Obama's Legacy, as Aides Assure Trump All Is Fine," *the Daily Beast*, **July 19, 2017**

For Trump, anger serves as a way to manage staff, express his displeasure or simply as an outlet that soothes him. Often, aides and advisers say, he'll get mad at a specific staffer or broader situation, unload from

the Oval Office and then three hours later act as if nothing ever oc-
curred even if others still feel rattled by it. Negative television coverage
and lawyers earn particular ire from him.

*White House officials and informal advisers say the triggers for
his temper are if he thinks someone is lying to him, if he's caught by
surprise, if someone criticizes him, or if someone stops him from trying
to do something or seeks to control him.*

**Nancy Cook and Josh Dawsey, "'He Is Stubborn and Doesn't Realize How
Bad This Is Getting,'" *Politico*, August 16, 2017**

As the examples provided in this chapter demonstrate,
the Toddler in Chief's dark moods are frequent. Indeed, this
trait had become so widely reported that by 2018 the *New
York Times'* Marc Leibovich noted, "The Trump-mood-story
genre has, by now, acquired its own conventions. Print articles inevitably rely on several interviews with 'sources close
to the president' who spoke 'on the condition of anonymity
in exchange for their candor discussing the president.' . . .
Trump is commonly described as 'bristling' over unflattering
assessments. . . . The stories typically begin with an anecdote,
often featuring the president's being upset or defensive about
something."[1]

White House and former campaign aides have tried to make sure
Trump's media diet includes regular doses of praise and positive stories to keep his mood up—a tactic honed by staff during the campaign
to keep him from tweeting angrily.

Shane Goldmacher, "How Trump Gets His Fake News," *Politico*, May 15, 2017

Former advisers say Trump also appears to lack any understanding
of the impact his often sharp-tongued tirades can have on aides. One
adviser recalled being berated by Trump in the Oval Office, in front of
multiple colleagues, in particularly humiliating fashion. The next day,

Trump called the adviser on the phone and started joking as though the previous day's outburst had never happened.

Jonathan Lemire and Julie Pace, "Expressing Empathy Remains a Challenge for Trump," Associated Press, October 7, 2017

Frustrated by his Cabinet and angry that he has not received enough credit for his handling of three successive hurricanes, President Trump is now lashing out, rupturing alliances and imperiling his legislative agenda, numerous White House officials and outside advisers said Monday....

Trump in recent days has shown flashes of fury and left his aides, including White House chief of staff John F. Kelly, scrambling to manage his outbursts....

One Trump confidant likened the president to a whistling teapot, saying that when he does not blow off steam, he can turn into a pressure cooker and explode. 'I think we are in pressure cooker territory,' said this person.

Robert Costa, Philip Rucker, and Ashley Parker, "A 'Pressure Cooker': Trump's Frustration and Fury Rupture Alliances, Threaten Agenda," *Washington Post*, October 9, 2017

There are two ways to interpret Trump's fits of presidential pique. First, this could be a hallmark of Trump's populist style of leadership. Second, it could be that Trump demonstrates all the psychological markers of a toddler, and toddlers are less emotionally regulated and therefore more prone to fits of temper. Regardless of the reason, the effects are dangerous.

Populists do not possess a monopoly on anger in politics, but most populist politicians project anger as part of their leadership style.[2] They are adept at exploiting the (often justified) resentment that voters possess toward the elites in charge before their own rise to power. The effect is reciprocal: evoking anger among citizens is a surefire way to get individuals to trust institutions less.[3] No wonder that during one of the 2016 GOP primary debates, Trump said, "I will gladly accept the mantle of anger."[4]

Of course, there are downsides to exploiting anger in politics. The post-2008 wave of populist anger reverses a centuries-long Western effort to contain that emotion in world politics.[5] Recent scholarship on emotions in politics suggest that sustained levels of anger carry severe risks. Anger was valorized in societies with strong honor cultures and warrior castes, biologically conditioning citizens toward that feeling. As the political scientist Neta Crawford notes, "Threats that evoke anger (if they are associated with perceived insults) tend to decrease the perception of a threat and simultaneously heighten risk-taking behaviors on the part of those who feel angry."[6]

The dangers of angry rhetoric can be heightened through misperception and mistranslation. Conventional leaders are prepped to stay within the lanes of "accepted" diplomatic discourse. This permits them to avoid accidentally triggering a crisis as well as enabling them to employ shifts in rhetoric to send a clear foreign policy signal. In contrast, angry populists scorn diplomatic language as exercises in sophistry and hypocrisy. Angry populists with easy access to social media will use undiplomatic language frequently. They will say things like "fire and fury" and "enemy of the people" designed to appeal to their base, increasing the likelihood that outside observers misconstrue their words. Angry tirades from leaders like Trump have been mistranslated abroad—and usually in a direction that paints the leader as more bellicose than intended.[7] Populist leaders will be reluctant to correct such misperceptions, because that would require them to engage in the nuanced diplomatic discourse they have previously derided. When Trump has been forced to walk back his diplomatic faux pas—such as his misbegotten Helsinki summit with Vladimir Putin—he has done so in such a ham-handed way that he amplifies his original misstep.

Some of Mr. Trump's own advisers privately said they were shocked by the president's performance, including his use of the phrase "witch hunt" to describe the special counsel investigation while standing beside Mr. Putin.

Aboard Air Force One back to Washington, Mr. Trump's mood grew foul as the breadth of the critical reactions became clear, according to some people briefed on the flight. Aides steered clear of the front of the plane to avoid being tapped for a venting session with Mr. Trump.

Julie Hirschfield Davis, "Trump, at Putin's Side, Questions U.S. Intelligence on 2016 Election," *New York Times*, **July 16, 2018**

As news outlets began chipping away at the [Mexico migration] agreement's veneer, pointing out that it wasn't the game-changer that Trump made it out to be, the president started lashing out, painting himself as a victim and insisting that he's not getting the credit he deserves....

The cycle of lashing out and hitting back is a familiar pattern for Trump. As his presidency reaches the 2.5-year mark, he is more aggrieved than ever, telling advisers that he believes he'll never get fair treatment from the media and establishment politicians that he believes hate him....

"He has this insatiable need to impress people and demonstrate accomplishments and notch achievements," a former White House official said. "When he feels like he's done something that should be recognized as a success and people are not recognizing it that way, it poses an existential threat to his sense of self—and this is what you get."

Andrew Restuccia, "'He Needs Some Victories': Trump Lashes Out over His Mexico Deal," *Politico*, **June 10, 2019**

Displays of righteous indignation might play well with a populist leader's domestic base. Some even argue that developing the reputation for having a temper can be a good bargaining strategy. Negotiators who represent angry leaders can try a variation of the good cop–bad cop strategy, warning interlocutors to make concessions now, otherwise they cannot guarantee what their frustrated leader will do. Former French ambassador to the United States Gérard Araud got at this when he advised his superiors on how to respond to Trump's public insults: "Do nothing because he will always outbid you. Because he can't accept appearing to lose. You have restraint on your side, and he has no restraint on his side, so you lose. It is escalation dominance."[8]

There was a lengthy debate inside the Trump administration about [attending] the [East Asia] summit, but officials close to Trump were concerned the president did not want to stay in the region for so long and worried he could get cranky, leading to unpredictable or undiplomatic behavior.

Josh Rogin, "Trump to Skip Key Asia Summit in Philippines to Go Home Earlier," *Washington Post*, October 24, 2017

A call about trade and migration between US President Donald Trump and French President Emmanuel Macron soured last week after Macron candidly criticized Trump's policies, two sources familiar with the call told CNN.

"Just bad. It was terrible," one source told CNN. *"Macron thought he would be able to speak his mind, based on the relationship. But Trump can't handle being criticized like that."*

Michelle Kosinski and Maegan Vazquez, "Trump's Phone Call with Macron Described as 'Terrible,'" CNN, June 4, 2018

In actuality, the international effect of angry outbursts is to narrow the zone of possible cooperation between countries. If a leader unleashes an angry tirade against another country, that is sure to gain considerable public attention in both nations. This automatically raises the "audience costs" for both leaders. The larger the audience that is paying attention to any dispute, the greater the political costs a leader can suffer by backing down in that dispute.[9] Displays of temper make it harder for the populist to compromise, but it will also make it more politically difficult for the object of the tirade to make any concessions. Angry provocations therefore make negotiations more costly and conflict escalation more likely.[10] Trump's inability to secure significant concessions on trade agreements and arms control treaties reflect this dynamic.

France pledged on Sunday to stand by the G7 summit statement disowned by Donald Trump and took a swipe at the U.S. president by declaring that international cooperation could not depend on "fits of anger" or "little words.". . . .

"We spent two days to obtain a text and commitments. We will stand by them and anyone who would depart from them, once their back was turned, shows their incoherence and inconsistency," said the statement, quoted by *Le Monde*, which did not mention Trump by name but was clearly referring to his actions.

"*International cooperation cannot depend on fits of anger or little words. Let us be serious and worthy of our people*," the statement said.

Maïa De La Blume, "France Blasts 'Incoherent' Trump after G7 Fiasco," ***Politico*, June 10, 2018**

President Trump stormed out of a White House meeting with congressional leaders on Wednesday after Speaker Nancy Pelosi said she would not fund a border wall even if he agreed to reopen the govern-

ment, escalating a confrontation that has shuttered large portions of
the government for 19 days and counting.

Nicholas Fandos, Michael Tackett, and Julie Hirschfeld Davis, "Trump
Storms Out of White House Meeting with Democrats on Shutdown," *New
York Times*, January 9, 2019

The other possible explanation for Trump's short temper is
that he has the emotional maturity of a two-year-old. Plenty
of officials who interacted with the Toddler in Chief have
noticed this tendency. FBI Deputy Director Andrew McCabe
described a phone conversation with Trump after the President had fired James Comey. Trump was furious that McCabe
had authorized an FBI plane to ferry Comey from California
to Washington DC after he had been fired. As McCabe put
it, "The ranting against Comey spiraled. I waited until he
had talked himself out." Similarly, GOP members of Congress
often talk about the President's public policy views as a function of his mood. As the examples in this chapter attest, it is
striking how often Trump's allies and supporters describe his
temper as being out of control. As a populist, Trump is happy
to exploit anger; as the Toddler in Chief, however, he is a slave
to his own temper.

Shortly after learning in May that a special counsel had been appointed to investigate links between his campaign associates and Russia,
President Trump berated Attorney General Jeff Sessions in an Oval
Office meeting and said he should resign, according to current and
former administration officials and others briefed on the matter. . . .

Accusing Mr. Sessions of "disloyalty," Mr. Trump unleashed a string
of insults on his attorney general.

Ashen and emotional, Mr. Sessions told the president he would quit
and sent a resignation letter to the White House, according to four

people who were told details of the meeting. Mr. Sessions would later tell associates that the demeaning way the president addressed him was the most humiliating experience in decades of public life.

Michael S. Schmidt and Maggie Haberman, "Trump Humiliated Jeff Sessions after Mueller Appointment," *New York Times*, **September 14, 2017**

President Trump publicly pushed back Thursday against a characterization by White House Chief of Staff John F. Kelly that the president's views on a southern border wall had "evolved" and privately fumed about the episode. . . . *Several Trump associates said the president was furious with his chief of staff both for what he said and for the tone he used, which Trump thought made it appear he was a child who had to be managed.*

John Wagner, Josh Dawsey, and Robert Costa, "Trump Pushes Back on Chief of Staff's Claims That Border Wall Pledges Are 'Uninformed,'" *Washington Post*, **January 18, 2018**

Opportunistic aides and advisors who know their leader is easily triggered will have an incentive to exploit that emotion. Members of any ruling clique who perceive that they are losing an internecine policy dispute could provoke the leader's anger to short-circuit a decision-making process in which they would lose. This has been standard operating procedure during the Trump administration. According to the *Daily Beast*, "It was common practice for aides to slide into the Oval Office and distract and infuriate the president with pieces of negative news coverage." Former staffer Omarosa Maningault Newman presented stories to Trump that "would often enrage the president, and resulted in [his] spending at least the rest of the day fuming."[11] White House staffers Peter Navarro and Stephen Miller also riled Trump up to sabotage any attempt to fashion compromises on trade or immigration policy.[12] One senior White House official told *Politico*, "People would put articles on the president's desk that were things he didn't need to see, things that were meant to gin him up or get him mad at somebody."[13] While this tactic temporarily slowed during John Kelly's tenure as White House Chief of Staff, it returned as Kelly's influence ebbed.[14]

According to two officials, Trump's decision to launch a potential trade war was born out of anger at other simmering issues and the result of a broken internal process that has failed to deliver him consensus views that represent the best advice of his team. On Wednesday evening, the president became "unglued," in the words of one official familiar with the president's state of mind.

Stephanie Ruhle, "Trump Was Angry and 'Unglued' When He Started a Trade War, Officials Say," NBC News, March 2, 2018

Inside the White House, aides over the past week have described an air of anxiety and volatility—with an uncontrollable commander in chief at its center.

These are the darkest days in at least half a year, they say, and they worry just how much further President Trump and his administration may plunge into unrest and malaise before they start to recover. As one official put it: "We haven't bottomed out."

Trump is now a president in transition, at times angry and increasingly isolated. He fumes in private that just about every time he looks up at a television screen, the cable news headlines are trumpeting yet another scandal.

Philip Rucker, Ashley Parker, and Josh Dawsey, "'Pure Madness': Dark Days inside the White House as Trump Shocks and Rages," *Washington Post*, March 3, 2018

Inside the White House, Mr. Trump—furious after the F.B.I. raided his longtime personal lawyer, Michael D. Cohen—spent much of the day brooding and fearful and near what two people close to the West Wing described as a 'meltdown.'. . . .

Mr. Trump's mood had begun to sour even before the raids on his lawyer. People close to the White House said that over the weekend, the president engaged in few activities other than dinner at the Trump International Hotel. He tuned into Fox News, they said, watched reports about the so-called deep state looking to sink his presidency and became unglued."

Julie Hirschfield Davis and Maggie Haberman, "At the White House, Trump Takes Selfies and Seethes over Mueller," *New York Times,* **April 10, 2018**

Trump does not stand out from other Presidents because he gets mad. What stands out is how often his temper emerges, and how frequently it has sabotaged his administration. Trump's tantrums emerge more prominently during moments of severe political stress—the simultaneous publication of Bob Woodward's book *Fear: Trump in the White House* and an anonymous *New York Times* op-ed from a high-ranking Trump official being the most obvious flashpoint. President Trump yelled at Chief of Staff John Kelly so viciously that according to the *New York Times* Kelly told his staff that "he had never been spoken to like that during 35 years of serving his country."[15] Trump screamed at Attorney General Jeff Sessions so loudly that Sessions later described it as "the most humiliating experience in decades of public life."[16] The President called up National Security Advisor H. R. McMaster once for the sole purpose of screaming at him.[17] If all Trump's meltdowns from the #ToddlerinChief thread had been included in this chapter, it would be double the length.

A Most Angry Week

Trump's Reactions to Bob Woodward's Fear *and the Anonymous* New York Times *Op-Ed*

In curating the #ToddlerinChief thread, it was easy to spot instances in which Trump's temper spiked. It happened when he received blowback from his Charlottesville comments in August 2017, in March 2018 when he dispatched with many of his initial crop of White House advisers, in November 2018 after the GOP setback in the midterms, and in April 2019 after the release of the Mueller report. Without question, however, his longest temper tantrum was in response to the near-simultaneous publication of Bob Woodward's *Fear* and the anonymous *New York Times* op-ed from a senior administration official:

Behind the scenes, White House aides and others in Trump's orbit largely steeled themselves for what they privately predicted would be the president's all-but-inevitable explosion, which they predicted would occur as cable news channels switched from coverage of Supreme Court nominee Brett M. Kavanaugh's confirmation hearings to juicy tidbits from the [Woodward] book. By early Tuesday evening, Trump was furious and asking people who spoke to Woodward, an outside adviser said.
—ASHLEY PARKER AND JOSH DAWSEY, "Trump, White House Attack New Book from Bob Woodward," *Washington Post*, September 4, 2018

Trump reacted to the [anonymous New York Times *op-ed] with* "volcanic" anger and was "absolutely livid" *over what he considered a treasonous act of disloyalty . . . according to two people familiar with his private discussions.* — PHILIP RUCKER, ASHLEY PARKER, AND JOSH DAWSEY, "'The Sleeper Cells Have Awoken': Trump and Aides Shaken by 'Resistance' Op-Ed," *Washington Post*, September 5, 2018

One senior administration official described a White House in "total meltdown" *by Wednesday evening, after the president went on television to directly attack the author and the Times, an assessment corroborated in interviews with more than a dozen current and former White House officials and outside advisers....*

Trump was furious about the anonymous official's account, according to people close to him. The op-ed prompted the president to launch into an angry rant against the Times, CNN, and the rest of the "dishonest media" during a Wednesday White House event with sheriffs from across the country.

—ANDREW RESTUCCIA, ELIANA JOHNSON, CHRISTOPHER CAD-ELAGO, AND ANNIE KARNI, "'It's Open Season on the President': Op-Ed Unleashes West Wing Meltdown," *Politico*, September 5, 2018

Trump himself insisted the Times must "turn over" the writer for "National Security purposes," if the writer and senior official does "indeed exist." The op-ed contained not even a hint of classified information, providing no national security justification for Trump's tacit threat.

Behind the scenes, sources say, Trump wasn't holding up much better. According to people familiar with his response, the president, in the words of one adviser, "exploded" to those close to him on Wednesday, demanding to know who this anonymous senior official could be.—ERIN BANCO, SPENCER ACKERMAN, ASAWIN SUEBSAENG, AND LACHLAN MARKAY, "The Rebels of Trump's Internal Resistance Are 'Fist-Bumping' Each Other," *Daily Beast*, September 6, 2018

Trump lashed out at his Cabinet, and Nielsen in particular, when told that the number of people arrested for illegally crossing the Mexico border topped 50,000 for the second consecutive month. The blowup lasted more than 30 minutes, according to a person with knowledge of what transpired, as Trump's face reddened and he raised his voice, saying Nielsen needed to "close down" the border....

Trump's tirade went on so long that many present began fidgeting in their seats and flashing grimaces, White House aides said. Eventually, the topic moved on to health care, bringing relief to many in the room.

Josh Dawsey and Nick Miroff, "Trump Unloads on Homeland Security Secretary in Lengthy Immigration Tirade," *Washington Post*, **May 10, 2018**

Trump's fury with [Attorney General Jeff] Sessions is so ever-present it has taken to darkening his moods even during otherwise happy moments. On Thursday, Trump was on Air Force One returning from a trip to Texas, reveling in both a successful day of fundraising and the heads-up he had received from economic adviser Larry Kudlow that the next day's jobs report would be positive.

But when an aide mentioned Sessions, Trump abruptly ended the conversation and unmuted the television in his office broadcasting Fox News, dismissing the staffer to resume watching cable, according to a person familiar with the exchange.

Jonathan Lemire, "Trump Tweet Reflects Anticipation for Clinton Probe Report," **Associated Press, June 5, 2018**

Trump's temper tantrums have also led to poor decision-making and pathological staff strategies for coping with it. Anger leads to short-term, impulsive decision-making that might feel good in the moment but soon leads to disastrous consequences. Trump's uncontrollable temper also ties into the issues of poor impulse control and lack of executive func-

tioning that I discuss in chapter 3. Trump's anger led him
to fire FBI Director James Comey, triggering an independent investigation by Special Counsel Robert Mueller that
dominated headlines for two years. Trump's fits so rattled
his foreign policy team that his Secretary of State, National
Security Advisor, Secretary of Defense, and Chief of Staff all
disparaged him in ways that made it into the media. An irate
Trump took on-camera responsibility for the longest federal
government shutdown in history, an action that eventually
led to his backing down without getting any of his demands
fulfilled by Congress. The President's out-of-control temper
has caused staffers to delay or shorten their own travel, as well
as that of the President, in order to avoid setting him off.[18] It
has also contributed to a burn rate that is the highest in the
history of White House staffs.[19]

     Trump's temper has limited government transparency.
According to several senior Pentagon officials, the Defense
Department halted televised briefings because they were worried President Trump would get angry if he saw something he
disliked.[20] Trump officials asked former White House Counsel
Don McGahn to falsely state that he never believed the President obstructed justice, in the hopes that this would calm the
President down.[21] Most disturbingly, his temper is so bad that
it has clearly warped the information that his staff provide to
him on anything ranging from political analysis to national
security intelligence. No President likes to hear bad news.
In Trump's case, his temper has deterred his subordinates
from providing him with necessary information. Then, when
he learns of it, he gets even more angry. McGahn told GOP
Senate aides after he had stepped down that he "spent the
last couple of years getting yelled at" by Trump.[22] The result
has been a persistent and dangerous doom loop of anger and
ignorance.

Trump's always formidable temper has been shorter-fused than usual, his willingness to listen less than normal. Some White House officials have stopped speaking up in meetings, knowing it won't make any difference because Trump is counting on a shrinking circle of those he trusts. Nothing anyone on the National Security Council staff, in the counsel's office or from across government can outweigh what the President hears from conservatives on cable television or from his social media maven and communications adviser.

Philip Elliott, "Inside Donald Trump's Twitter-Fueled Weekend Meltdown," *Time,* **February 20, 2018**

What is most troubling, say these officials and others in government and on Capitol Hill who have been briefed on the [intelligence briefing] episodes, are Trump's angry reactions when he is given information that contradicts positions he has taken or beliefs he holds. Two intelligence officers even reported that they have been warned to avoid giving the President intelligence assessments that contradict stances he has taken in public.

John Walcott, "'Willful Ignorance': Inside President Trump's Troubled Intelligence Briefings," *Time,* **February 5, 2019**

CHAPTER TWO

Short Attention Span

Around ages two and three, children naturally are very active and impulsive and have a short attention span. All children occasionally seem overactive or easily distractible—for example, when they're very tired, excited about doing something 'special,' or anxious about being in a strange place or among strangers.

AMERICAN ACADEMY OF PEDIATRICS,
CARING FOR YOUR BABY AND YOUNG CHILD

When European diplomats meet these days, they often swap stories about Trump—and how to manage their volatile new ally. *"The president of the United States has a 12-second attention span,"* NATO Secretary-General Jens Stoltenberg told a former senior official in April after meeting Trump in the Oval Office. Not only that, this person told me, the president seemed unprepared and ill-informed, turning the conversation to North Korea and apparently unaware that NATO is not a part of the ongoing North Korea saga.

Susan Glasser, "'People Here Think Trump Is a Laughingstock,'" *Politico*, May 19, 2017

Political leadership cannot be exercised on a whim. Almost by definition, problems that rise to the top of the policy queue are intractable ones. This is particularly true for problems that require congressional buy-in. Even when a President's party controls both houses of Congress, it is no small thing to get legislation passed. It requires drive, determination, sustained focus, investments of political capital, and the art of persuasion.[1] A President needs to be able to signal to other policymakers in the executive and legislative branches which issues are key priorities.

To say that President Trump can be easily distracted would be an understatement. One former high-ranking government official, who met with Trump during the transition period to discuss a possible cabinet position, told me that their hour-long conversation was really a series of 60 one-minute conversations. This was because the President-elect's attention wandered constantly. Trump would ask a question and then less than a minute later would ask a completely unrelated question: "What do you think about climate change? Is NATO worth it? How big is an aircraft carrier?" This jibes with how others view Trump. One foreign diplomat who met with Trump later told BuzzFeed, "He just bombed us with questions: 'How many people do you have? What's your GDP? How much oil does [that country] produce? How many barrels a day? How much of it is yours?'"[2] Former George W. Bush economic advisor Lawrence Lindsay told GOP lawmakers that Trump had the long-term decision-making ability of "an empty chair."[3]

Conversations with some officials who have briefed Trump and others who are aware of how he absorbs information portray a president with a short attention span.

He likes single-page memos and visual aids like maps, charts, graphs and photos.

National Security Council officials have strategically included Trump's name in "as many paragraphs as we can because he keeps reading if he's mentioned," according to one source, who relayed conversations he had with NSC officials.

Steve Holland and Jeff Mason, "Embroiled in Controversies, Trump Seeks Boost on Foreign Trip," Reuters, May 17, 2017

Trump biographers and collaborators also stress this aspect of his behavior. Wayne Barrett, the author of *Trump: The Deals and the Downfall*, warned *Politico* that Trump "doesn't have the attention span" to handle the day-to-day rigors of the presidency.[4] Tim O'Brien told the *New York Times*, "The reason he gets surprised by these political problems is because he's not detail-oriented. He has a really short attention span, and he's profoundly impatient."[5] Tony Schwartz, who wrote Trump's *The Art of The Deal*, told the *New Yorker* that "if he had to be briefed on a crisis in the Situation Room, it's impossible to imagine him paying attention over a long period of time."[6]

The president often doesn't read the usual briefing books and relies on in-person briefings, the officials said, so aides also have written a list of tweet-length sentences that summarize the main points Trump could bring up with Putin.

Brian Bennett, "Stakes Are High for Trump's Meeting with Putin. Here's What to Expect," *Los Angeles Times*, July 4, 2017

In classified briefings, Trump would frequently flit between subjects. "We moved very quickly from news to intelligence to policy with very little clarity on which lanes we were in," said a U.S. official who took part in the briefings. "McMaster would act like the tangents didn't happen and go back to Point 2 on his card."

Trump had little time for in-depth briefings on Afghanistan's history, its complicated politics or its seemingly endless civil war. Even a single page of bullet points on the country seemed to tax the president's attention span on the subject, said senior White House officials.

"I call the president the two-minute man," said one Trump confidant. *"The president has patience for a half-page."*

Greg Jaffe and Philip Rucker, "National Security Adviser Attempts to Reconcile Trump's Competing Impulses on Afghanistan," *Washington Post,* **August 4, 2019**

"You have to understand that you are dealing with a guy whose most fundamental, minute-by-minute fear in life is of boredom," said a friend [of Trump's]. *"He's decided that the presidency is the best way in the world not to be bored."*

Howard Fineman, "The 'State' of Donald Trump? He Thinks It Couldn't Be Better." NBC News, January 30, 2018

Since Trump has been President, officials have also noted this toddler-like trait. Former FBI Director James Comey, in a January 2017 memorandum for the file, characterized a meeting with the President as "chaotic, with topics touched, left, then returned to later, making it very difficult to recount in a linear fashion." Comey concluded, "It really was a conversation-as-jigsaw-puzzle in a way, with pieces picked up, then discarded, then returned to."[7] Secretary of Defense James Mattis told colleagues that Trump was a good listener—unless you strayed onto one of his third rails, after which he was likely to go off on a tangent that would last a good long while.[8] GOP Senator Charles Grassley told reporters, "I'm not sure if you talk to him face to face, he hears everything you say."[9]

This is the life of a modern president of the United States in the month of December—and Donald Trump hates every minute of it. While he is known to enjoy hosting large social events and rallies, current and for-

mer White House staffers say he regards presidential Christmas parties with a special loathing and goes out of his way to escape early. . . .

*"It's just a lot," a senior White House official told me. "They're host-
ing all these people, half of whom they don't know," the official said.
"He just gets impatient. He likes to go go go. Sitting through things,
he gets restless."*

Olivia Nuzzi, "Donald Trump Hates Christmas Parties," *New York*, **December 17, 2018**

As Trump has been in office longer, the gripes about his
attention span from his own staff have grown louder. In *Fear*,
Bob Woodward recounted Gary Cohn complaining to White
House Staff Secretary Rob Porter:

> Things are just crazy here. They're so chaotic. He's never
> going to change. It's pointless to prepare a meaningful,
> substantive briefing for the president that's organized,
> where you have a bunch of slides. Because you know he's
> never going to listen. We're never going to get through it.
> He's going to get through the first 10 minutes and then
> he's going to want to start talking about some other topic.
> And so we're going to be there for an hour, but we're never
> going to get through this briefing.[10]

Trump's inability to demonstrate sustained focus on any
particular set of issues has had a pronounced effect on how
he has been staffed. The most obvious effect has been in the
way that subordinates have briefed the President on emergent
issues. Over the course of his presidency, his staff has contin-
ually reduced the amount of briefing materials, reduced the
length of briefings, and added as much visual material as possible. To be sure, the concise transmission of information is a
good thing regardless of who is the President. As the examples in this chapter demonstrate, however, Trump's briefings

have been far too brief. Even so, there is every indication that the Toddler in Chief does not do his homework and read his briefing books.[11] White House officials have acknowledged that Trump does not read even short memos. At one point Trump's Chief of Staff John Kelly, in response to a reporter's query about whether the President had read a particular 10-page memo, responded, "He has it. It's pretty lengthy. We'll get some people down to brief him on it."[12]

White House aides also have talked about having a rotating cast of staff brief the media, a group that could include officials such as national security adviser H. R. McMaster. Having several aides share the briefing responsibilities could help prevent Trump—who has a notoriously short attention span—from growing bored or angry with any one staff member."

John Wagner, Robert Costa, and Ashley Parker, "Trump Considers Major Changes amid Escalating Russia Crisis," *Washington Post*, May 27, 2017

For much of the past year, President Trump has declined to participate in a practice followed by the past seven of his predecessors: He rarely if ever reads the President's Daily Brief, a document that lays out the most pressing information collected by U.S. intelligence agencies from hot spots around the world.

Trump has opted to rely on an oral briefing of select intelligence issues in the Oval Office rather than getting the full written document delivered to review separately each day, according to three people familiar with his briefings.

Reading the traditionally dense intelligence book is not Trump's preferred "style of learning," according to a person with knowledge of the situation. . . .

Soon after Trump took office, analysts sought to tailor their intelligence sessions for a president with a famously short attention span, who is known for taking in much of his information from conservative

Fox News Channel hosts. The oral briefings were augmented with photos, videos and graphics.

Carol Leonnig, Shane Harris, and Greg Jaffe, "Breaking with Tradition, Trump Skips President's Written Intelligence Report and Relies on Oral Briefings," *Washington Post*, **February 9, 2018**

When Trump assumed office, N.S.C. staffers initially generated memos for him that resembled those produced for his predecessors: multipage explications of policy and strategy. But "an edict came down," a former staffer told me: "'Thin it out.'" The staff dutifully trimmed the memos to a single page. "But then word comes back: 'This is still too much.'" A senior Trump aide explained to the staffers that the President is "a visual person," and asked them to express points "pictorially."

"By the time I left, we had these cards," the former staffer said. They are long and narrow, made of heavy stock, and emblazoned with the words "THE WHITE HOUSE" at the top. Trump receives a thick briefing book every night, but nobody harbors the illusion that he reads it. Current and former officials told me that filling out a card is the best way to raise an issue with him in writing. *Everything that needs to be conveyed to the President must be boiled down, the former staffer said, to "two or three points, with the syntactical complexity of 'See Jane run.'"*

Patrick Radden Keefe, "McMaster and Commander," *New Yorker*, **April 23, 2018**

To be fair, Presidents have so much on their plate that reading even a 10-page memo comes with opportunity costs. It could be argued that brevity in briefing is not always a bad thing, and it forces staffers to distill their documents into the most vital briefs possible. The flaw in this argument is that Trump's knowledge deficits compound the problem of his short attention span.[13] More than any other President, Trump lacks the basic background information to understand the complexities of, say, health care policy or the history of US interventions in Latin America. Tony Schwartz's warning proved to be prescient; the 45th President cannot sit through a normal briefing, much less the lengthier-than-average briefings that he actually needs. Most of the time, the Toddler in Chief is operating on very little information, and he lacks the mental capacity to learn what he needs to learn in order to do his job properly.

How do you devise messaging for Trump, who will blow up the strategy without warning with a single early-morning tweet? "One hour you'll be talking about immigration reform. The next you'll be talking about the NFL. The next you'll be talking about gun policy. The next you'll be talking about tax cuts. And then, you know, circle back around to who lied on *Morning Joe* that day," a second former White House official told New York, comparing the experience in the press shop to being, "on speed."

Olivia Nuzzi, "Inside the Cutthroat Battle to Be the Next Hope Hicks," *New York*, March 28, 2018

Amid the scramble to put together the Kim profile [in the run-up to the Singapore summit], the U.S. officials said another challenge was determining how much information to give Trump—known to have little patience for detailed briefings or lengthy documents—and then persuading him not to act purely on gut instinct, as he often does with foreign leaders.

Briefers are expected to limit their presentation to an abridged version, accompanied by photos, maps, drawings and video, the officials said.

Matt Spetalnick, David Brunnstrom, and John Walcott, "Understanding Kim: Inside the U.S. Effort to Profile the Secretive North Korean Leader," Reuters, April 26, 2018

After arriving in Singapore on Sunday, an antsy and bored Trump urged his aides to demand that the meeting with Kim be pushed up by a day—to Monday—and had to be talked out of altering the long-planned and carefully negotiated summit date on the fly, according to two people familiar with preparations for the event.

"We're here now," the president said, according to the people. "Why can't we just do it?"

Ashley Parker, Josh Dawsey, Carol Leonnig, and Karen DeYoung, "'Why Can't We Just Do It?': Trump Nearly Upended Summit with Abrupt Changes," *Washington Post*, **June 14, 2018**

Because of the Toddler in Chief's inability to focus, staffers are unclear on which action items the President cares about and which are transient whims. Regardless of who occupies the Oval Office, all White House officials act to protect Presidents from their own worst impulses. A common tactic for staffs of modern Presidents, when their boss issues a dubious order, is to delay action to see if the President was serious or just in a bad mood. If a President truly cares about the subject, they will revisit it with follow-up requests.

Trump's short attention span, however, means that he is constantly popping off about a kaleidoscope of issues. Without any sustained focus, it is easy for bureaucratic actors to slow-walk or delay implementation of an idea to see if the President's attention shifts elsewhere. Indeed, Trump's White House staff has repeatedly used delaying tactics in response to direct orders; as the *Washington Post*'s Ashley Parker and Greg Jaffe reported in 2017: "In the White House, when advisors hope to prevent Trump from making what they think is an unwise decision, they frequently try to delay his final verdict—hoping he may reconsider after having time to calm down."[14] This delaying tactic makes sense for Trump's individual whims. Collectively, however, it leads to a dysfunctional administration. A repeated theme of this administration is the President's desire to do something, followed by staff inaction, followed by a tweet announcing a shift in policy, followed by staff confusion about what to do in response, and then the uncertainty of whether Trump will follow through or not. The result is a series of policy announcements that end with poor follow-through and bad implementation.[15]

A related problem is the difficulty of briefing the Toddler in Chief on salient issues if he is not interested in them. For example, according to the *New York Times*, Homeland Security officials were aware of a rising tide of white nationalism but could not brief the President about it: "Officials at the department have felt they could not broach topics like domestic terrorism and white supremacist violence with Mr. Trump because he was not interested in those concerns."[16] When then-DHS Secretary Kirstjen Nielsen sought to regularly brief the President on issues of domestic terrorism, the White House rebuffed her request.

During negotiation sessions, Trump's attention has veered wildly. At one such meeting with Pelosi and Schumer in the White House Situation Room earlier this month, the president went on a long diatribe about unrelated topics. He trashed the Iran nuclear deal, telling Democrats they should give him money for the wall because, in his view, they gave President Barack Obama money for the agreement with Tehran. He boasted about his wisdom in ordering the withdrawal of U.S. troops from Syria. And he raised the specter of impeachment, accusing Pelosi of wanting to try to force him from office—which she denied.

Eventually, he was moved back to the budget talks.

Robert Costa, Josh Dawsey, Philip Rucker, and Seung Min Kim, "'In the White House Waiting': Inside Trump's Defiance on the Longest Shutdown Ever," *Washington Post*, **January 12, 2019**

At times, Trump evinced less rage than a lack of interest. Sims recounts one time when Ryan was in the Oval Office explaining the ins and outs of the Republican health-care bill to the president. As Ryan droned on for 15 minutes, Trump sipped on a glass of Diet Coke, peered out at the Rose Garden, stared aimlessly at the walls and, finally, walked out.

Ryan kept talking as the president wandered down the hall to his private dining room, where he flicked on his giant flat-screen TV. Apparently, he had had enough of Ryan's talk. It fell to Vice President Pence to retrieve Trump and convince him to return to the Oval Office so they could continue their strategy session.

Philip Rucker, "'Absolutely Out of Control': Cliff Sims's Book Depicts Life in Trump's White House," *Washington Post*, **January 21, 2019**

Mulvaney told donors about his instructions to one White House policy adviser, who was scheduled to brief the president on budget cuts, government spending and regulations. Mulvaney warned that no one gets through a presentation without being interrupted multiple times by the president.

This official did manage to deliver his full briefing, Mulvaney told the crowd. But instead of asking a follow-up question, Trump asked the White House aide who he would be in the world, if he could be anyone — himself or, say, Tiger Woods?

Nancy Cook, "Ivanka Tells Donors She Got Her Moral Compass from Her Dad," *Politico*, **September 13, 2019**

Finally, on the global stage, Trump's short attention span has been a diplomatic disaster. Part of the President's job is to attend summits, meet with heads of state, and participate in other ceremonial functions. For Trump, this means having to sit through other leaders giving speeches. Trump's inability to sit still and focus, however, hurts US standing in two ways. First, Trump's short attention span means he can miss nuanced shifts in another country's position on an issue. Second, Trump's restlessness can often lead to violations of diplomatic protocol, which other foreign leaders view as a sign of disrespect. For example, at the June 2018 NATO Summit, the *New York Times* reported that "during the middle of a speech by Ms. Merkel, Mr. Trump again broke protocol by getting up and leaving, sending ripples of shock across the room, according to American and European officials who were there."[17] Trump's awkward first visit with Queen Elizabeth II generated similar reactions. Unfortunately, given the Toddler in Chief's short attention span, he is unlikely to factor in the perceptions of others when he violates protocol.

From the start of Trump's presidency, the CIA and the Office of the Director of National Intelligence began streamlining the PDB [Presidential Daily Brief], reducing it to a collection of bullet points and images or graphics. U.S. officials have made additional adaptations over the past two years.

They generally refrain from sending analysts who are deep experts on a specific subject, instead dispatching generalists for meetings with a president whose attention tends to wander.

Analysts have learned to emphasize economic issues that resonate with Trump and to employ eye-catching graphics. Even so, briefers often return from the White House voicing concern.

"Either it doesn't resonate or there is a lack of comprehension," the U.S. official said. "You feel frustration and helplessness in a way. What else can you do?"

Greg Miller, "Gap Continues to Widen between Trump and Intelligence Community on Key Issues," *Washington Post*, **December 11, 2018**

Summer arrives this week with [Venezuelan president Nicolás] Maduro still in place, and little indication that he is imminently on his way out, or that the Trump administration has a coherent strategy to remove him. The president, officials said, is losing both patience and interest in Venezuela. . . .

Trump has clearly been frustrated about a foreign policy issue he "always thought of ... as low-hanging fruit" on which he "could get a win and tout it as a major foreign policy victory," the former official said. "Five or six months later ... it's not coming together."

Since early last month, Trump has rarely spoken publicly about Venezuela or his "all options" promise to use military force if necessary to achieve U.S. goals there.

Karen DeYoung and Josh Dawsey, "With Maduro Entrenched in Venezuela, Trump Loses Patience and Interest in Issue, Officials Say," *Washington Post***, June 19, 2019**

[CIA Director Gina] Haspel has often joined Coats and a career senior intelligence official in the Oval Office for the president's intelligence briefings, semi-regular sessions that bear little resemblance to the deep dives on pressing issues that earlier presidents have taken. According to officials familiar with the briefings, Haspel and company boil them down to a few key points that they think Trump absolutely needs to know. Trump favors pictures and graphics over text. And Haspel is careful not to contradict the president or argue with him about his opinions.

Shane Harris, "The Quiet Director: How Gina Haspel Manages the CIA's Volatile Relationship with Trump," *Washington Post***, July 30, 2019**

The biggest problem with Trump's short attention span? He will be incapable of paying attention to anyone who tells him that his short attention span is a real problem.

In his new role, Coats was responsible for walking a president he hardly knew through his daily intelligence briefing. He quickly found his boss had a short attention span for the information he was providing, current and former administration officials said. Coats struggled with how to respond when Trump veered off on unrelated tangents or bluntly disagreed with the intelligence he presented—as he often did, the current and former senior administration officials said.

Coats found it particularly hard to hide his exasperation with Trump's insistence in the weeks after taking office that Obama had wiretapped him during the 2016 campaign, according to the officials. Over and over again Trump raised the issue, and over and over Coats told him he wasn't wiretapped, officials said, but the president didn't want to hear it.

"It was a recurring thing and began early on," a senior administration official who observed the exchanges said. *"You could tell that Coats thought the president was crazy."*

Carol E. Lee and Courtney Kube, "Mike Pence Talked Dan Coats Out of Quitting the Trump Administration," NBC News, March 28, 2019

CHAPTER THREE

Poor Impulse Control

From the child's perspective, these are the terrific twos because they are so excited about all the new things they are able to do developmentally. It's as if they are saying 'Look what I can do!' As a result, all toddlers get frustrated at anyone or anything limiting their ability to do what they wish to do, even if they are not capable of it. This lack of independence leads to immediate and intense frustration and loss of control.

AMERICAN ACADEMY OF PEDIATRICS,
CARING FOR YOUR BABY AND YOUNG CHILD

The Twitter disruptions were emblematic of a president operating on a tornado of impulses—and with no clear strategy—as he faces some of the most consequential decisions of his presidency, including Syria, trade policy and the Russian interference probe that threatens to overwhelm his administration. . . .

Senior U.S. officials describe a president who is operating largely on impulse, with little patience for the advice of his top aides. *"A decision or statement is made by the president, and then the principals—Mattis or Pompeo or Kelly—come in and tell him we can't do it,"* said one senior administration official. *"When that fails, we reverse-engineer a policy process to match whatever the president said."*

Ashley Parker, Seung Min Kim, and Philip Rucker, "Trump Chooses Impulse over Strategy as Crises Mount," *Washington Post*, **April 12, 2018**

In 2017 Kellyanne Conway, counselor to the President, told White House reporters that that "the hallmark of leadership is a deliberative process, not an impulsive reaction."[1] Unfortunately, it would appear that Conway failed to impart that advice to President Trump. A consistent feature of the Toddler in Chief's leadership style has been to act on impulse. Jack O'Donnell, the former President of the Trump Plaza Hotel and Casino in Atlantic City, told reporters that during his business career, "When he's under pressure is when he tends to do this impulsive stuff."[2] Trump biographer Tim O'Brien observes that Trump "doesn't regulate his own emotions, he's not a disciplined thinker." He further warned, "Donald lacks any kind of sophisticated strategic planning. I think he's simply a force of nature. He's Mr. Id, and he just plows forward into any situation in which he can get attention."[3] GOP strategist Rick Wilson put it more pungently: "Donald Trump has the attention span of a gnat on meth. If he was stonked to the gills on Adderall, he might achieve the attention span of a toddler."[4]

Trump would impulsively want to fire someone like Attorney General Jeff Sessions; create a new, wide-ranging policy with far-flung implications, like increasing tariffs on Chinese steel imports; or end a decades-old deal like the North American Free Trade Agreement. Enraged with a TV segment or frustrated after a meandering meeting, the president would order it done immediately.

Delaying the decision would give Priebus and others a chance to change his mind or bring in advisers to speak with Trump—and in some cases, to ensure Trump would drop the idea altogether and move on. . . .

Trump would sometimes lash out at Priebus for not doing what he wanted immediately, though, several officials said.

Josh Dawsey, "White House Aides Lean on Delays and Distraction to Manage Trump," *Politico*, **October 9, 2017**

Indeed, for Trump this style of leadership is a feature, not a bug. In a November 2018 interview with the *Washington Post*, he said, "I have a gut, and my gut tells me more sometimes than anybody else's brain can ever tell me."[5] President Trump's supporters and opponents alike have described him as a "gut politician." Trump's trust in his own instincts and impulses is so strong that it has profoundly shaped how his White House operates. Trump disdains any form of strategic planning. As one of his advisors explained, "He gets frustrated when there *is* a plan. He's not a guy who likes a plan. . . . There's an animosity towards planning, and there's a desire to pick fights that have nothing to do with us."[6] There have been very few instances during Trump's presidency in which one can identify a deliberative policy process at work.[7] Gérard Araud, the former French ambassador to the United States, concluded that "the interagency process [is] totally broken and decisions [are] taken from the hip basically."[8] Many of Trump's high-profile decisions—renouncing the Iran deal, withdrawing forces from Syria, his summits with North Korean leader Kim Jong Un, the government shutdown—were made impulsively.

The former official pointed to another time when Trump surprised his advisers by levying tariffs: In March 2018, in off-the-cuff remarks during a meeting with steel and aluminum executives, Trump announced the beginning of a global trade war by promising a 25 percent tariff on steel imports and a 10 percent tariff on aluminum imports. In this case, the former official said, Trump's snap decision was not so much a way to distract from a particular news cycle as it was the result of *"feeling good in the moment"* as he bantered cheerfully with the executives.

Elaina Plott, "Trump's Two Crutches," *Atlantic,* **June 4, 2019**

White House officials often refer to the *"shiny-object phenomenon"* when discussing the president or those closest to him—the tendency for Trump and Kushner, mainly, to find themselves consumed by whatever the hot topic of the day is, and not much else.

Elaina Plott and Peter Nicholas, "How a Forgotten White House Team Gained Power in the Trump Era," *Atlantic,* **June 27, 2019**

One could argue that there are moments when a political leader—or any human being, for that matter—is better off acting on gut instinct. In crisis situations, leaders often need to make decisions with incomplete information. Acting decisively can be superior to a long, deliberative process. A quick decision can be more valuable than making a better choice after it is too late. If a bear is charging my campground, I am better off immediately fleeing the scene than wasting precious seconds contemplating which items from the campground I should take with me.

That said, impulse control is a key marker for emotional and intellectual maturity. An important part of growing up is the development of "executive functioning," defined in the psychology literature as "a range of assumed higher order cortical functions, such as goal-directed behavior, attentional control, temporal organization and planning."[9] A key component of executive functioning is inhibition: "one's ability to deliberately inhibit dominant, autonomic, or prepotent responses when necessary."[10] In other words, impulse control. An inability to demonstrate impulse control implies that the person in question does not possess significant executive functioning abilities.[11] Limited executive functioning also retards an individual's ability to develop a theory of mind—a trait that is essential for an individual's ability to critically assess and evaluate new information.[12] As I discuss in the concluding chapter, Trump's poor impulse control helps to explain his malformed theory of mind.

What is true for human development in general holds with even greater force for political leaders. A hallmark of political leadership is resisting emotional impulses long enough to think through the implications of rash actions. For one thing, sometimes the impulse is wrong, or premised on biased information. Most adults can think of decisions they made in haste or things they said in the heat of the moment that they wish they could take back. A good decision-making process leads to fewer poor decisions, and lower political costs for decisions that play out badly. A bad decision is a bad decision, but if the decision-making process is viewed as sound, politicians can pay less of a price. If leaders say or do something that turns out to have been a mistake, they can at least fall back on the strength of the decision-making process to justify or explain their actions. An impulsive act, on the other hand, automatically places all the political burden on the decision-maker. Sometimes those gut instincts can work. If they do not, leaders have no one to blame but themselves.

"No one knows what to expect from him anymore," one former White House official, who spoke on the condition of anonymity to discuss internal conversations about the president, told Insider.

They added: "His mood changes from one minute to the next based on some headline or tweet, and the next thing you know his entire schedule gets tossed out the window because he's losing his s---."
Sonam Sheth, "'He's Losing His S---': Trump's Advisers Are Increasingly Worried about His Mental State following Days of Erratic Behavior," *Business Insider*, September 6, 2019

Another source . . . said that some around the president anticipate he will engage in more "impulsive" behavior, with pressure expected to build on him daily during the impeachment inquiry.

That's sparking worries that Trump could display increasingly unpredictable behavior and lash out in unexpected ways — both a presidential and a political concern in an election year.

Shannon Pettypiece, Kristen Welker, Hallie Jackson and Carol E. Lee, "'Total Panic' as 'Shell-Shocked' White House Struggles to Find Impeachment Footing," NBC News, September 26, 2019

President Trump's own top aides didn't think he fully understood what he had done last Sunday, when he fired off a trio of racist tweets before a trip to his golf course. . . .

As is often the case, Trump acted alone—impulsively following his gut to the dark side of American politics, and now the country would have to pick up the pieces. The day before, on the golf course, he hadn't brought it up. Over the coming days, dozens of friends, advisers and political allies would work behind the scenes to try to fix the mess without any public admission of error because that was not the Trump way.

Michael Scherer, Josh Dawsey, Ashley Parker, and Seung Min Kim, "'He Always Doubles Down': Inside the Political Crisis Caused by Trump's Racist Tweets," *Washington Post,* **July 21, 2019**

Emotional impulses can cloud cost-benefit analyses, a fact that has debilitated even the most successful Presidents. In 1985, Ronald Reagan met with the families of US hostages being held in Lebanon. His staff had assiduously tried to avoid these meetings; they were worried that Reagan would become so emotionally affected that he would demand an ill-conceived policy response. Both Reagan's biographer and his National Security Advisor concluded that this meeting led the President to endorse the arms-for-hostages approach to Iran.[13] This mushroomed into Iran-Contra, a scandal that derailed most of Reagan's second term. Poor impulse control affects even the best leaders; it eviscerates poor leaders.

A political leader with poor impulse control will likely prove to be a bad negotiator. Many bargaining strategies require a leader to act in a strategic manner and conceal one's tactics and preferences. A leader with poor impulse control, however, will often reveal their preferences because they simply cannot restrain themselves. Trump has done this on numerous occasions. The most prominent example would be Afghanistan. The Trump administration has been negotiating with the Taliban for an orderly withdrawal of most US troops. The problem for US negotiators, however, is that the Toddler in Chief cannot keep quiet about what he wants. According to *Politico*, "His public statements and leaks of his closed-door demands have weakened the hand of his negotiators by making it clear just how desperately the president wants a deal." One observer of the negotiations confirmed, "The Taliban have been rather rude with the US throughout the peace process because they have the impression that a withdrawal deal is a desperate desire of the USA, not the Taliban."[14] Senior advisors, including H. R. McMaster and Mike Pompeo, have vented to colleagues that their best-laid plans are often blown up from a single Trump tweet.[15] If international negotiations are like a high-stakes game of poker, Trump is the kind of person who bluffs and then loudly tells the other players, "I'm bluffing."

As President Trump appears to lurch from crisis to crisis on the world stage, Defense Secretary James N. Mattis and Secretary of State Rex Tillerson have quietly maneuvered to constrain an impulsive commander in chief, the latest sign of a national security team that is increasingly challenging the president.

Officials say the two senior Cabinet officers have slow-rolled requests for options on a wide range of policy goals, including exiting the Iran nuclear disarmament deal, reacting to missile strikes into Saudi Arabia by Iran-backed rebels in Yemen, pressuring longtime ally Pakistan by cutting U.S. military aid, and possible limited airstrikes on North Korea's nuclear infrastructure. . . .

"They are going to hide the ball from the president to keep him from doing stupid [stuff], there's no doubt about it," said another former official, a national security expert who served in the Trump administration transition and asked not to be identified discussing internal deliberations.

Brian Bennett, "McMaster Caught in the Middle as Mattis and Tillerson Maneuver to Constrain Trump on National Security Issues," *Los Angeles Times*, March 4, 2018

Another reason for politicians to keep their impulses under control is that leadership requires some degree of long-term thinking, and a lack of impulse control cuts against that vision. Even a self-interested focus on reelection usually requires a President to think months or years into the future. A decision that feels and looks good in the moment can boomerang in the medium to long run. Trump's initial claims, for example, that his administration competently handled Hurricane Maria in Puerto Rico failed to hold up over time. One study revealed that the estimated number of deaths to be more than 70 times the official estimate.[16] In response, Trump tried to deny the validity of the study, a claim that even his close political allies rejected.[17] Since then, Trump has had to face repeated negative news cycles about his alleged vindictiveness toward the commonwealth.[18] A similar dynamic played out in Trump's 2019 attacks on minority Democratic members of Congress. Trump's own staffers scoffed at the media speculation that these attacks were a political strategy; they knew that this was Trump acting on impulse.[19] This leads to an additional problem for Presidents with poor impulse control: it is easy to ensnare them in fights that they should avoid. A President's bully pulpit can dominate and frame debates in the media. Used adroitly, that is an important tool of power for any President. If someone has poor impulse control, however, then they can be goaded into engaging in disputes and debates that do not help their political fortunes. One of the reasons Democrats won the 2018/19 government shutdown stand-off was that Senate Minority Leader Chuck Schumer goaded Trump into taking ownership of it.[20]

Per source, Trump was "mostly aggravated with Schumer," the fellow New Yorker, and his refusal to look at POTUS while directing his comments to the pool cameras. Aides, however, were more rattled that he'd just accepted responsibility for a possible shutdown. . . . Very little of substance took place after the pool cameras were finally ushered out. *"Once the president has been aggravated to that level, there's no coming back from that and re-focusing."*
Los Angeles Times Reporter Eli Stokols (@EliStokols), Twitter, December 11, 2018, 5:17 p.m.

Trump's short attention span often plays hand-in-hand with this lack of impulse control, as when he disrupts news cycles that are favorable to him. After the Barr summary of the Mueller report revealed that the special counsel would not charge Trump with a crime, the President seemed to be catching a positive wave. He pivoted quickly to health care, however, stepping on favorable headlines and creating new controversies.[21] Worse, Trump can "extend the shelf life" of a scandal, in the words of his own staff, because he cannot help but talk about it in his interactions with the press.[22] This happened in the wake of his August 2017 Charlottes-ville comments, his bigoted comments about four freshman Democrats in the summer of 2019, and his errant hurricane warning to the state of Alabama in September 2019.

This dynamic has also played out in reaction to every book from a reporter or White House staffer that criticizes Trump. Prudently, Trump's staff has not wanted him to engage with the news cycles covering these book releases, because doing so would only extend the coverage. In every instance, however—from Michael Wolff's *Fire and Fury* to James Comey's *A Higher Loyalty* to Omarosa Maningault Newman's *Unhinged* to Bob Woodward's *Fear* to Cliff Sims's *Team of Vipers*—Trump surrendered to his impulse to fight back. In each case, he elevated a book that might have lasted only one news cycle into a narrative lasting weeks.

Perhaps the most important reason for leaders to avoid acting on impulse is that such moves undercut their ability to make credible commitments. In both domestic politics and foreign policy, a leader's word matters a great deal. Contrary to folk wisdom, leaders rarely lie in world politics, because they do not want to damage their reputation in international negotiations.[23] Trump's impulse control has been so poor that foreign diplomats have learned to discount many of his threats. As one Mexican diplomat put it, "He has shown us that what's black at 9 a.m. can be gray at 3 p.m. and white at 7 p.m."[24] Similarly, in domestic politics, leaders cannot impulsively change their minds if legislators have expended political capital to endorse a now-outdated position. Members of Congress do not want to cast unpopular votes and then learn that the President has pulled the rug out from under them.

Trump's advisers have at times tried to curb his media appearances, worried he will step on his message. "They were not helpful to us," one senior administration official said. "There was no point to do all of them."

White House officials said privately there was no broader strategy behind the interviews. GOP strategists and Capitol Hill aides were puzzled by it all. "I have no idea what they view as a successful media hit," said one senior GOP consultant with close ties to the administration. *"He just seemed to go crazy today,"* a senior GOP aide said.

Josh Dawsey, "Trump's Dizzying Day of Interviews," Politico, May 1, 2017

Even under normal circumstances, members of Congress like to have policy and political certainty from a president, especially chief executives of the same party. Trump's habit of changing his mind after giving his blessing to an emerging deal, or a piece of legislation—often based on conversations with family members or allies outside the White House—is unnerving for GOP lawmakers.

David M. Drucker, "Republicans' Frustration with Trump Resurfaces over Immigration," *Washington Examiner*, June 22, 2018

Trump's increasingly erratic behavior over the past 12 days—since he first threatened to seal the border in a series of tweets on March 29—has alarmed top Republicans, business officials and foreign leaders who fear that his emotional response might exacerbate problems at the border, harm the U.S. economy and degrade national security.

David Nakamura, Josh Dawsey, and Seung Min Kim, "Twelve Days of Chaos: Inside the Trump White House's Growing Panic to Contain the Border Crisis," *Washington Post*, April 9, 2019

Little wonder, then, that Trump's lack of impulse control has exasperated GOP lawmakers. In early 2018 Charlie Dent, then a GOP House Representative, told the Associated Press, "The spontaneity and lack of impulse control are areas of concern for lots of members on both sides of the aisle. Disorder, chaos, instability, uncertainty, intemperate statements are not conservative virtues in my opinion "[25] In early 2019, Senate Majority Whip John Cornyn said about the Toddler in Chief: "It's always difficult when the person you're negotiating with is someone who changes their mind."[26] Trump's impulsive moves have shredded his credibility even within his own party's caucus in Congress.[27]

Trump's lack of impulse control has clearly affected the way he has been staffed. Trump chafes at being "handled," but as the examples in this chapter demonstrate, his closest staffers do not trust him to be alone with negotiating partners, for fear that he will impulsively agree to a deal that is not in his best interests. The examples range from Trump's meetings with congressional Democrats to his meetings with Russian dignitaries to his summits with North Korean ruler Kim Jong Un. Similarly, congressional leaders take pains to praise Trump in their interactions. As GOP political consultant Rick Wilson explains, "Their praise of Trump isn't some esoteric mystery; it's the cost of doing business and a way of distracting the Toddler in Chief with shiny objects."[28]

There is a growing sense that Mr. Trump seems unwilling or unable to do the things necessary to keep himself out of trouble and that the presidency has done little to tame a shoot-from-the-hip-into-his-own-foot style that characterized his campaign.

Some of Mr. Trump's senior advisers fear leaving him alone in meetings with foreign leaders out of concern he might speak out of turn.

Glenn Thrush and Maggie Haberman, "At a Besieged White House, Tempers Flare and Confusion Swirls," *New York Times*, May 16, 2017

Perhaps the greatest example of Trump's poor impulse control has been his use of Twitter. Trump himself has acknowledged that some of his tweets have not been "Presidential"—and yet he frequently crosses the line anyway.[29] The instantaneous nature of Twitter makes it almost impossible for Trump to contain himself. In his first year in office, Reince Priebus and Hope Hicks attempted to create a White House committee to compose Trump's tweets, but that idea quickly foundered.[30] In multiple instances, a planned formal announcement was scrambled because Trump had tweeted the news out prematurely.[31] In July 2019, the President announced ICE raids of major cities in advance, thereby putting potential targets on notice. Trump's tweets were so unprecedented that the Acting DHS Secretary pushed to delay the raids.[32]

One senior official noted that though some of the president's outbursts on the issue have seemed "nutty," this kind of public behavior and feuding on the president's part are all but expected and "standard." Another official simply observed that @realDonaldTrump's NFL-related tantrums were less likely to cause an international incident than tweets about Kim Jong Un.

Asawin Suebsaeng, "Team Trump Forced to Defend His 'Nutty' NFL Tweets ... Again," *Daily Beast*, **September 24, 2017**

Numerous GOP officials have complained about Trump's tweets. US Representative Mike Simpson told the *Wall Street Journal* in 2017, "Most of us are tired of apologizing for the tweets that he sends out every day and trying to defend him."[33] Priebus explained to the *New York Times*, "I told him, 'Some of it's not helpful, it causes distraction. We can get thrown off our message by tweeting things that aren't the issues of the day.' ... Everybody tried at different times to cool down the Twitter habit—but no one could do it. Not me, Jared, Ivanka, Hope."[34] Even in a polarized country, an overwhelming majority of Americans disapprove of Trump's use of Twitter. An August 2017 Marist poll found that 72 percent of Americans believed Trump's communication through Twitter to be "reckless and distracting." An October 2017 Quinnipiac poll found that 70 percent of Americans wanted Trump to stop tweeting from his personal account. A May 2018 Morning Consult poll found that 72 percent of Americans believed that Trump's use of Twitter was excessive—including 58 percent of Republicans.[35]

In some instances, information has been withheld from

Trump for fear that he would blurt it out to interlocutors or on Twitter. When Gary Cohn was running the National Economic Council, he kept jobs numbers from the President until just before they were announced publicly in order to avoid such incidents. After Cohn departed, the President did indeed prematurely announce jobs numbers by tweet, in June 2018. A Trump ally acknowledged to the *Wall Street Journal* that this was due to "a breakdown in [Trump's] conduct."[36] Deputy White House Chief of Staff Joe Hagin kept sensitive logistical details about key summits from the President because of concerns that the Toddler in Chief might tweet about them and upend plans.[37]

Several advisers and others close to Trump said they wouldn't be surprised if Trump gave information he shouldn't have [to Russia dignitaries in the Oval Office].

One adviser who often speaks to the president said the conversation was likely freewheeling in the Oval Office, and he probably wanted to impress the officials.

"He doesn't really know any boundaries. He doesn't think in those terms," this adviser said. "He doesn't sometimes realize the implications of what he's saying."

Josh Dawsey, Eliana Johnson, and Josh Meyer, "Trump's Handling of Classified Info Brings New Chaos to White House," *Politico,* **May 15, 2017**

The result is the worst of all worlds: a President who is ill-informed, reacting impulsively to events rather than planning ahead.

CHAPTER FOUR

Oppositional Behavior

When your three-year-old is faced with specific learning challenges, you'll find her reasoning still rather one-sided. She can't yet see an issue from two angles, nor can she solve problems that require her to look at more than one factor at the same time.

AMERICAN ACADEMY OF PEDIATRICS,
CARING FOR YOUR BABY AND YOUNG CHILD

Aides say the quickest way to get Trump to do something is to tell him he can't, or argue that it's contrary to tradition.

Mike Allen, "How Trump Thinks about Pardons," Axios, July 23, 2017

Trump's 2016 campaign staff developed an unofficial diagnosis, "defiance disorder," to describe Trump's inclination to ignore the collective advice of his advisors and double down on whatever counterproductive gambit he had settled on. As Fox News' Howard Kurtz noted in his book on Trump and his advisors, "Whenever Trump went off script, the coverage was often universally negative. Most politicians would backtrack, admit error, or change the subject. Trump invariably dug in his heels."[1] Similarly, *New York Times* reporter Maggie Haberman, the print journalist who knows Trump the best, tweeted in June 2017 about Trump's oppositional behavior: "Trump doesn't want to be controlled. In [the] campaign,

[he] would often do opposite of what he was advised to do, simply because it was opposite."[2]

A senior White House official once [said] there are three ways to get Trump to do something, all of which we're seeing this week (with his tariffs announcement as well):

Tell him it's never been done before.

Tell him the lawyers would never allow it.

Tell him the establishment would go crazy.

Jonathan Swan and Mike Allen, "Trump's Highest-Stakes Improvisation," Axios, March 9, 2018

Oppositional behavior is also a common toddler trait.[3] As one book of parenting advice notes, "Toddlers tend to hear strongly worded commands as something to DO. If you yell, 'Stop running around the pool!' what is likely to register with your toddler is: 'Run around the pool!'"[4] Putting it more bluntly, *The Daily Show's* Trevor Noah said, "This whole thing with Trump leads me to a question: have you ever argued with a toddler? . . . Toddlers will say the most outlandish shit and the more you argue with them, the more they become entrenched in their views."[5]

Trump's oppositional behavior could be related to his deep reluctance to take responsibility for mistakes. Trump biographer Michael D'Antonio explained to the *Washington Post* that the 45th President has possessed this trait since he was a small child. In grade school, he would continue to act out even if teachers complained about his behavior: "He has always—always—been terrified of having been found to be responsible for something, and the pursuit of alternative explanations has been intense at every step of his life. There had to be a conspiracy at work, some criminality, some hidden hand."[6]

It could also be related to Trump's implicit theory of power. According to Bob Woodward, White House Staff Secretary Rob Porter "observed that anytime anybody challenged Trump—in a policy debate, in court, in the public square—his natural instinct seemed to be that if he was not exerting strength, he was failing."[7] This belief forces Trump to stand firm even when he is factually wrong or has made a catastrophic error in political judgment. For Trump, doubling down on a wrong decision can also be a display of power. To some, the fact that he can persist in a poor decision for a sustained period is evidence of his power and will.

"We will have to see what Trump does when he returns to the United States because he is distracted at the moment," the Republican said. *"One can imagine he is going to weigh in the opposite of what the establishment wants [Roy] Moore to do."*
Sarah Westwood, "All Eyes on Trump as Roy Moore Allegations Pile Up," *Washington Examiner*, **November 14, 2017**

President Trump has long mused about doing what he wants, when he wants, how he wants. He wanted tariffs on steel and aluminum—big ones—now. He wanted to negotiate with Congress—in public, on his court, surprise and shock, all for the cameras. He wanted to ditch any P.C. pretenses and consider Singapore-style death for all drug dealers. He wanted to play by his rules alone. . . .

His staff at times managed to talk him off the ledge. No more. Tired of the restraints, tired of his staff, Trump is reveling in ticking off just about every person who serves him.
Mike Allen and Jonathan Swan, "Man of Steel: Trump's Secret Fantasies Realized," Axios, March 2, 2018

The president's decision last Thursday to announce steep new tariffs on aluminum and steel—and gleefully tout a possible trade war—

caught almost his entire team, including some of his top trade advisers, by surprise.

Earlier in the week, Cohn was telling people he was going to continue stalling Trump on tariffs. He described the tariffs as "obviously stupid," in the recollection of one person who spoke to him.

"Gary said to him, you can't do this, you can't do that," a senior administration official said. "The more you tell him that, the more he is going to do what he wants to do."

Philip Rucker, Ashley Parker, and Josh Dawsey, "'Pure Madness': Dark Days inside the White House as Trump Shocks and Rages," *Washington Post,* **March 3, 2018**

One could make a case that among Trump's toddler traits, oppositional behavior might be the most useful for exercising political leadership. A common trope in the political psychology literature is about the dangers of "groupthink" among policymaking elites.[8] Groupthink occurs when policymakers form an unspoken consensus about a policy problem, causing them to stifle their own objections and ostracize officials who do dissent. This can lead political leaders to agree to policy recommendations that have not been fully vetted. During the Cuban Missile Crisis, President Kennedy resisted his advisors' consensus recommendation to launch an airstrike on Cuba, thereby successfully defusing a crisis that could have resulted in the exchange of nuclear weapons. One can argue that some of the biggest US policy miscues of the past half-century—Vietnam and Iraq—were made under conditions of groupthink.

Indeed, one of the few core themes of Trump's 2016 campaign was his desire to disrupt the consensus of elite policymakers. In his most significant foreign policy speech during the campaign, Trump argued, "It's time to shake the rust off America's foreign policy. It's time to invite new voices and new visions into the fold." He went on to state that his foreign policy advisors would not be "those who have perfect résumés but very little to brag about except responsibility for a long history of failed policies and continued losses at war."[9] An oppositional thinker can shatter a failed policy consensus. Only Trump would have met with North Korean dictator Kim Jong Un without any preconditions or called off an airstrike on Iran that his entire national security team supported.

President Trump did not follow specific warnings from his national security advisers Tuesday when he congratulated Russian President Vladimir Putin on his reelection—including a section in his briefing materials in all-capital letters stating "DO NOT CONGRATULATE," according to officials familiar with the call.

Trump also chose not to heed talking points from aides instructing him to condemn the recent poisoning of a former Russian spy in Britain with a powerful nerve agent, a case that both the British and U.S. governments have blamed on Moscow.

Carol Leonnig, David Nakamura, and Josh Dawsey, "Trump's National Security Advisers Warned Him Not to Congratulate Putin. He Did It Anyway." *Washington Post,* **March 20, 2018**

"If you go into a meeting and say we can't do that, or that's not the way it's been done, you can be assured he's going to want to do it," says one senior National Security Council official. *"He thinks the way it's been done is wrong and stupid and won't work."* But lately Trump has become increasingly energized by the idea that he's shattering precedent, and feels vindicated by the results of his risky moves, according to interviews with more than a dozen friends, aides and former officials.

Brian Bennett, "This Is What Trump's Impulsive Diplomacy Looks Like," *Time,* **June 14, 2018**

The episode at the G-20 conference, an annual gathering of the world's 20 biggest economies, will do nothing to ease the long-standing perception that Trump is too friendly toward Russia—a relationship that has alarmed Democrats and Republicans alike and led to congressional investigations.

But it could have been expected, according to his current and former advisers. Trump often bristles at being told what to say or do, they say. So when pushed, the president simply mocks what is expected of him, even when it comes to Russia.

And each time he refuses to conform to expected behavior toward Russia, it inevitably causes a firestorm in Washington.

Anita Kumar, "Trump Can't Help Himself When It Comes to Putin," *Politico*, **June 28, 2019**

There are considerable downsides to Trump's strain of oppositional behavior, however. For one thing, it permits the President to develop and cement a misperception despite all evidence to the contrary. Beliefs about issues on which there is a range of disagreement are one thing; beliefs about facts not in evidence are another thing entirely. Trump's oppositional thinking makes it particularly difficult to combat his predilection for conspiracy theories. Trump started his political career by erroneously claiming that Barack Obama was not born in the United States. He has articulated a variety of other crackpot theories during his political career. These include the notion that vaccines cause autism and other health issues, that Senator Ted Cruz's father was involved in the Kennedy assassination, and that the Chinese had fabricated climate change to gain a competitive edge over the US economy.[10]

Throughout his presidency, Trump has articulated false beliefs and refused to acknowledge his errors. Trump has persisted in the claim that millions of votes were cast fraudulently in 2016. He has insisted to friends that it was not his voice on the infamous *Access Hollywood* tape.[11] He told GOP fundraisers that he had not called Apple CEO Tim Cook "Tim Apple," despite video evidence to the contrary.[12] He has insisted that wind turbines cause cancer, and that regulations make highways too curvy.[13] Trump has claimed to confidants that his actual poll numbers are 20 percent higher than what has been published. When these friends have pushed back on this notion, Trump has simply tuned them out.[14] These are only the most obvious of the thousands of times Trump has made demonstrably false statements.[15] One person close to Trump explained it simply: "Trump doesn't deal in reality. He creates his own reality and he actually believes it."[16] Former White House Communications Director Anthony Scaramucci acknowledged that Trump "definitely has a reality distortion field around himself where he curves facts toward himself."[17]

The U.S. official said Trump was specifically briefed not to raise the issue [of invading Venezuela] and told it wouldn't play well, but the first thing the president said at the dinner [with four Latin American presidents] was, "My staff told me not to say this." Trump then went around asking each leader if they were sure they didn't want a military solution, according to the official, who added that each leader told Trump in clear terms they were sure.

Eventually, McMaster would pull aside the president and walk him through the dangers of an invasion, the official said.

Joshua Goodman, "Trump Pressed Aides on Venezuela Invasion, US Official Says," Associated Press, July 4, 2018

Ahead of the meeting, staffers provided Trump with some 100 pages of briefing materials aimed at laying out a tough posture toward Putin, but the president ignored most of it, according to one person familiar with the discussions, who spoke on the condition of anonymity to disclose internal deliberations. Trump's remarks were "very much counter to the plan," the person said.

"Everyone around Trump" was urging him to take a firm stance with Putin, according to a second person familiar with the preparations. Before Monday's meeting, the second person said, advisers covered matters from Russia's annexation of Crimea to its interference in the U.S. elections, but Trump "made a game-time decision" to handle the summit his way. . . .

The spectacle in Helsinki also underscored Trump's eagerness to disregard his own advisers, his willingness to flout the conclusions of his own intelligence community—that Russia interfered in the 2016 U.S. elections—and his apparent fear that pressing Putin on the subject might cast doubt on his electoral victory.

Trump had grown frustrated that his own government had been so negative about meeting with Putin and wanted a one-on-one meeting so it would not leak, aides said. *One senior White House official described Trump's public remarks as striking a deliberately "contrarian" tone."*

Ashley Parker, Josh Dawsey, and Carol Leonnig, "'Very Much Counter to the Plan': Trump Defies Advisers in Embrace of Putin," *Washington Post*, July 16, 2018

According to two people familiar with the day's events, the president was still absorbing well into Tuesday much of the brutal coverage and commentators' assessments of the Trump-Putin joint press conference and was visibly annoyed at the near-uniformity of stunningly negative media reactions to his performance.

He stewed and dug in his heels for hours, resenting that he was widely portrayed as "weak" and having been "played" by Russian President Vladimir Putin, and that he wasn't getting the kudos he felt he deserved. . . .

By Tuesday evening, as Trump retreated to the residence, it became increasingly clear that—even after participating in a painfully staged attempt at clarification from the White House—he would not be getting the credit and plaudits from the media to which he feels entitled.

"[He's] going to hate this," a West Wing official bluntly assessed Tuesday afternoon, predicting yet more fuming and rage-tweeting over this in the coming days, if not hours.

Asawin Suebsaeng and Lachlan Markay, "Trump Tanks His Own Putin Walk-Back during One of the 'Worst Moments of His Presidency'" *Daily Beast,* **July 17, 2018**

President Trump continues to reject the judgments of U.S. spy agencies on major foreign policy fronts, creating a dynamic in which intelligence analysts frequently see troubling gaps between the president's public statements and the facts laid out for him in daily briefings on world events, current and former U.S. officials said.

The pattern has become a source of mounting concern to senior U.S. intelligence officials who had hoped that Trump, as he settled into office, would become less hostile to their work and more receptive to the information that spy agencies spend billions of dollars and sometimes put lives at risk gathering.

Instead, presidential distrust that once seemed confined mainly to the intelligence community's assessments about Russia's interference in the 2016 election has spread across a range of global issues. Among them are North Korea's willingness to abandon its nuclear weapons program, Iran's nuclear and regional ambitions, the existence and implications of global climate change, and the role of the Saudi crown prince in the killing of a dissident journalist.

Greg Miller, "Gap Continues to Widen between Trump and Intelligence Community on Key Issues," *Washington Post,* **December 11, 2018**

Trump's insistence that he must be right despite all evidence to the contrary has had repercussions in how he has been staffed. It has profoundly affected his intelligence briefings. In one instance in January 2019, Trump canceled his daily intelligence briefing after top intelligence officials contradicted his statements on Iran in Congressional testimony.[18] More frequently, Trump's intelligence briefers have had to tread carefully when briefing him about issues on which his public pronouncements have been wrong.[19] This problem has allowed distrust between Trump and the US intelligence community to fester.

Earlier this week, he ignored the advice his national-security staff and congratulated Vladimir Putin on another term of office as Russia's president.... *One White House official said the advisers erred by "telling him you should think and do this," rather than letting him improvise. "That's a cardinal mistake with him," the official said.*

Peter Nicholas, Michael C. Bender, and Rebecca Ballhaus, "Trump Relishes Off-Script Approach," *Wall Street Journal,* **March 23, 2018**

When Trump believes something to be true, U.S. officials tell NBC News, it's extremely difficult for them to dissuade him, even if they have a mountain of evidence he is wrong. And when he doubts something they are telling him, he often requires iron-clad proof of a type that is rarely available from intelligence collection.

Elyse Perlmutter-Gumbiner, Ken Dilanian, and Courtney Kube, "On Trump's Calendar, Just 17 Intelligence Briefings in 85 Days," NBC News, February 6, 2019

A related problem is that the 45th President's resistance to negative feedback raises the stakes for anyone required to deliver bad news. There were several reasons that Trump grew weary of H. R. McMaster as his National Security Advisor, but one of them was simple: McMaster was the person who had to deliver news that Trump didn't want to hear on a regular basis.[20] The Toddler in Chief felt a similar irritation

with Mick Mulvaney once he became Acting White House
Chief of Staff.[21]

[A] Republican operative and unofficial White House adviser was more
definitive, saying that no matter how respected or talented Kelly may
be, his first 2½ weeks on the job demonstrated an essential truth about
the Trump White House: The president will act as he so pleases, even
despite—and sometimes to spite—the efforts of his aides.

**Ashley Parker and Robert Costa, "Trump's Lack of Discipline Leaves New
Chief of Staff Frustrated and Dismayed,"** *Washington Post*, **August 16, 2017**

Trump's stubbornness, combined with his lack of knowledge, also complicated some of his interactions with interest
groups. In one bizarre case, Trump met with the leaders of
various veterans groups in the White House. While talking
about their issues, one vet brought up the need for VA access
for those suffering from Agent Orange poisoning. At that
point, Trump asked if Agent Orange was "that stuff from that
movie." After realizing that Trump meant *Apocalypse Now*,
they explained to the President that was confusing Agent
Orange with napalm. Trump refused to accept that he was
mistaken and kept insisting that he was right. This occupied
so much of the meeting that Trump was unable to get to all
the attendees in the room, annoying and confusing many of
the participants.[22]

His oppositional behavior has also been responsible for
many of his political own-goals. His insistence that "both
sides" were responsible for the ugliness in Charlottesville
in August 2017 turned into a weeks-long saga. His refusal
to extend standard presidential courtesies after the passing
of Senator John McCain, despite entreaties from everyone
on his staff, generated days of negative press coverage. His
refusal to apologize for his summer 2019 tweets telling four

junior minority Democratic congresswomen to "go back" to the "totally broken and crime infested places from which they came" led to a multiweek controversy. In each of these instances, Trump eventually made partial concessions to political reality, seething at the necessity of doing it.[23]

Many of the problems come from Trump, who assures his legal team that he understands their advice but then disregards it, several White House officials and advisers said. *"They say, don't do this, don't do that, and then he tweets,"* one White House adviser said. "And then the conversation happens again."

Josh Dawsey, "Trump's Lawyers Try to Control Unruly White House," *Politico,* **July 13, 2017**

Trump has, on several occasions, walked down to the Oval Office in the morning and told aides he knew they didn't like the tweets he'd sent earlier.

"They're not presidential, I know," he said, *with a mocking tone on the word "presidential,"* according to one person familiar with his comments.

Then, the next day, he'd wake up and send more tweets they didn't like.

Josh Dawsey, "White House Aides Lean on Delays and Distraction to Manage Trump," *Politico,* **October 9, 2017**

Perhaps Sharpiegate is the best example of how Trump's refusal to admit error gets him into deeper trouble. His September 1, 2019 tweet claiming that Alabama was under threat of Hurricane Dorian long after meteorologists ruled out that possibility required an immediate correction from the National Weather Service. Over the next ten days, the president insisted that he had been right despite all evidence to the contrary. To bolster his case, he ordered his subordinates to muzzle government scientists and used a Sharpie to deface a hurricane map that he showed to the White House press corps. The result has been a flurry of congressional queries and at least two official investigations of political interference in scientific work.[24]

Staffers have also learned to exploit Trump's defiance disorder to manipulate him into making decisions that they want. This has been apparent from the first week of Trump's presidency, when President Trump approved a botched raid into Yemen that killed a member of SEAL Team 6 as well as multiple civilians. According to press reports, Secretary of Defense James Mattis and the Chairman of the Joint Chiefs of Staff Joseph Dunford helped convince Trump to approve the raid by hinting that President Obama would have been too cautious to approve it.[25]

Trump's foreign policy is chiefly driven by an obsession with unravelling Barack Obama's policies. "It's his only real position," one European diplomat said. "He will ask: 'Did Obama approve this?' And if the answer is affirmative, he will say: 'We don't.' He won't even want to listen to the arguments or have a debate. He is obsessed with Obama."

Alberto Nardelli, "This Is What European Diplomats Really Think about Donald Trump," BuzzFeed, August 9, 2017

In isolation, Trump's habit for oppositional behavior and oppositional thinking would not be his worst trait as President. Unfortunately, it exacerbates all his other toddler traits. Because of his knowledge deficits, Trump is far more likely to double down based on a paucity of information. His subsequent temper tantrums raise the costs for staffers trying to correct him. When the Toddler in Chief makes mistakes—and he makes them frequently—his oppositional mindset exacerbates their political and policy costs.

Trump so resists being led that his instinct is nearly always to upend prevailing opinion.

"He is reflexively contrary," another of the generals told me.

Mark Bowden, "Top Military Officers Unload on Trump," *Atlantic*, November 2019

The entire 44-year vision of the G-7 gathering, according to the non-U.S. participants, is to hash out global issues among like-minded democracies. So the discussion quickly turned even more fundamental: Whether the leaders should assign any special weight to being a democracy, officials said.

Most of the other participants forcefully believed the answer was yes. Trump believed the answer was no. The pushback against him was delivered so passionately that the U.S. president's body language changed as one leader after another dismissed his demand, according to a senior official who watched the exchange. He crossed his arms. His stance became more combative.

Michael Birnbaum and Philip Rucker, "Trump Advocates for Putin at G-7 Summit in Move to Soften Russia's Pariah Status," *Washington Post*, August 27, 2019

CHAPTER FIVE

Knowledge Deficits

If we were to single out the major intellectual limitation at this age, it would be your child's feeling that everything that happens in his world is the result of something he has done. . . . Reasoning with your two-year-old is often difficult. After all, he views everything in extremely simple terms.

AMERICAN ACADEMY OF PEDIATRICS,
CARING FOR YOUR BABY AND YOUNG CHILD

One of the biggest differences between a toddler and an adult is also one of the simplest: an adult knows a lot more about the world. This is a simple question of brain development; the ability to retain knowledge, or even to grasp the concept of object permanence, is limited in babies. In his pioneering theory of cognitive development, Jean Piaget suggests that while infants develop some degree of object permanence by age seven months, the ability to think symbolically about the world takes far longer. One toddler parenting manual explains, "During the toddler stage . . . higher mental processes simply haven't developed yet." A leading child development textbook puts it similarly: "Although children's capacity to relate symbols to each other in a meaningful way increases dramatically during the preschool years, it does not include the ability to relate them in a consistently logical way."[2] It is difficult for toddlers to understand cause-and-effect relationships—that is, that α causes β—when they barely know what α and β actually are.

The President visited Calexico, California, where he said, "We're full, our system's full, our country's full—can't come in! Our country is full, what can you do? We can't handle any more, our country is full. Can't come in, I'm sorry. It's very simple."

Behind the scenes, two sources told CNN, the President told border agents to not let migrants in. Tell them we don't have the capacity, he said. If judges give you trouble, say, "Sorry, judge, I can't do it. We don't have the room."

After the President left the room, agents sought further advice from their leaders, who told them they were not giving them that direction and if they did what the President said they would take on personal liability. You have to follow the law, they were told.

Jake Tapper, "Trump Pushed to Close El Paso Border, Told Admin Officials to Resume Family Separations and Agents Not to Admit Migrants," CNN, April 9, 2019

Several times in the first year of his administration, President Donald Trump wanted to call Japanese Prime Minister Shinzo Abe in the middle of the afternoon. But there was a problem. Midafternoon in Washington is the middle of the night in Tokyo—when Abe would be fast asleep.

Trump's aides had to explain the issue, which one diplomatic source said came up on "a constant basis," but it wasn't easy. . . .

"He wasn't great with recognizing that the leader of a country might be 80 or 85 years old and isn't going to be awake or in the right place at 10:30 or 11 p.m. their time," said a former Trump NSC official. "When he wants to call someone, he wants to call someone. He's more impulsive that way. He doesn't think about what time it is or who it is," added a person close to Trump. . . .

Trump's desire to call world leaders at awkward hours is just one of many previously unreported diplomatic faux pas Trump has made since assuming the presidency, which go beyond telephone etiquette to include misconceptions, mispronunciations and awkward meetings. Sometimes the foibles have been contained within the White House. In one case, Trump, while studying a briefer's map of South Asia ahead of a 2017 meeting with India's prime minister, mispronounced Nepal as "nipple" and laughingly referred to Bhutan as "button," according to two sources with knowledge of the meeting.

Daniel Lippman, "Trump's Diplomatic Learning Curve: Time Zones, 'Nambia' and 'Nipple,'" *Politico*, August 13, 2018

During a meeting with German car executives this month, Mr. Trump threatened to impose higher fuel efficiency standards on their imported cars than required on American vehicles even though aides told him he could not do that.

Peter Baker and Maggie Haberman, "For Trump, 'a War Every Day,' Waged Increasingly Alone," *New York Times*, December 22, 2018

Less than two hours after Defense Secretary Jim Mattis went to the White House on Thursday to hand a resignation letter to President Trump, the president stood in the Oval Office and dictated a glowing tweet announcing that Mr. Mattis was retiring "with distinction" at the end of February.

But Mr. Trump had not read the letter. As became apparent to the president only after days of news coverage, a senior administration official said, Mr. Mattis had issued a stinging rebuke of Mr. Trump over his neglect of allies and tolerance of authoritarians. The president grew increasingly angry as he watched a parade of defense analysts go on television to extol Mr. Mattis's bravery, another aide said, until he decided on Sunday that he had had enough.

Helene Cooper, "Trump, Angry over Mattis's Rebuke, Removes Him 2 Months Early," *New York Times*, December 23, 2018

To be fair to toddlers, however, they lack the cognitive capacity to learn through conventional educational means.[3] They are simply too young. As children mature, they develop the ability to sit in a classroom setting and imbibe knowledge. Expecting this of most preschoolers would seem unfair. After all, they call it "preschool" for a reason.

Donald Trump may have the cognitive capacity of an adult, but when it comes to what he knows about politics, public policy, and international affairs, he shares a toddler's limitations. His short attention span makes it difficult for him to learn facts in a conventional manner, according to Tony Schwartz, who shadowed Trump for 18 months to write *The Art of the Deal*. Schwartz explained that Trump possessed "a stunning level of superficial knowledge and plain ignorance," attributing the deficit to a short attention span. He added, "I seriously doubt that Trump has ever read a book straight through in his adult life."[4] Similarly, biographer Michael D'Antonio warned after Trump's election that "he's going to be very frustrated with the flow of information if they try to press it upon him in the way that staff would press information upon a normal President. And I could see him lashing out and sending people out of his office because he doesn't want to deal with data."[5] Senate Majority Leader Mitch McConnell acknowledged, "This is a guy who is largely unfamiliar with a whole lot of stuff, as we know."[6] Trump's economic advisors have repeatedly complained to the press that his knowledge of international economics is meager at best. One of his former advisors told a reporter, "Frankly I don't think he really understands any of this."[7]

Trump has sometimes expressed confusion about what agencies and secretaries are in charge of what duties, a senior administration official said. For example, this official said, he has complained to [EPA Administrator Scott] Pruitt about regulatory processes for construction projects, although the EPA is not in charge of the regulations.

Ashley Parker, Josh Dawsey, Philip Rucker, and Carol Leonnig, "Trump Decides to Remove National Security Adviser, and Others May Follow," ***Washington Post*, March 15, 2018**

In private conversations with aides, Trump said he wanted to sign a full immigration bill as part of an executive order, which one administration official described as "a pretty insane idea." The president was told by government lawyers that he could not change immigration law by fiat, said a person familiar with the discussions.

Devlin Barrett, Josh Dawsey, and Nick Miroff, "Arguments, Confusion, Second-Guessing: Inside Trump's Reversal on Separating Migrant Families," ***Washington Post*, June 22, 2018**

President Trump had a suggestion for how Spain could deal with Europe's migration crisis during a recent meeting with Foreign Minister Josep Borrell, according to reports in the Spanish media.

The idea was simple: "Build a wall across the Sahara.". . . .

Borrell said that he did not support a wall along the border between the United States and Mexico and that Spanish diplomats had told Trump that the situation was considerably different in scale anyway. Trump disagreed, according to Borrell's recollection, adding that "the Sahara border can't be bigger than our border with Mexico."

Adam Taylor, "Trump Suggested a Wall across the Sahara, According to Spain's Foreign Minister," ***Washington Post*, September 19, 2018**

These assessments jibe with Trump's unintentional displays of ignorance as the Commander in Chief. In his first 1,000 days as President, Trump made well over 13,000 false or misleading claims.[8] Some of these falsehoods are conscious lies; some are, to use a technical term of philosophy, complete bullshit.[9] In many instances, it would appear that Trump genuinely does not know what he is talking about. Daniel Dale, a journalist who has meticulously fact-checked Trump for his entire time in office, notes that, "a solid chunk of [Trump's false claims] seem confused or uninformed rather than deliberate."[10] Trump's appalling lack of knowledge across a wide array of issues guarantees that he will also get a lot wrong in his public statements. When asked about subjects ranging from Frederick Douglass to school busing, his answers reveal a lack of contextual knowledge. He frequently relies on phrases like "we're looking into it" and "we'll see what happens" to cover for his ignorance.[11]

As late as one hour before the decision [to end DACA] was to be announced, administration officials privately expressed concern that Mr. Trump might not fully grasp the details of the steps he was about to take, and when he discovered their full impact, would change his mind.

Michael D. Shear and Julie Hirschfield Davis, "Trump Moves to End DACA and Calls on Congress to Act," *New York Times*, **September 5, 2017**

In one of their first phone calls, the chancellor explained to the president why Ukraine was a vital part of the trans-Atlantic relationship. Mr. Trump, officials recalled, had little idea of Ukraine's importance, its history of being bullied by Russia or what the United States and its allies had done to try to push back Mr. Putin.

German officials were alarmed by Mr. Trump's lack of knowledge, but they got even more rattled when White House aides called to complain afterward that Ms. Merkel had been condescending toward the new president.

Mark Landler, "Trump, the Insurgent, Breaks with 70 Years of American Foreign Policy," *New York Times*, **December 28, 2017**

Over their year of living dangerously with Trump, foreign leaders and diplomats have learned this much: The U.S. president was ignorant, at times massively so, about the rudiments of the international system and America's place in it, and in general about other countries. He seemed to respond well to flattery and the lavish laying out of red carpets; he was averse to conflict in person but more or less immovable from strongly held preconceptions. And given the chance, he would respond well to anything that seemed to offer him the opportunity to flout or overturn the policies endorsed by his predecessors Barack Obama and George W. Bush.

The European diplomat who was told to practice "strategic patience" did not find it all that useful in the several face-to-face meetings with Trump he ended up sitting in on. "*We were struck by the absence of knowledge of the president*," he said. Another takeaway: Trump made commitments he then did not deliver on. "On some things, he accepted the argument, and we thought now it is resolved, only to find out later he uses the same phrases and arguments as he did before," the diplomat said.

Susan Glasser, "Donald Trump's Year of Living Dangerously," *Politico*, January/February 2018

Trump also has demonstrated a tendency, once he learns a basic fact, to repeat that fact as if no one else were aware of it. When he said "nobody knew that health care could be so complicated" in early 2017, it prompted widespread derision because of course everyone in Washington knew it.[12] As the *Washington Post*'s Jenna Johnson observed, "Trump's public remarks are filled with dozens of similar comments. They often begin with some variation of the phrase 'Most people don't know ... ' and end with a nugget of information that many of those surrounding him—fellow world leaders, diplomats, journalists, politicians or aides—do indeed already know."[13] On issues ranging from France being America's first ally to Lincoln being a Republican, the Toddler in Chief tries to sound like the smartest person in the room while unintentionally revealing his very small knowledge base. As the examples in this chapter demonstrate, there are significant gaps in Donald Trump's factual knowledge. Unlike any of his predecessors, Trump possessed zero experience in any branch or level of government. His only legal experience has been suing others and being sued, which did not prep him for the finer points of constitutional law. Trump's lack of interest in the intricacies of legislation or executive management compound the problem.[14] As a result, Trump has repeatedly commanded his staffers and Cabinet Secretaries to do things that, as President, he has no legal authority to do.[15] A few weeks after coming on as White House Chief of Staff, John Kelly said, "The president just really doesn't understand anything about that. He doesn't know what he's talking about." By 2018, he had condensed his assessment to "he's an idiot. It's pointless to convince him of anything."[16] Kelly was hardly the only Trump official to reportedly make that assessment. Secretary of State Rex Tillerson, Treasury Secretary Steven Mnuchin, Chief of Staff Reince Priebus, and National Security Advisor H. R. McMaster all called him some variation of "idiot."[17]

National Security Adviser H. R. McMaster mocked President Trump's intelligence at a private dinner with a powerful tech CEO, according to five sources with knowledge of the conversation.

Over a July dinner with Oracle CEO Safra Catz—who has been mentioned as a candidate for several potential administration jobs—McMaster bluntly trashed his boss, said the sources, four of whom told BuzzFeed News they heard about the exchange directly from Catz. *The top national security official dismissed the president variously as an "idiot" and a "dope" with the intelligence of a "kindergartner," the sources said.*

Joseph Bernstein, "Sources: McMaster Mocked Trump's Intelligence at a Private Dinner," BuzzFeed, November 20, 2017

White House Chief of Staff John F. Kelly told Democratic lawmakers Wednesday that some of the hard-line immigration policies President Trump advocated during the campaign were "uninformed," that the United States will never construct a wall along its entire southern border and that Mexico will never pay for it, according to people familiar with the meeting.

Ed O'Keefe, "Trump Pushes Back on Chief of Staff Claims That Border Wall Pledges 'Uninformed,'" *Washington Post*, **January 18, 2018**

Trump's lack of public service and knowledge of governance is compounded by a complete absence of practical lived experience. Trump's privileged upbringing shielded him from "common sense" knowledge about how the other half lives. During the January 2019 government shutdown, Trump suggested that furloughed government workers would be fine, because local grocers would extend them temporary credit.[18] He appears to know the fictional world of *Mayberry R.F.D.* better than 21st- century America. He avoided military service during the Vietnam era with a medical diagnosis of bone spurs, written by a podiatrist as a favor to Trump's father.[19] Trump claimed that his attendance of a secondary-school military academy was tantamount to military experience. Steve Bannon, an actual Navy veteran, countered that Trump was incapable of handling the families of soldiers killed in combat: "He's not that guy. He's never really been around the military. He's never been around military family. Never been around death."[20]

Trump's lack of experience is matched only by his lack of knowledge about foreign policy. In his initial interviews with the *Washington Post* and *New York Times* during the 2016 presidential campaign, Trump displayed a weak understanding of world politics; follow-up interviews on the topic suggested little subsequent learning.[21] In GOP primary debates, Trump demonstrated ignorance of concepts like the nuclear triad or the Trans-Pacific Partnership. On the campaign trail, Trump backtracked, prevaricated, and flip-flopped on key foreign policy issues numerous times.[22] In his first few weeks as President, Trump continued to demonstrate ignorance on numerous foreign policy matters ranging from the particulars of his own executive orders to a refugee deal with Australia to the contents of a nuclear arms treaty with Russia.[23]

Trump's lack of preparation has added a further level of unpredictability to his interactions with foreign leaders, the officials said. The president rarely reads his nightly briefing book, which focuses on issues likely to come up in meetings, a second senior U.S. official said. To slim down Trump's workload, aides have sometimes put the most critical information in a red folder, the official said. . . .

Some White House officials worry that Putin, who has held several calls with Trump, plays on the president's inexperience and lack of detailed knowledge about issues while stoking Trump's grievances. . . .

Greg Jaffe, Josh Dawsey, and Carol Leonnig, "Ahead of Nato and Putin Summits, Trump's Unorthodox Diplomacy Rattles Allies," *Washington Post*, **July 6, 2018**

Christie had made sure that Trump knew the protocol for his discussions with foreign leaders. The transition team had prepared a document to let him know how these were meant to go. The first few calls were easy—the very first was always with the prime minister of Great Britain—but two dozen calls in you were talking to some kleptocrat and tiptoeing around sensitive security issues. Before any of the calls could be made, however, the president of Egypt called in to the switchboard at Trump Tower and somehow got the operator to put him straight through to Trump. "Trump was like . . . *I love the Bangles! You know that song Walk Like an Egyptian*?" recalled one of his advisers on the scene.

Michael Lewis, "'This Guy Doesn't Know Anything': The inside Story of Trump's Shambolic Transition Team," *Guardian*, September 27, 2018

Trump's lack of policy understanding has pronounced effects on the way he is staffed. Even before he was inaugurated, Steve Bannon warned incoming CIA Director Mike Pompeo that Trump "has a steep learning curve."[24] Trump's first Secretary of State, Rex Tillerson, invoked that phrase repeatedly when discussing Trump in his May 2019 congressional testimony.[25] White House advisors have voiced uneasiness with leaving Trump without supervision during negotiations. Stephen Miller, for example, was convinced in January 2018 that Trump would agree to a grand bargain on immigration if he were left alone with Senators pushing for that deal. At a key meeting—the one in which Trump referred to West African countries as "shitholes"—Miller took care to pack the Oval Office with as many immigration hawks as possible.[26] Similarly, John Kelly repeatedly expressed fears in January 2018 that if Trump were left alone with Senate Minority Leader Chuck Schumer, he would acquiesce on immigration.[27] As Secretary of State, Mike Pompeo demonstrated similar uneasiness over Trump spending too much time alone with North Korean leader Kim Jong Un.

The Europeans spent months negotiating with the State Department about supplements to the Iran deal that would accommodate concerns Trump expressed in January. By late April, senior officials on all sides said they were close to agreement.

Yet when Macron, Merkel and Johnson traveled to Washington in the days and weeks before Trump's announcement, all came away with the feeling Trump had not read the five-page document they had prepared and perhaps was even unaware of the effort.

Karen DeYoung, "Allies Fume over Trump's Withdrawal from Iran Deal but Have Few Options to Respond," *Washington Post,* **May 14, 2018**

The aides are also concerned about what kind of grasp Mr. Trump has on the details of the North Korea program, and what he must insist upon as the key components of denuclearization. Mr. Moon and his aides reported that Mr. Kim seemed highly conversant with all elements of the program when the two men met, and Secretary of State Mike Pompeo has made similar comments about Mr. Kim, based on his two meetings with him in Pyongyang, the North's capital.

But aides who have recently left the administration say *Mr. Trump has resisted the kind of detailed briefings about enrichment capabilities, plutonium reprocessing, nuclear weapons production and missile programs that Mr. Obama and President George W. Bush regularly sat through.*

David E. Sanger, "Trump Grappling with Risks of Proceeding with North Korea Meeting," *New York Times,* **May 20, 2018**

To be fair, no one enters the presidency with firsthand experience of the job. This century's other Presidents—George W. Bush and Barack Obama—were also inexperienced compared to their predecessors. And most Presidents have gaps in their policy knowledge, particularly in foreign affairs. The difference, however, is that prior Presidents could recognize and attempt to compensate for their shortcomings. George W. Bush, for example, demonstrated a willingness to be tutored on foreign policy questions. Obama took care to hire seasoned foreign policy experts before launching his presidential campaign. Almost all Presidents prior to Trump possessed the self-awareness to know, to some degree, what they did not know. Furthermore, they were all genuinely interested in the presidency as an institution. In contrast, Trump admitted in the summer of 2016 that he had never read a single biography of a President and had no intention to do so in the future.[28]

The Toddler in Chief lacks the necessary metacognition to know what he does not know. Like a small child who thinks that no one is wise to him, Trump has consistently claimed expertise on subjects that he clearly knows nothing about.[29] During the 2016 campaign, Trump boasted that, on foreign policy, "My primary consultant is myself and I have a good instinct for this stuff."[30] Despite Trump's rather limited tech savviness, he has claimed expertise about wind energy, the aeronautics of Boeing planes, and self-driving cars.[31] He repeatedly brags that he is a "very stable genius"; as one former White House official explained, "Part of it comes from his insecurities about not being perceived as intelligent."[32] These insecurities make it difficult for his staff compensate for his lack of knowledge. Such efforts always run the risk of setting off his temper. Trump is the President with the least experience in government in American history and also the one most hostile to expert advice.

Citing multiple in-person episodes, these intelligence officials say *Trump displays what one called "willful ignorance" when presented with analyses generated by America's $81 billion-a-year intelligence services.* The officials, who include analysts who prepare Trump's briefs and the briefers themselves, describe futile attempts to keep his attention by using visual aids, confining some briefing points to two or three sentences, and repeating his name and title as frequently as possible. . . .

The problem has existed since the beginning of Trump's presidency, the intelligence officials say, and for a time they tried to respond to the President's behavior in briefings with dark humor. After a briefing in preparation for a meeting with British Prime Minister Theresa May, for example, the subject turned to the British Indian Ocean Territory of Diego Garcia. The island is home to an important airbase and a U.S. Naval Support Facility that are central to America's ability to project power in the region, including in the war in Afghanistan.

The President, officials familiar with the briefing said, asked two questions: Are the people nice, and are the beaches good?

John Walcott, "'Willful Ignorance.' Inside President Trump's Troubled Intelligence Briefings," *Time*, **February 5, 2019**

A series of recently published presidential schedules show that he has been in just 17 intelligence briefings over the last 85 days. That's about the same frequency as two of his predecessors, Barack Obama and Bill Clinton, according to a former CIA briefer who has written a book on the subject. But unlike those former presidents, Trump does not regularly read the written intelligence briefing sent over each day to the White House, U.S. officials tell NBC News, and in private he frequently questions the integrity and judgment of the intelligence officials who are giving him secret information.

Elyse Perlmutter-Gumbiner, Ken Dilanian, and Courtney Kube, "On Trump's Calendar, Just 17 Intelligence Briefings in 85 Days," NBC News, February 6, 2019

While Mr. Trump is confident in his approach, his decision to add new trade barriers with China—in the form of higher tariffs—has confounded analysts and some business groups that have otherwise praised his handling of the economy. . . .

Many of those groups say growth would be even stronger this year if Mr. Trump had reached a deal with China and averted a prolonged government shutdown. They blame Mr. Trump's fundamental misunderstanding of tariffs—which he believes are lifting the economy—for driving the country into a danger zone.

Jeanna Smialek, Jim Tankersley, and Mark Landler, "Trump's Trade War Escalation Will Exact Economic Pain, Adviser Says," *New York Times*, **May 12, 2019**

The president's deep ignorance leaves him more vulnerable to conspiracy theories and data shaped by advisors leery of upsetting him. Trump's first Homeland Security Advisor, Tom Bossert, repeatedly tried to convince Trump that Ukraine did not meddle in the 2016 election, but the Toddler in Chief persisted in his belief.[33] Even as the economy started cooling off in the summer of 2019, Trump's White House advisors continued their practice of only showing him rosier economic assessments. According to the *Washington Post*, "Trump has a somewhat conspiratorial view, telling some confidants that he distrusts statistics he sees reported in the news media and that he suspects many economists and other forecasters are presenting biased data to thwart his reelection."[34]

Monitoring his information consumption—and countering what Mr. Kelly calls "garbage" peddled to him by outsiders—remains a priority for the chief of staff and the team he has made his own. Even after a year of official briefings and access to the best minds of the federal government, Mr. Trump is skeptical of anything that does not come from inside his bubble.

Some advisers, like the Treasury secretary, Steven Mnuchin, consider this a fundamentally good thing. "I see a lot of similarities between the way he was running the campaign and the way he is as president," Mr. Mnuchin said. *"He really loves verbal briefings. He is not one to consume volumes of books or briefings."*

Other aides bemoan his tenuous grasp of facts, jack-rabbit attention span and propensity for conspiracy theories.

Maggie Haberman, Glenn Thrush, and Peter Baker, "Inside Trump's Hour-by-Hour Battle for Self-Preservation," *New York Times,* **December 9, 2017**

Trump's ignorance of international affairs has also negatively affected his relations with allied leaders. In the run-up to the 2017 G-7 summit, Trump's staffers warned foreign leaders that contradicting or lecturing the President on climate change would be counterproductive.[35] Nonetheless, Trump's knowledge deficits have prompted leaders to fact-check him—a gambit certain to irk the 45th President. President Trump complained about British Prime Minister Theresa May's "schoolmistress" tone, particularly when she corrected him in public.[36] He has been similarly hostile to German Chancellor Angela Merkel's lectures.[37] Some might argue that frosty personal relationships with world leaders are a function of diverging interests. This contradicts Trump's own views, however. Multiple accounts suggest that he believes foreign relations are all about strong personal ties between leaders. Indeed, nearly all of Trump's interactions with world leaders are premised on his belief that his ability to charm and cajole foreign leaders is more important than policy goals or strategic aims.[38]

Accepted protocol dictates that alliance members do not discuss internal business in front of nonmembers. But as is frequently the case, Mr. Trump did not adhere to the established norms, according to several American and European officials who were in the room.

He complained that European governments were not spending enough on the shared costs of defense, leaving the United States to carry an outsize burden. He expressed frustration that European leaders would not, on the spot, pledge to spend more. And he appeared not to grasp the details when several tried to explain to him that spending levels were set by parliaments in individual countries, the American and European officials said."

Julian E. Barnes and Helene Cooper, "Trump Discussed Pulling U.S. from NATO, Aides Say amid New Concerns over Russia," *New York Times*, **January 14, 2019**

The president's aides were not the only ones who felt the need to clarify or contradict Trump during the G-7 summit — several fellow leaders stepped in at times during the day, often gently, to make clear they were not agreeing with a point made by Trump.

The president indicated that North Korea's Kim Jong Un, with whom Trump is eager to strike a nuclear deal, had not broken "an agreement" by repeatedly conducting missile tests in recent weeks that have U.S. allies in Asia growing nervous. Japanese Prime Minister Shinzo Abe, sitting in the chair beside him, said otherwise.

Josh Dawsey, "Trump Admits to Having 'Second Thoughts'—A Scramble Ensues to Explain What He Meant," *Washington Post*, **August 25, 2019**

Trump's defenders might argue that the 45th President's deal-making abilities compensate for his ignorance, that well-informed advisors can compensate. These arguments do not hold up. Trump's lack of knowledge erodes his ability to lead. Indeed, his ignorance enables his subordinates to pursue policies independently, including those at variance with Trump's broader wishes. As Georgetown political scientist Elizabeth Saunders has demonstrated, inexperienced leaders are less able to constrain their subordinates from engaging in bureaucratic conflicts or pursuing risky actions.[39] Their lack of direct experience and knowledge makes it more difficult for them to effectively monitor their subordinates. Saunders concludes that "a base of substantive, domain-specific knowledge is important, and is distinct from procedural experience and acumen (such as good organizational or bargaining skills)."[40] The Toddler in Chief does not possess that base of knowledge.

Manifestly clear is that Trump's ignorance about policy and process make it harder for both him and his staff to do their jobs properly. In his first 1,000 days Trump stumbled repeatedly on questions of policy. Briefing him was next to impossible. In his House testimony, former Secretary of State Rex Tillerson said, "I had to adapt to the fact that it wasn't going to be useful to give him something and say this is, you know, this is an article worth reading or this is a brief." While he acknowledged that this was very different from how he operated, he explained, "The task for the rest of us was to learn how to operate in a way that supported him given that that's his style. It wasn't our job to try to change the way he does things."[41] His staff, if anything, exacerbated the problem. They declined to correct his public assertions when they were factually incorrect, because they feared making him look uninformed. In August 2019 Trump asserted, "The First Lady has gotten to know Kim Jong Un and I think she'd agree with me, he is a man with a country that has tremendous potential." Trump's claim was patently false, since Melania Trump had never met the North Korean dictator. White House Press Secretary Stephanie Grisham's clarification was that, while the First Lady had never met Kim, "the President feels like she's gotten to know him too."[42]

The result has been akin to letting a proud toddler make decisions: a radically uninformed President fully confident that he knows everything he needs to know.

Trump operates almost purely on gut instinct. "He never wanted to be briefed all that much before these foreign leader meetings," a former senior administration official said. "He was annoyed when [former national security adviser H. R.] McMaster would come in and say here's what we need to do and give him note cards and all the information."

"Trump lives by improvisation," said another source who has seen Trump at close quarters in foreign leader meetings. "He believes he doesn't need to prepare, that he performs best when he flies by the seat of his pants and stays flexible. He believes this approach has always worked for him in business and so far at least, politics."

Jonathan Swan, "Inside Trump's Shock and Brawl Strategy with Foreign Leaders," Axios, May 11, 2018

When former National Economic Council director Gary Cohn's staffers prepared a presentation for Trump about deficits, Cohn told them no. It wouldn't be necessary, he said, because the president did not care about deficits, according to current and former officials.

Trump also repeatedly told Cohn to print more money, according to three White House officials familiar with his comments.

"He'd just say, run the presses, run the presses," one former senior administration official said, describing the president's Oval Office orders. "Sometimes it seemed like he was joking, and sometimes it didn't.". . . .

Chief of Staff John F. Kelly has told others about watching television with Trump and asking the president how much the chairman of the Joint Chiefs of Staff earns. Trump guessed $5 million, according to people who were told the story by Kelly, startling the chief of staff. Kelly responded that he made less than $200,000. The president suggested he get a large raise and noted the number of stars on his uniform.

Josh Dawsey and Damian Paletta, "Trump Demands Action to Reduce Deficit, Pushes New Deficit Spending," *Washington Post*, **December 2, 2018**

CHAPTER SIX

Too Much Screen Time

Most media use is passive. Sitting and watching TV all the time, for example, does not help your child acquire the most important skills and experiences she needs at this age, such as communication, creativity, fantasy, judgment, and experimentation.

AMERICAN ACADEMY OF PEDIATRICS,
CARING FOR YOUR BABY AND YOUNG CHILD

Top White House officials tell me the key to forcing a more disciplined President Trump (like the one onstage overseas) is limiting his screen time. In Trump's case, it's curtailing his time watching TV and banging out tweets on his iPhone.

Trump himself has been pushing staff to give him more free time. But staff does everything it can to load up his schedule to keep him from getting worked up watching cable coverage, which often precipitates his tweets.

Mike Allen, "Trump's iPhone Has One App: Twitter," Axios, May 25, 2017

The American Academy of Pediatrics recommends that children under the age of two not be exposed to any television at all, and that children older than two be exposed only to limited amounts of quality television.[1] The World Health Organization has reached similar conclusions about all screens.[2] The reasons proffered are straightforward.[3] Young children with heavy exposure to screens are more at risk for delayed language development. Television reduces a child's focused attention by approximately 75 percent and leads to a decrease in classroom engagement.[4] Ample amounts of screen time are positively correlated with obesity. Too much screen time in the evening can interfere with the body's natural release of melatonin, which facilitates sleep. A lot of television programs that are marketed as "educational" or useful for a child's cognitive development are actually devoid of such value. Most important in terms of cognitive development, there are far better activities for a toddler to pursue than watching television. As the American Academy of Pediatrics warns, "passive screen time is not a substitute for reading, playing, or problem solving."[5] Despite these warnings, most parents in the United States let their toddlers watch television or play with tablets. Most parents also acknowledge that this is not the greatest mode of parenting.

The Toddler in Chief watches a lot of television. Trump himself has denied this, claiming at one press gaggle, "People that don't know me, they like to say I watch television—people with fake sources." He went on: "But I don't get to watch much television. Primarily because of documents. I'm reading documents. A lot."[6] People close to Trump have flatly contradicted that claim, estimating that he spends between four to eight hours a day in front of a television.[7] That would be an above average amount of screen time for an ordinary American. For a President tasked with far more responsibility and authority, it is an extraordinary amount of time. As Trump's "Executive Time" has increased over the course of his presidency, so has his television viewing. It has spread to his business hours as well. In meetings with Vice President Mike Pence, Speaker of the House Paul Ryan, and other GOP allies, Trump has been repeatedly distracted by whatever is on television.[8]

Advisers have tried to curtail Trump's idle hours, hoping to prevent him from watching cable news or calling old friends and then tweeting about it. That only works during the workday, though—Trump's evenings and weekends have remained largely his own.

"It's not like the White House doesn't have a plan to fill his time productively but at the end of the day he's in charge of his schedule," said one person close to the White House. "He does not like being managed."

Josh Dawsey, Shane Goldmacher, and Alex Isenstadt, "The Education of Donald Trump," *Politico*, **April 27, 2017**

We do not need to rely on insider accounts of Trump's television watching to have it confirmed. Trump's Twitter feed offers an excellent real-time data source of the President's heavy television diet. Since the fall of 2017, Media Matters for America's Matthew Gertz has monitored the correlation between Trump's tweets and what is on cable news.[9] He has demonstrated that most of Trump's early morning and evening tweets correlate directly to Fox News and Fox Business Channel programming. Trump's early morning tweets are usually about whatever *Fox & Friends* has covered; his evening tweets correspond to content on *Hannity* and *Lou Dobbs Tonight*. *The Art of the Deal* ghostwriter Tony Schwartz claims that television is Trump's primary information source.[10] The examples cited in this chapter back up that claim. According to *Time*, "Nothing anyone on the National Security Council staff, in the counsel's office or from across government can outweigh what the President hears from conservatives on cable television."[11]

On the first couple's recent trip overseas, Melania Trump's television aboard Air Force One was tuned to CNN. President Trump was not pleased.

He raged at his staff for violating a rule that the White House entourage should begin each trip tuned to Fox—his preferred network over what he considers the "fake news" CNN—and caused "a bit of a stir" aboard Air Force One.

Katie Rogers and Maggie Haberman, "Spotting CNN on a TV aboard Air Force One, Trump Rages against Reality," *New York Times,* **July 24, 2018**

Aides said there was no grand strategy to the president's actions, and that he got up each morning this week not knowing what he would do. Much as he did as a New York businessman at Trump Tower, Mr. Trump watched television, reacted to what he saw on television and then reacted to the reaction.

Mark Landler and Julie Hirschfield Davis, "After Another Week of Chaos, Trump Repairs to Palm Beach. No One Knows What Comes Next," *New York Times,* **March 23, 2018**

While at the White House, he will often keep the TV tuned to business channels and watch the Dow's minute-to-minute movements, people close to the White House say. He would get excited about triple-digit gains in a single day and question aides about how certain actions might influence the market, people familiar with the matter said. Asked about Mr. Trump's attention to the stock market, one person close to the White House said: "He's glued to it."

Vivian Salama, "As Trade Battle Unfolds, Trump Keeps Close Focus on Markets," *Wall Street Journal,* **December 7, 2018**

Much as some parents defend certain kinds of screen time as "educational," however, Trump defenders have developed justifications for his copious cable news consumption. If television is the best way for Trump to process information, why not let him watch it? Perhaps fair and balanced content from Fox News can provide sources of information superior to a stodgy intelligence briefing from the Deep State?

The flaws in this argument are legion. First and foremost, watching television during the day compromises an individual's ability to focus. Among children, media multitasking is negatively correlated with academic performance, emotional regulation, and cognitive control.[12] Even adults who attempt to multitask usually find themselves doing poorly on maintaining focus and attention.[13] In Trump's case, his short attention span compounds the problem. Having a television on in the background dramatically reduces the 45th President's ability to focus on whatever is happening in the foreground. At times this has caused Trump to misinterpret what he saw on the screen. Early in his administration, he was meeting with some advisors on North Korea when he saw footage of North Korean missiles being fired. Trump thought this was happening in real time. Lindsey Graham had to reassure the President that he was watching was old footage and therefore did not in fact need to respond to an imminent missile strike.[14]

By all accounts, Mr. Trump's consumption of cable television has actually increased in recent months as his first scheduled meetings of the day have slid back from the 9 or 9:30 a.m. set by Reince Priebus, his first chief of staff, to roughly 11 many mornings. During 'executive time,' Mr. Trump watches television in the residence for hours, reacting to what he sees on Fox News. *While in the West Wing, he leaves it on during most meetings in the dining room off the Oval Office, one ear attuned to what is being said.*

Peter Baker and Maggie Haberman, "For Trump, 'a War Every Day,' Waged Increasingly Alone," *New York Times*, December 22, 2018

For decades, presidents and vice presidents have held regular one-on-one lunches with no aides present. The ritual helps build trust and, because only two people are at the table, prevents leaks, veterans of past White Houses said.

Trump ditched that tradition. Instead he has invited to the lunches both his and Pence's top aides. At the meals in the small dining room off the Oval Office, Trump keeps a big-screen TV tuned to cable news. Aides who have walked in have seen Trump yelling at the TV as he sits with Pence and their deputies over plates of chicken and cheeseburgers. When he sees something on the screen that he dislikes, Trump on occasion will interrupt the lunch and summon aides to discuss a response, people familiar with the lunches said.

Peter Nicholas, "A Survival Guide for the Trump White House," *Atlantic*, **April 14, 2019**

On several occasions, Trump was watching Fox News when old sections of border barrier would flash on the screen. Thinking it was new construction, he called Nielsen and other officials in a fury, according to people familiar with their exchanges, only to be told that Fox was running 'B-roll'—old footage of pre-existing sections.

Jason Zengerle, "How America Got to 'Zero Tolerance' on Immigration: The Inside Story," *New York Times Magazine*, **July 16, 2019**

Second, Trump is not really watching the news part of Fox News, but rather the opinion programs: *Fox & Friends* and *Hannity*. The former show can be described as a Trump-friendly program in which, in the words of one *Washington Post* columnist, "opposing viewpoints are piped in infrequently, and usually in discrete sound bites . . . that can then be dismissed without having to delve too deeply into unpleasant arguing."[15] In many instances, *Fox & Friends* or *Hannity* have broadcast uninformed speculation on breaking news, causing in turn the Toddler in Chief to tweet out unsubstantiated rumors rather than rely on his own intelligence officials for information.[16] One Trump White House official admitted, "Sometimes on Fox, a lot of stories are embellished, and they don't necessarily cover the big news stories of the day.

When they cover the smaller stories, if that gets the President riled up, then that becomes an issue. Whenever he tweets, all of us do a mad dash or mad scramble to find out as much information about that random topic as possible."[17] Like many toddlers, Trump has difficult distinguishing between reality and fantasy when watching television.

As the meeting [with pro-Trump surrogates and media commentators] wound down, President Trump made sure to approach people one-on-one to commend them for their performances and appearances on live TV. In some cases, he cited specific TV interviews and segments from the past weeks that he found particularly compelling and fun to watch. Some attendees were surprised at how closely the president of the United States had been watching them. For others, it was simply additional confirmation of "how much of a [TV] addict" Trump is, according to another person at the White House meeting.

Asawin Suebsaeng and Lachlan Markay, "Sean Hannity Has Been Advising Donald Trump on the Nunes Memo, Because of Course He Has," *Daily Beast***, February 1, 2018**

President Trump often gets agitated—and stirred to action—by random things he hears on TV or from shoot-the-bull conversations with friends.

Why it matters: It drives staff nuts because they are responding to things that are either inaccurate, highly distorted or flat-out don't exist.

Mike Allen and Jonathan Swan, "Trump's Land of Make-Believe," Axios, March 28, 2018

After more than two years in office, Trump continues to view his presidency through TV ratings and news coverage, while assessing the worthiness of his allies by how they perform during cable news hits. . . .

Republican lawmakers have grown accustomed to Trump's predilection to obsess over TV and the coverage of him—and have adapted.

While negotiating with Democrats in December on a potential deal to reopen the government, Sen. Lindsey O. Graham (R-S.C.) said Trump did not yet know the details of his new immigration idea. He planned to first pitch the idea to Laura Ingraham—whose show he would go on later that week—and Sean Hannity and Lou Dobbs, among other TV hosts. . . .

One reason [Speaker of the House Paul] Ryan struggled with Trump was because the president would often call him early in the morning to talk about what was on "Fox and Friends," and Ryan was not usually watching or versed on the particulars of the show.

Josh Dawsey and Seung Min Kim, "Trump's Barometer for Success following Russia Investigation's End—TV Ratings," *Washington Post*, **March 30, 2019**

Third, because Fox News and Fox Business Channel cater to conservative viewers, Trump uses it to gauge what his base is thinking. This can cause him to alter his positions in response to criticism aired on those channels. Keeping in touch with political constituencies is a traditional task of a politician. Because Trump relies on television so heavily, however, it allows activists to skew the President's perceptions by scheduling constant appearances. In early 2017 House Freedom Caucus leader Jim Jordan instructed his congressional staff to put him on television more "because you're talking to the president" when on television.[18] Trump nearly vetoed a March 2018 omnibus spending bill after seeing negative coverage of it on Fox News. In December 2018 he flip-flopped on signing another spending bill because Fox News aired criticisms from Ann Coulter and Rush Limbaugh.[19] That led to a government shutdown that accomplished none of Trump's stated aims.

In the White House communications shop, officials rotate going on [Fox News' Jeanine] Pirro's show because they know Trump will be watching—and partially to prevent him from calling in himself, several officials said, as he did earlier this year.

"*Someone has to be on the show every week*," an official said.

Josh Dawsey, "Trump's Must-See Tv: Judge Jeanine's Show and Her Positive Take on the President," *Washington Post*, April 5, 2018

White House officials had an appointment with their television remotes at 9 p.m. on Saturday. At that hour, they worried, Fox News' "Justice with Judge Jeanine" might sway Donald Trump's pick for the Supreme Court and undo everything officials have spent weeks working on.

Philip Elliott, "Inside Donald Trump's Supreme Court Deliberations," *Time*, July 8, 2018

Fourth, and finally, in watching so much television, Trump is ceding his agenda-setting powers to producers at Fox News. While this might please Trump's conservative base, it can also lead to imbroglios that distract from administration priorities. For example, in the summer of 2019 President Trump decided to attack US Representative Elijah Cummings after watching a Saturday morning Fox and Friends segment that characterized Cummings' district as trash-ridden. Over the next week, the Trump White House was forced to defend the president against accusations of racism and bipartisan criticism of Trump's comments. As Axios's Jonathan Swan noted as the controversy died down, "Nobody knew it was coming, nobody knew how to handle it, and a week later, senior White House officials have their fingers crossed that the president won't turn their week upside-down once again with another tweet about a "Fox and Friends" segment. . . . Baltimore Week illuminates how things often work inside the Trump White House: The president watches TV, he tweets, and the machinery of government scrambles into action to deal with an emergency of the president's own creation."[20] A senior administration official acknowledged, "I've seen him go from Point A to Point B in minutes. . . . Usually what does it is something on TV like a [Democratic] politician or commentator saying he's the one to blame that sets him off."[21]

President Donald Trump's racist attack on four Democratic congress-women is undisciplined impulsiveness now being dressed up as insightful "strategy" by his supporters, Republican political consultants said, arguing it will likely make his reelection campaign even harder.

"There was no strategy," acknowledged one former Trump aide on condition of anonymity. "This is just a Sunday morning reaction to 'Fox and Friends.'"

S. V. Dáte, "Trump Campaign Trying to Rebrand Racist Attacks as Clever 'Strategy,'" *Huffington Post*, July 17, 2019

Despite this, Trump has not dialed down his television consumption. If anything, it has increased during his time in office. He enjoys the feedback loop between his tweets/statements and their being reported on the news. He judges his subordinates based on how well they perform on television. He also likes to appoint people he believes fit "central casting," which often means prior experience on television. Matthew Whitaker was a CNN commentator before being hired to be Chief of Staff and then Acting Attorney General at the Justice Department. Heather Nauert migrated from Fox News anchor to spokesperson for the State Department. Trump fired Border Patrol Chief Mark Morgan during the first few weeks of his presidency, but after Morgan appeared on Fox News and voiced vociferous support for the President's hardline policies, he was rehired at the Department of Homeland Security.[22] At total of 19 people have migrated from working at Fox News to serve in the Trump administration.[23] The President has regularly looped Lou Dobbs into White House policy debates on immigration, and he listens to Tucker Carlson on Iran policy.[24] Trump talks regularly with Sean Hannity and invited him to speak at one of his campaign rallies. According to one source close to the White House press office, Trump hired Anthony Scaramucci to be the White House Communications Advisor because he "wanted to give Scaramucci something to do because he likes him on TV."[25] Trump initially wanted John Ratcliffe to replace Dan Coats as Director of National Intelligence without a full vetting because of his television appearances.[26]

Trump's aides frequently ask him for the status of certain Cabinet officials so they will not say anything inaccurate publicly. Not checking frequently can leave an aide "looking dumb" with yesterday's information, according to one former senior White House official. For instance, Trump told aides for several weeks that he was planning to oust McMaster. After a story said that, he told aides to deny it—and then moved to replace him less than a week later.

Trump will see a segment on TV and begin musing for someone in a job, creating uncertainty. For example, he saw Labor Secretary Alexander Acosta on "Fox & Friends" one morning and asked an aide if he could be the next attorney general.

Lisa Rein, Josh Dawsey, and Emily Wax-Thibodeaux, "'He Knows He Is Done': Veterans Affairs Chief Lies Low amid Rumors He'll Be Ousted," *Washington Post*, **March 27, 2018**

Trump's Cabinet, a collection of corporate heavyweights, decorated generals and influential conservatives, has been beset by regular bouts of turnover and scandal. A Cabinet member's standing with Trump—who's up, who's down; who's relevant, who's not —is closely tied to how that person or their issue is playing in the press, especially on cable TV....

Trump has had more turnover of Cabinet-level positions than any president at this point in their tenure in the last 100 years.

But what has angered Trump more than the substance of the scandals are the bad images they produced, according to four White House officials and outside advisers. *The president has complained to confidants that more members of his Cabinet "weren't good on TV."* He fumed to one ally in the spring, at the height of the ethical questions surrounding Pruitt, Zinke and Housing and Urban Development head Ben Carson, that he was only seeing his Cabinet on TV for scandals and not for fulfilling campaign promises.

Trump has also complained that he wants to see more of them on cable television defending his administration and showcasing his accomplishments. In recent months, the White House has pushed Cabinet members to make more public shows of support.

Jonathan Lemire, Catherine Lucey, and Zeke Miller, "Life in Trump's Cabinet: Perks, Pestering, Power, Putdowns," Associated Press, July 5, 2018

President Trump's reliance on television as his primary source of information has had a profound effect on how staffers, advisors, and other politicians attempt to influence him. Like most exasperated parents, their first instinct was to limit his screen time. His staffers tried to limit his access to television programs that they believed would set him off. White House staff dreaded rainy Sundays, because that meant the Toddler in Chief would be watching television and tweeting rather than playing golf.[27] Trump's first Chief of Staff Reince Priebus described rainy Sunday afternoons as "the devil's play shop," and Sunday evenings—when Trump was likely to watch CNN or MSNBC—as "the witching hour." He began to schedule Trump's return from weekend golf trips later in the day, so Trump would not be able to watch the more political programs.[28]

The ammunition for his Twitter war is television. No one touches the remote control except Mr. Trump and the technical support staff—at least that's the rule. During meetings, the 60-inch screen mounted in the dining room may be muted, but Mr. Trump keeps an eye on scrolling headlines. What he misses he checks out later on what he calls his "Super TiVo," a state-of-the-art system that records cable news. . . .

To an extent that would stun outsiders, Mr. Trump, the most talked-about human on the planet, is still delighted when he sees his name in the headlines. And he is on a perpetual quest to see it there. One former top adviser said Mr. Trump grew uncomfortable after two or three days of peace and could not handle watching the news without seeing himself on it.

During the morning, aides monitor "Fox & Friends" live or through a transcription service in much the way commodities traders might keep tabs on market futures to predict the direction of their day.

If someone on the show says something memorable and Mr. Trump does not immediately tweet about it, the president's staff knows he may be saving Fox News for later viewing on his recorder and instead watching MSNBC or CNN live—meaning he is likely to be in a foul mood to start the day.

Maggie Haberman, Glenn Thrush, and Peter Baker, "Inside Trump's Hour-by-Hour Battle for Self-Preservation," *New York Times***, December 9, 2017**

That tactic largely failed, so in response the staff has tried to shape the content that Trump watches on television. Even those advisors who have considerable "face time" with Trump will also attempt to deploy allies onto television programs that they know the President will watch. The *Washington Post* reported that "aides sometimes plot to have guests make points on Fox that they have been unable to get the president to agree to in person. 'He will listen more when it is on TV,' a senior administration official said."[29] This is also true of ambitious politicians. In December 2017, Trump waded into the GOP primary for Florida governor to endorse Ron DeSantis over several other potential candidates. He did this without much knowledge of state party dynamics; rather, it was because he saw DeSantis on Fox News.[30]

Cable television news hosts and commentators are among the first voices that Trump hears in the morning and the last he listens to at night. Now he is increasingly relying on those voices in making decisions—often running afoul of his actual advisers in the process. . . .

That Trump reacts so frequently to what he sees on television, rather than what he is reading or being told by aides, underscores the outsize role that commentators and cable programming decisions play in Trump's administration. . . .

Aides, in turn, try to influence the cable hosts who influence the president.

When Treasury Secretary Steven Mnuchin led a delegation to China in May, he announced on "Fox News Sunday" that the United States was "putting the trade war on hold." But soon after, others in the delegation, including China hawk Peter Navarro, found an alternative audience with Dobbs to criticize Mnuchin's message.

Then Dobbs's criticisms were picked up on "Fox & Friends" the following day by host Brian Kilmeade. Before long, and on the basis of those media messages, the president made an abrupt change in policy, said an adviser who was not authorized to speak to the news media.

Anne Gearan and Sarah Ellison, "How Trump Relies on His Cable News Cabinet as Much as the Real One," *Washington Post*, August 28, 2018

According to one White House advisor, the influence of White House officials and other administration personnel on Trump was "exactly equal" to what emanated from Fox News.[31] It is unsurprising that so many observers have labeled the Trump administration as a "reality show presidency." Trump's television addiction permits him to weigh in on breaking news. Unfortunately, it also exacerbates almost every other toddler trait discussed in this book.

Senior White House officials, taking their cues from chief of staff John Kelly, insist that they can't—and won't—control what the president does on social media. Asked last week what he does when Trump unleashes provocative tweets, one senior White House official said simply, "Ignore them."

Another senior administration official said efforts to exert control over Trump's tweeting were a "lost cause," adding that aides have also had little success limiting the president's TV-watching habit. "TV is what it is," the official said.

Andrew Restuccia, "Trump's Uncontrollable Tweeting Triggers Deeper Anxiety among Advisers," *Politico*, **December 3, 2017**

CHAPTER SEVEN

Potpourri; or, A Toddler Sampler

Preschoolers are very eager to take control. They want to be more independent than their skills and safety allow, and they don't appreciate their limits. They want to make decisions, but they don't know how to compromise, and they don't deal well with disappointment or restraint.

AMERICAN ACADEMY OF PEDIATRICS,
CARING FOR YOUR BABY AND YOUNG CHILD

Most of the preceding chapters focus on a specific toddler behavior or characteristic that Donald Trump frequently exhibits. Each of these traits—temper tantrums, short attention span, impulse control, oppositional behavior, knowledge deficits—are those that all toddlers demonstrate to some degree. While they last, these traits have pronounced effects on a toddler's theory of mind and executive functioning capabilities.

There are other behavioral traits, however, that are not uniformly present in all toddlers but still seem rather toddler-like. For example, when President Trump inspected a firetruck on the White House South Lawn, he went into the driver's seat, pulled the horn, and said, "Where's the fire? I'll put it out fast."[1] Not every toddler would pretend to be a firefighter when presented with the opportunity, but an awful lot of them would. They have that in common with the Toddler in Chief.

This chapter examines behavioral traits that some but not all toddlers possess. There is the aversion to new foods, for example. Although some small children are delighted to experiment with new food tastes, we tend to associate an insistence on specific favorite foods with toddlerdom. As it turns out, this is a quality they share with the Toddler in Chief. Even before Trump was President, he demonstrated a deep aversion to new foods. In the mid-1990s, when his businesses teetered near bankruptcy, he reluctantly agreed to visit Hong Kong to close a deal on New York real estate. Once there, Trump awkwardly avoided eating most of the sumptuous feast that his business partners had prepared for him. His Trump Organization subordinate explained to the *New York Times*, "He didn't like the food, and couldn't use chopsticks."[2] Trump's appetite for fast food, on the other hand, matches that of any three-year-old. Campaign staffers David Bossie and Corey Lewandowski wrote that Trump's four major food groups are "McDonald's, Kentucky Fried Chicken, pizza, and Diet Coke." They stressed that "the orchestration and timing of Mr. Trump's meals was as important as any other aspect of his march to the presidency."[3]

When Trump travels overseas as President, he has repeatedly insisted on eating his own preferred cuisine instead of dining on local delicacies. During his first trip as President to Saudi Arabia, his hosts were well aware of the Toddler in Chief's aversion to travel and new foods. To avoid tantrums, the caterers ensured that the President received his favorite meal—well-done steak and ketchup—alongside the lamb and rice dishes traditionally served to foreign dignitaries.[4] Similarly, on Trump's November 2017 trip to Japan, he opted for a well-done hamburger rather than the local food after playing a round of golf with Japanese Prime Minister Shinzo Abe.[5] White House advance teams have taken care to ensure that host governments avoid serving Trump food that might seem challenging, such as fish heads.[6] Even within Washington, the Trump White House has abandoned the Obama White House's practice of inviting DC chefs in to prepare new food.[7] Trump's appetite for fast food is so strong that he once sent a longtime staffer out to fetch McDonald's because he did not like the White House kitchen staff's approximation of their burgers, and he has repeatedly served fast food to White House guests.[8] The Toddler in Chief, like many small children, prefers what he knows.

Toddlers are often at their most difficult during long trips. In addition to experiencing the stress of being in a strange place, children are particularly susceptible to the disruption that time zone changes cause to sleep cycles and daily routines. It would appear that the Toddler in Chief is equally sensitive. The White House has taken pains to limit the length of overseas trips to reduce the likelihood that Trump will have a temper tantrum. Staffers have also complained about Trump's behavior on Air Force One during these long sojourns. Trump refuses to sleep much and instead watches television, forcing his staffers to watch with him. The experience is so unpleasant that some of his subordinates actively avoid accompanying him overseas. One staffer complained, "It's like being held captive." Another lamented, "He will not go to sleep."[9]

Most small children do not want to tour museums or historical sites. They find these trips boring, often fail to pay attention, and might make rude or inappropriate remarks. It would appear that the Toddler in Chief shares their disinterest. In a January 2017 visit to the National Museum of African American History and Culture, Trump's aides warned the museum's founding director that Trump "was in a foul mood and that he did not want to see anything 'difficult.'" When he saw an exhibit that portrayed the Dutch role in the slave trade, he responded by telling his guide, "You know, they love me in the Netherlands."[10] An April 2018 visit to Mount Vernon produced similar results. Trump was unimpressed by George Washington's house, uninterested in the guided tour, and was most animated about whether Washington was, in his words, "really rich."[11]

Trump also appears to share some toddlers' relationship with imaginary play. According to the American Academy of Pediatrics, "From time to time, expect your preschooler to introduce you to one of her imaginary friends. Some children have a single make-believe companion for as long as six months."[12] As a candidate and as President, Trump has similarly invoked apparently imaginary playmates. When he talked about Paris in campaign rallies before and after his inauguration, for example, he recounted that his friend "Jim" had explained to him how parts of the City of Lights have been infiltrated by Islamic extremists. According to the Associated Press, "Whether Jim exists is unclear. Trump has never given his last name."[13] In other speeches, Trump has referenced another friend who is a CEO; the White House has refused to corroborate the existence of this friend either.[14]

Finally, some small children who are not quite toilet-trained like to rebel against parental strictures by pretending that their parents do not exist. The Toddler in Chief is also a fan of the silent treatment; according to the *New York Times*, "[Trump's] most cutting insult is to pretend someone does not exist or that he barely knows them."[15] According to the Mueller report, Trump grew so upset with National Security Advisor Michael Flynn that he stopped looking at him during his intelligence briefings.[16] Similarly, Trump was so enraged with Gary Cohn's *Financial Times* op-ed criticizing his Charlottesville response that the President spent weeks refusing to speak with Cohn and ignoring him at meetings.[17]

This chapter briefly examines four additional examples of the Toddler in Chief's behavior that not every toddler demonstrates, but many do: his tendency to make fun of people he does not like, his tendency to misbehave with certain playdates, the ways he is easily impressed by flattery, and his special interests as President.

NICKNAMES AND IMPRESSIONS

Ironically, despite your child's being most interested in himself, much of his playtime will be spent imitating other people's mannerisms and activities. Imitation and "pretend" are favorite games at this age.

AMERICAN ACADEMY OF PEDIATRICS,
CARING FOR YOUR BABY AND YOUNG CHILD

In trying to make sense of the world and navigate it, young children will rely on the limited tools at their disposal. If they cannot pronounce a long word, they might use a nickname instead. If they see a behavioral tic that they find amusing, they are likely to mimic it to make other people laugh. As the American Academy of Pediatrics explains, "These play activities . . . serve as valuable rehearsals for future social encounters."[18] Most of the time, these activities are innocuous. Even young children, however, can tease each other. And some children will use imitation not as a form of flattery but as a form of bullying. For the Toddler in Chief, impressions and nicknames are a form of bullying. As one friend of Trump explained, "Trump believes that if you can encapsulate someone in a phrase or a nickname, you can own them."[19]

Although Trump called Kim "Rocket Man" in his first address to the United Nations, he thought it was not an insult and could even be seen as a compliment, Trump said at the dinner, according to attendees. But after Kim issued a statement calling Trump a "dotard," Trump upped the ante.

Josh Rogin, "In Private Remarks, Trump Opines on North Korea, Afghanistan and Catapults," *Washington Post,* **September 26, 2017**

In a meeting at the White House last month with House and Senate leaders from both parties . . . Trump upset Senate Majority Leader Mitch McConnell (R-Ky.) and House Speaker Paul D. Ryan (R-Wis.) by cutting a deal with Democrats. In subsequent days behind closed doors, the president mocked the reactions of McConnell and Ryan from the meeting with an exaggerated crossing of his arms and theatrical frowns.

Ashley Parker and Greg Jaffe, "Inside the 'Adult Day-Care Center': How Aides Try to Control and Coerce Trump," *Washington Post,* **October 16, 2017**

Behind the scenes, Trump has derisively referred to Sessions as "Mr. Magoo," a cartoon character who is elderly, myopic and bumbling, according to people with whom he has spoken.

Devlin Barrett, Josh Dawsey, and Rosalind S. Helderman, "Mueller Investigation Examining Trump's Apparent Efforts to Oust Sessions in July," *Washington Post,* **February 28, 2018**

Trump quickly soured on Tillerson and made no secret of his dislike. He mocked his mannerisms and Texas drawl, saying his secretary of state talked too slowly.

Ashley Parker, Philip Rucker, Josh Dawsey, and Carol Leonnig, "'It Was a Different Mind-Set': How Trump Soured on Tillerson as His Top Diplomat," *Washington Post,* **March 13, 2018**

Trump had for months complained that McMaster's briefing style was irritating and would do impressions of the three-star general bellowing out a list of points in staccato, his body puffing up and down as he spoke, the officials said.

Carol E. Lee, Courtney Kube, Kristen Welker, and Stephanie Ruhle, "Kelly Thinks He's Saving U.S. from Disaster, Calls Trump 'Idiot,' Say White House Staffers," NBC News, May 1, 2018

Seized by paroxysms of anger, Trump has intermittently pushed to fire his attorney general since March 2017, when Sessions announced his recusal from the Russia investigation. If Sessions' recusal was his original sin, Trump has come to resent him for other reasons, griping to aides and lawmakers that the attorney general doesn't have the Ivy League pedigree the president prefers, that he can't stand his Southern accent and that Sessions isn't a capable defender of the president on television—in part because he "talks like he has marbles in his mouth," the president has told aides.

Eliana Johnson and Elana Schor, "Trump Personally Lobbying GOP Senators to Flip on Sessions," *Politico*, August 29, 2018

Trump considered reappointing [Janet] Yellen to the post, and she impressed him greatly during an interview, according to people briefed on their encounter. But advisers steered him away from renominating her, telling him that he should have his own person in the job.

The president also appeared hung up on Yellen's height. He told aides on the National Economic Council on several occasions that the 5-foot-3-inch economist was not tall enough to lead the central bank, quizzing them on whether they agreed, current and former officials said.

Philip Rucker, Josh Dawsey, and Damian Paletta, "Trump Slams Fed Chair, Questions Climate Change and Threatens to Cancel Putin Meeting in Wide-Ranging Interview with the Post," *Washington Post*, November 27, 2018

Whenever Trump is souring on the DNI [Dan Coats] he privately calls "Mister Rogers"—because he won't implement a directive or has left the impression he thinks the president is irrational—Pence has encouraged Trump to stick with Coats, according to the current and former officials.

Carol E. Lee and Courtney Kube, "Mike Pence Talked Dan Coats Out of Quitting the Trump Administration," NBC News, March 28, 2019

Mr. Trump, who talks with members of his own Secret Service detail, had soured on [Secret Service Director Randolph "Tex"] Alles a while ago, convinced that as an outsider he was not popular among the agents, officials said. The president even made fun of the director's looks, calling him Dumbo because of his ears.

Peter Baker, Maggie Haberman, Nicholas Fandos and Zolan Kanno-Youngs, "Trump Purge Set to Force Out More Top Homeland Security Officials," *New York Times*, April 9, 2018

During a Republican retreat at Camp David last year, President Trump seemed particularly enthralled as Gary Cohn, then his chief economic adviser, delivered a briefing on infrastructure. The president impressed the assembled lawmakers with his apparent interest in the presentation, nodding along and scribbling furious notes.

But Trump's notes "had nothing to do with infrastructure," journalists Jake Sherman and Anna Palmer write in their new book, "The Hill to Die On."

Instead, Trump had scrawled "Sloppy Steve" atop his index card, followed by "copious notes" criticizing Stephen K. Bannon, his former chief strategist whom he had fired several months earlier.

Ashley Parker, "New Book Details Trump's Topsy-Turvy Relationship with Congress," *Washington Post*, April 3, 2019

In one tense meeting in the Oval Office, the president told Mr. Mattis he didn't know what he was doing and implored him to stop talking, then made fun of him for talking as if he had marbles in his mouth, according to two people familiar with the exchange.

Vivian Salama, Gordon Lubold, and Nancy A. Youssef, "Generals Fall Out of Favor as Trump Advisers," _Wall Street Journal_, July 15, 2019

UNSUPERVISED PLAY

Children under five should play on equipment separate from older children.

AMERICAN ACADEMY OF PEDIATRICS,
CARING FOR YOUR BABY AND YOUNG CHILD

Once toddlers reach 24 months, they are likely to be interested in playing with other children their own age. This can be a great relief for parents and caregivers, as children learn to entertain themselves. The problem is that young children can still get into trouble. As one parenting manual observes, "While grown-ups generally have a clear set of rules about how children are supposed to play with other children . . . toddlers operate under an entirely different set of rules."[20] Left unsupervised, some toddlers can goad each other into more and more reckless behavior. For the Toddler in Chief, there are groups of friends who appear to bring out the worst in him, a fact that vexes his staffers to no end.

Kelly has developed a Mar-a-Lago strategy to prevent Trump from soliciting advice from members and friends (In February [2017] Trump turned his dinner table into an open-air Situation Room when North

Korea test-fired a ballistic missile.) Sources briefed on Kelly's plans said he will attempt to keep Trump "out of the dining room."

Gabriel Sherman, "Amid a Widening Rift, John Kelly Has a Mar-a-Lago Strategy to Contain Trump," *Vanity Fair,* **October 9, 2017**

Trump feels especially liberated when he is at Mar-a-Lago, his lush seaside resort in Palm Beach, Fla., where he spent the Thanksgiving holiday, according to his friends. There, Trump enjoys a less structured and disciplined environment than at the White House, where Kelly attempts to tightly control whom the president sees and what information he receives.

In Palm Beach, friends and club members can approach Trump at will and plant ideas in the president's head, which he sometimes repeats or acts on.

Two outside advisers to Trump suspected it was no coincidence that he returned to Washington on Sunday night and soon thereafter struck a pugnacious tone in his public comments.

"Mar-a-Lago stirs him up," said one of the advisers, who spoke on the condition of anonymity to be candid.

Philip Rucker and Ashley Parker, "Trump Veers past Guardrails, Feeling Impervious to the Uproar He Causes," *Washington Post,* **November 29, 2017**

White House aides have also expressed worry that they can control Trump less at his palatial Florida estate, where he is known to seek out counsel from club members and get revved up by their at-times provocative advice.

Jonathan Lemire and Catherine Lucey, "What's in Those Seized Records? Trump's Biggest New Worry," Associated Press, April 16, 2018

White House aides and outside advisers to the president had long expected this kind of outburst from the president during his Mar-a-Lago visit. Trump has been known to let loose during his trips to the private South Florida club, where he has more time to talk to friends who validate his concerns and to escape the regimentation of the White House.

Andrew Restuccia, "Trump Lashes Out as Legal Risks Pile Up," *Politico*, **April 21, 2018**

White House aides have always been leery of Trump's visits to Bedminster where, as at Mar-a-Lago, he can mingle with members without staff "handlers" surrounding him. Also, there are fewer staff to try to keep him upbeat and, with some luck, away from the television.

The New Jersey golf club is where a brooding Trump unleashed several of his most inflammatory attacks and where, in spring 2017, he made the final decision to fire FBI Director James Comey, the move that triggered the special counsel's probe into Russian election meddling. During last summer's Bedminster break, he debuted his threat to unleash "fire and fury" against North Korea and then made his first tepid response to the racial violence in Charlottesville, Virginia.

This year, Trump's tweets have included scientifically dubious theories about the raging California wildfires and an insult to NBA superstar LeBron James that to some read as a racial dog whistle.

Jill Colvin and Jonathan Lemire, "Trump, at Golf Club, Intent on Projecting He's Hard at Work," Associated Press, August 11, 2018

Trump delights in decamping to his properties, especially Mar-a-Lago, his private Florida club, where he is expected to spend the upcoming holidays. The trips give him more time to bounce ideas off outside allies and friends without the regimentation of even his loose daily White House schedule, which he increasingly bristles against.

But White House aides and outside advisers acknowledge privately that Trump is often more impulsive when he's on the road and out of sight of senior staffers.

"He's more free and liberated there. He's able to do more things according to his style, on his own timetable—more like he did in the private sector," a former White House official said. "He doesn't have the same guardrails."

Andrew Restuccia, "Trump to Ditch Washington Restraints as 2018 Closes," *Politico,* **November 8, 2018**

Typically, Trump is accompanied by only a small staff entourage, sometimes with mid-level aides, on his weekend jaunts to Florida. But on Friday, several senior White House officials, including acting chief of staff Mick Mulvaney and press secretary Sarah Sanders, flew with him to Florida—in part so Trump would be surrounded by people he knows and trusts and therefore be less likely to do something rash, according to two people close to the president who spoke on the condition of anonymity to reveal internal details.

Philip Rucker, Robert Costa, Josh Dawsey, and Ashley Parker, "The Battle over the Mueller Report Begins as Trump Allies Claim Victory," *Washington Post,* **March 23, 2019**

FANCY PARADES AND FANCY LETTERS

It's . . . important to recognize that at this age his friends are not just playmates. They also influence his thinking and behavior. He'll desperately want to be just like them, even when their actions violate rules and standards.

AMERICAN ACADEMY OF PEDIATRICS,
CARING FOR YOUR BABY AND YOUNG CHILD

It can be very easy to impress babies. A simple game of "peeka-boo" will elicit squeals of delight. For toddlers, somewhat bigger displays are required to make an impression. Nonetheless, they will be attracted to superficial displays such as fireworks or fancy presents. In some instances, the impression will be so lasting that they will want to recreate the moment, or to obsess about their new toy.

Long before he became President of the United States, Donald Trump liked to show off his fancy toys. Being the President means being exposed to even fancier toys. Some of them have left a lasting impression on the Toddler in Chief.

Trump, impatient with the Senate's glacial pace [on repealing Obamacare], asked for a candid assessment of the legislation's status from the veteran lawmakers, according to officials familiar with the meeting. He implored them to hurry up and get the bill to his desk. But it was Paris and the flag-waving festivities he had witnessed alongside French President Emmanuel Macron on Thursday and Friday that occupied much of his attention during the conversation, the officials said.

Robert Costa, Kelsey Snell, and Sean Sullivan, "'It's an Insane Process': How Trump and Republicans Failed on Their Health-Care Bill," *Washington Post*, July 17, 2017

Pentagon officials told NBC News that they will be able to pull off the extravaganza, but the lack of momentum is notable—and possibly indicative of low enthusiasm for the event outside the Oval Office.

"There is only one person who wants this parade," a senior U.S. official said, referring to Trump. . . .

Trump got the idea for the parade while viewing France's Bastille Day Parade last summer. Naturally, he wanted it to be really big-league.

"We're going to have to try to top it," he later told French President Emmanuel Macron.

Courtney Kube, "Planning for Trump's Military Parade Finally Getting Underway," NBC News, June 28, 2018

Attending the 2017 Bastille Day parade at the invitation of President Emmanuel Macron, Trump was dazzled by the soldiers, armored tanks and fighter jets that painted the French sky red, white and blue—and informed high-ranking defense officials upon his return that he wanted a parade of his own in Washington.

Officials scrambled to put something together and set a tentative date of November 11. But when estimates for Trump's military parade soared to nearly $100 million, officials realized they needed a backup plan to convince Trump a parade was too exorbitant. In the end, they persuaded him that dozens of other world leaders would be in Paris for the commemoration, and he needed to be, too.

Kevin Liptak and Kaitlin Collins, "Trump's Paris Trip Marked by Missed Moments—and a Dire Warning," CNN, November 12, 2018

It has become a favorite parlor trick of President Trump's, and on Wednesday, he was at it again, brandishing his latest letter from the North Korean dictator, Kim Jong-un.

"Those few people that I've shown this letter to," Mr. Trump told reporters during a cabinet meeting, his voice trailing off as he waved three typewritten sheets in front of the cameras. "They've never written letters like that. This is a great letter. We've made a lot of progress with North Korea and Kim Jong-un."

If history is any guide, he will end up showing Mr. Kim's letter to more than a few people. Mr. Trump delights in sharing with visitors the correspondence he has received from North Korea's leader since they began writing to each other last year.

Typically, according to people who have witnessed such displays, Mr. Trump calls to an assistant sitting just outside the Oval Office to bring him "the letters," which he then fans out across the Resolute Desk so the people facing him can get a glimpse.

Mark Landler and Maggie Haberman, "The Pen Proves Mighty for an Unlikely Trump Correspondent," *New York Times*, January 2, 2019

One of the sources familiar with the contents of the latest letter tells CNN that Kim seems to send letters to Trump when he feels like things have gone quiet or when he wants to remind Trump about the strong rapport they struck up in Singapore. Another source who has been told about the letter from Kim said this one was also "predictably effusive."

The view of some in the administration is that Kim is sending the letters to keep Trump enthusiastic about their relationship, appeal to Trump's ego and provide a buffer for when Pompeo and others tell him that North Korea is failing to follow through on its Singapore commitments, so he can point to the letters and say he's developed this great relationship.

Kylie Atwood, Kevin Liptak, and Zachary Cohen, "US Scouting Sites for 2nd Trump-Kim Summit," CNN, January 3, 2019

The push for a second summit came almost entirely from the president himself, according to current and former White House officials—but Trump remains undeterred. He has gushed about the "wonderful letters" he has received from Kim, as well as the "good rapport" he has developed with the North Korean leader and the enormous media coverage the event in Vietnam's capital is likely to attract. Trump even bragged, in a phone call Tuesday with South Korean President Moon Jae-in, that he is the only person who can make progress on denuclearizing the Korean Peninsula, according to a person briefed on the conversation, and complained about negative news coverage he has received.

Eliana Johnson, "Trump Aides Worry He'll Get Outfoxed in North Korea Talks," *Politico*, February 22, 2019

SPECIAL INTERESTS

It's important for him to "show off" his home, family, and possessions
to other children. This will help him establish a sense of self-pride.

AMERICAN ACADEMY OF PEDIATRICS,
CARING FOR YOUR BABY AND YOUNG CHILD

Small children will often become obsessed about a topic for
days, weeks, or months on end. The topic could be predictable
(Disney princess stories) or more arcane (train schedules).
What matters are two things. First, the toddler's interest is
genuine and must be sated. Second, handled appropriately, a
special interest can be a godsend for caregivers. When small
children are occupied with their special interest, they are not
getting into trouble. In focusing on something that they can
master, they block out all the spheres of their life that seem
confusing or complex. Unsurprisingly, when parents take toddlers out to unfamiliar settings, they will let their child bring
a token of their special interest to occupy their attention.

One could hypothesize that Trump's staff has figured out
the value of this tactic. By the end of 2017, it had become clear
that the more Trump inserted himself into negotiations with
Congress, the less successful his administration. One reason
the health care legislation failed but the tax cut passed was
that Trump played more of a hands-off role in the latter process.[21] In his first few years in office, Trump's efforts to cajole
Congress mostly backfired.

What is the best way to get a hyperactive President not to
commit political self-harm? Divert his attention to his special
interests. Ordinarily, encouraging a President to microman-
age picayune tasks is a recipe for political disaster; Jimmy
Carter's supervision of the White House tennis court schedule
comes to mind. Donald Trump is a special kind of President,

however. As historian Matthew Dallek notes, "Where his pre-decessors sometimes knew so much that they got obsessed with the details, Trump knows so little that microscopic concerns seem almost to be ends in and of themselves."[22] Encouraging the Toddler in Chief to focus on his special interests means that Trump is causing less havoc in more important areas of policymaking. Fortunately for Trump's staff, he has a healthy number of special interests.

Trump is obsessed with the FBI building. For months now, in meetings with White House officials and Senate appropriators intended to discuss big-picture spending priorities, the president rants about the graceless J. Edgar Hoover Building in downtown Washington, D.C. . . .

Trump told Chief of Staff John Kelly he wants to oversee the project at an excruciating level of detail: the cost per square foot, the materials used, the renovation specs, etc.

Jonathan Swan, "Trump's Obsession with the 'Terrible' FBI Building,"
Axios, July 28, 2019

President Trump has effectively taken charge of the nation's premier Fourth of July celebration in Washington, moving the gargantuan fireworks display from its usual spot on the Mall to be closer to the Potomac River and making tentative plans to address the nation from the steps of the Lincoln Memorial, according to top administration officials. . . .

The president has received regular briefings on the effort in the Oval Office and has gotten involved in the minutiae of the planning—even discussing whether the fireworks should be launched from a barge in the Potomac River, administration aides said. The president has shown interest in the event that he often does not exhibit for other administration priorities, the aides added. . . .

Trump's focus on Independence Day reflects a broader pattern of focusing on the details of projects important to him personally. He grew obsessed, for example, with the renovation of FBI headquarters in Washington, asking for building specs, floor plans and even furniture and carpet schemes, current and former aides said.

Josh Dawsey, Juliet Elperin, and Peter Jamison, "Trump Takes over Fourth of July Celebration, Changing Its Location and Inserting Himself into the Program," *Washington Post*, May 10, 2019

At a moment when the White House is diverting billions of dollars in military funds to fast-track construction [of a wall along the Southern border], the president is micromanaging the project down to the smallest design details. But Trump's frequently shifting instructions and suggestions have left engineers and aides confused, according to current and former administration officials.

Trump has demanded Department of Homeland Security officials come to the White House on short notice to discuss wall construction and on several occasions woke former secretary Kirstjen Nielsen to discuss the project in the early morning, officials said.

Trump also has repeatedly summoned the head of the U.S. Army Corps of Engineers, Lt. Gen. Todd T. Semonite, to impart his views on the barrier's properties, demanding that the structure be physically imposing but also aesthetically pleasing. . . .

Trump often brought up the construction of the barrier at un-related meetings, and aides learned to bring prep books—and even sketches—to address his questions. He often grew frustrated when he would learn that more of the barrier was not built, the current and former officials said.

Nick Miroff and Josh Dawsey, "Trump Wants His Border Barrier to Be Painted Black with Spikes. He Has Other Ideas, Too." *Washington Post*, May 16, 2019

The president has insisted the structure be painted black and topped with spikes, while grumbling to aides that the Army Corps contracting process is holding back his ambitions. At the White House meeting

Thursday, he said he doesn't like the current design for the wall's gates, suggesting that instead of the hydraulic sliding gate design, the Army Corps should consider an alternative, according to an administration official: "Why not French doors?" the president asked.

Nick Miroff and Josh Dawsey, "'He Always Brings Them Up': Trump Tries to Steer Border Wall Deal to North Dakota Firm," *Washington Post***, May 23, 2019**

According to several former and current White House officials, Trump will grow visibly more animated or excited when the topic of meeting prominent members of royal families comes up, including the British royals. He makes a point of repeatedly asking aides about what he and others should wear during state visits and high-profile events with foreign countries' royalty, the sources said, and enthusiastically asks advisers about what kind of pomp and pageantry he should expect.

Tom Sykes and Asawin Suebsaeng, "William, Harry and Kate Deny Trump What He Wanted Most: A Photo Op," *Daily Beast***, June 4, 2019**

It appears the president, according to his own version of events, has helped choose design elements of the new Air Force One.

The natural question, of course, is, 'How does he find the time?' The answer, by all appearances, is that Trump isn't as busy as he probably should be, so he tackles tasks like these in between consuming hours of television.

And perhaps that's for the best. White House aides have told a variety of reporters that the key to keeping Trump out of trouble is keeping him busy and distracted. The more the Republican is focused on paint colors, the less time he'll have for more dangerous pursuits.

Steve Benen, "Trump Boasts about Personal Involvement in Air Force One Design," **MSNBC, June 14, 2019**

Trump, who had already ordered up a flyover by military aircraft including Air Force One and the Navy's Blue Angels, has pressed to expand his "Salute to America" event further with an F-35 stealth fighter and the involvement of Marine Helicopter Squadron One, which flies the presidential helicopter, according to government officials who spoke on the condition of anonymity to speak frankly. He also pushed to bring military tanks to the site of his planned speech at the Lincoln Memorial, prompting National Park Service officials to warn that such a deployment could damage the site, these individuals said. . . .

Trump has demonstrated an unusual level of interest in this year's Independence Day observance, according to three senior administration officials. He has received regular briefings about it from Interior Secretary David Bernhardt and has weighed in on how the pyrotechnics should be launched, how the military should be honored and more, according to people briefed on the discussions.

Juliet Elperin, Josh Dawsey, and Dan Lamothe, "Trump Asks for Tanks, Marine One and Much More for Grandiose July Fourth Event," *Washington Post*, **July 1, 2019**

Trump has pined for a national military parade since at least July 2017, when he watched French soldiers marching in Paris on Bastille Day. Speaking privately with French President Emmanuel Macron a couple of months later in New York at a United Nations General Assembly meeting, *Trump mentioned the display, turned to his delegation, and said "I want horses! I want horses!"* a former French official told me, speaking on the condition of anonymity to discuss the conversation.

Peter Nicholas, "Trump's Fourth of July Takeover Was Inevitable," *Atlantic*, **July 3, 2019**

CHAPTER EIGHT

When Caregivers Give Up

Staffing the Toddler in Chief

Without strong guidance, a very active child's energy can easily turn toward aggressive or destructive behavior. To avoid this, you need to establish clear and logical rules and enforce them consistently.

AMERICAN ACADEMY OF PEDIATRICS,
CARING FOR YOUR BABY AND YOUNG CHILD

Inside the White House, aides have grown calloused to the chaos. That the president managed to turn a simple question over a botched military operation into a week-long feud with a grieving military family, all while sullying his chief of staff's public image, didn't register as particularly eventful given the preceding nine months of drama.

Asawin Suebsaeng and Lachlan Markay, "Donald Trump Feels Zero Remorse over How the Week Went, Friends and Allies Say," *Daily Beast*, **October 20, 2017**

Every parent knows that taking care of toddlers can be exhausting. They are more mobile than babies and therefore more capable of putting themselves into peril. Toddlers require constant supervision. All the traits discussed in this book—poor impulse control, fits of temper, short attention spans, oppositional behavior, a profound lack of knowledge about how the world works—make toddlers particularly difficult to monitor in public. It is not surprising that parents of toddlers are often frazzled and overtired, particularly when shepherding them through air travel. Same with caregivers. Unsurprisingly, the low pay of many parts of the childcare sector leads to high rates of staff turnover.[1]

Compared to childcare service providers, White House staffers earn a higher salary, command greater respect, exercise more power, and participate in making history. The same logic holds with even greater force for cabinet secretaries. Traditionally, those who serve in the high ranks of an administration can expect a more rewarding future career track replete with honors, awards, and lucrative speaking engagements.[2] One would therefore expect there to be a bevy of Republicans eager to work for the 45th President. President Trump certainly assumed this during the campaign, pledging, "I'm going to surround myself only with the best and most serious people."[3]

And yet the opposite has been the case. Compared to previous administrations, the Trump White House has been much slower to fill presidential appointments across the federal government. According to the Partnership for Public Service, in its first seven months the Trump administration's process to fill presidential appointments was the slowest in 40 years. Of the 575 key policymaking positions he needed to fill, he'd secured Senate approval for only 50; Obama, in his first seven months as President, had confirmed more than four times as many.[4] Three years into Trump's presidency, the data show that his administration has taken far longer to announce nominees than his immediate predecessor. The poor quality of his choices has also lengthened the vetting process.[5]

Equally striking has been the high degree of turnover across

the upper ranks of the administration. The Trump administration had the highest first-year staff turnover in 40 years.[6]
By the end of his third year as President, Donald Trump was
on his third Chief of Staff, fourth National Security Advisor,
and sixth Communications Director. At one point in early
2019, Trump had five acting Cabinet Secretaries, and Mick
Mulvaney was serving concurrently as the Director of the
Office of Management and Budget, Director of the Consumer
Financial Protection Bureau, and Acting White House Chief
of Staff. According to the *New York Times*, the Trump staff had
experienced the highest turnover rate of 21 key White House
and cabinet positions during the post–Cold War era. In the
first 14 months of the Clinton administration, only three of
those positions turned over. In the Obama administration, it
was only two; with the George W. Bush administration, only
one. In contrast, nine of these positions turned over at least
once during the Trump administration during the same time
period.[7]

---

*"It's exhausting," says a midlevel aide. "Just when you think the pace
is unsustainable, it accelerates. The moment it gets quiet is when the
next crisis happens.". . . .*

Staffers are frustrated by leaks about staff turmoil coming from
Trump's extended circle of allies. But Trump has so far resisted attempts to impose order, insisting on long stretches of unstructured
time to watch television and call allies.

Michael Scherer and Alex Altman, "Trump's Loyalty Test," *Time,* **May 17,
2017**

West Wing aides privately admit they have no earthly idea what Trump
will do about *anything*—whether it be guns, immigration, their own
careers, or the fate of Chief of Staff John Kelly. . . .

Some aides feel the place is unraveling, that they can't trust their

colleagues, that they don't know what's going on, that there's no path
upward.

Jonathan Swan and Mike Allen, "In Trumpworld, Every Day Is Yesterday,"
Axios, February 23, 2018

Trump's first hires were a mixed bag at best. Some of his
cabinet picks, such as Secretary of Defense James Mattis,
Ambassador to the United Nations Nikki Haley, and Director
of National Intelligence Dan Coats, would have been predictable choices for any GOP administration. Many of the key
figures selected in the first few years, however, had skeletons
in their closet. This is best exemplified by White House Staff
Secretary Rob Porter. By all accounts he did a competent job
at handling Trump's paper flow and running the White House
policy process on trade, but he also was denied a permanent
security clearance because of his history of spousal abuse.[8]
The less said about the qualifications of Jared Kushner and
Ivanka Trump, the better.

The shoddy caliber of those who worked for the Trump
administration is demonstrated by how quickly their service
ended. Trump fired his first Chief of Staff and first Secretary of State by tweet. Multiple cabinet officials, including
Trump's first Secretary of Health and Human Services, EPA
Administrator, Interior Secretary, Secretary of Labor, and
Secretary of Veteran Affairs departed under clouds of scandal. Other Trump officials, including his first National Security Advisor, Michael Flynn, pleaded guilty to crimes. Even
on small matters, such as correct spelling in press releases,
the Trump White House has fallen short.[9] It is therefore
unsurprising that in an August 2018 Monmouth poll just
30 percent of respondents believed that Trump had hired
the best people, whereas 58 percent did not. Only 19 percent
of respondents expressed great confidence in the way that

White House advisors and staff handled their jobs.[10] Trump confidant Chris Christie, who ran Trump's transition planning during the 2016 campaign, characterized Trump's staff as a "revolving door of deeply flawed individuals—amateurs, grifters, weaklings, convicted and unconvicted felons—who were hustled into jobs they were never suited for, sometimes seemingly without so much as a background check via Google or Wikipedia."[11]

There are several possible explanations for why the Trump administration is such a negative outlier in terms of quality. It would be safe to describe the Trump team's personnel management as poor. From the moment Trump fired Chris Christie as his transition director the day after his election victory, his administration found itself woefully behind schedule on staffing.[12] The new transition team did a horrendous job of vetting, leading to many reversals and resignations after the press uncovered a nominee's past malfeasance.[13] Trump went so far as to claim that press coverage helped the administration in its vetting.[14]

Another problem—Trump's ideology and temperament was off-putting to many GOP stalwarts. Trump's brand of populist nationalism and "America First" slogan was somewhat at odds with longstanding Republican positions in support for balanced budgets, freer trade and an internationalist foreign policy. It was sufficiently polarizing that many Republican wonks eschewed working for him. This was particularly true in the foreign policy realm. During the 2016 campaign, GOP foreign policy experts signed multiple letters stressing Donald Trump's unfitness for higher office.[15] Secretary of State Rex Tillerson later told Congress that the Trump White House refused to even consider hiring any of the signatories to these petitions.[16] Because these names constituted a significant fraction of the GOP's bench strength in foreign policy and national security, it became that much more difficult to find appointees. The State Department was very slow in announcing political appointments; when Trump fired Tillerson in February 2018, only two of the top ten State Department political positions were occupied by a political appointee.[17]

In the past two months, President Donald Trump has repeatedly surprised many of his own closest advisers with the timing or substance of major public pronouncements: a potential troop withdrawal from Syria, steep new tariffs on key imports and the possibility of rejoining the Trans-Pacific Partnership trade agreement.

This week, it happened again, with U.S. Ambassador to the United Nations Nikki Haley—a Cabinet member—left dangling after Trump decided not to proceed with new Russia sanctions she'd already mentioned on national television.

These episodes have often left Trump's staff scrambling to get more information, moderate the president's position or change his mind altogether.

While people close to the president say Trump has always been mercurial, some of the president's allies attribute the recent spate of public disconnects to the departure of loyal aides who were skilled at translating his impulses into legible stances on key issues—and, perhaps more importantly, at keeping all the relevant White House and agency staffers in the loop on big decisions.

"There's nobody there that can say to him, 'Mr. President, you can't do that,'" said one former White House official.

Andrew Restuccia and Nancy Cook, "Trump Gets Lost in Translation amid West Wing Shuffle," *Politico,* **April 20, 2018**

For the past 18 months, Defense Secretary Jim Mattis and other top national security officials have mostly kept their heads down in public as they've tried to quietly counsel President Trump. But this low-key consultation process seems to be weakening, as a headstrong president becomes increasingly insistent about his judgment.

The Helsinki summit showed that Trump thinks he's his own best foreign policy adviser. The formal interagency process that traditionally surrounds such big events all but disappeared for the U.S.-Russia encounter, with no full National Security Council meetings to prepare for Helsinki and none last week to discuss its results.

"I don't think there is an interagency process now," cautioned one prominent Republican foreign policy expert. *"Trump glories in not listening to advisers. He trusts his instincts, as uninformed as they sometimes are."*

David Ignatius, "Trump Can't Win at Foreign Policy the Way He Wins at Golf," *Washington Post*, July 24, 2018

Over time, the toxic nature of Trump's presidency also complicated this administration's ability to attract talented staffers. With few exceptions, beleaguered Trump staffers contemplating their exit from government service did not find themselves overwhelmed with lucrative private-sector job opportunities.[18] The lack of promising jobs after serving in the Trump administration deterred many potential applicants. According to BuzzFeed, "Keeping their future career prospects in mind is also one of the reasons why Republicans are turning down opportunities to work in the administration."[19]

There is one other reason, however, why the 45th President has had such difficulties hiring the best people. Taking care of an ordinary toddler is hard work. Taking care of the Toddler in Chief is next to impossible. Reince Priebus, Trump's first Chief of Staff, explained that he agreed to the job to provide "a sane voice in the Oval Office": "There has to be a reasonable person in the room with him."[20] Imagine trying to rein in the Toddler in Chief nonstop, 24 hours a day, seven days a week.

That would exhaust even the best possible staffers, and the GOP was not sending its best to work for Trump.

Mr. Trump appeared heedless of his staff, unconcerned about Washington decorum, or the latest stock market dive, and confident of his instincts. He seemed determined to set the agenda himself, even if that agenda looked like a White House in disarray.

Inside the West Wing, aides described an atmosphere of bewildered resignation as they grappled with the all-too-familiar task of predicting and reacting in real time to Mr. Trump's shifting moods.

Mark Landler and Julie Hirschfield Davis, "After Another Week of Chaos, Trump Repairs to Palm Beach. No One Knows What Comes Next." *New York Times*, **March 23, 2018**

On some level, White House aides have simply reconciled themselves to the reality that they have little to no control over Trump's actions and instead remain prepared to explain them away or clean them up.

"Trump is truly serving as his own chief of staff, communications director, and policy maven," said a Republican strategist in frequent touch with the White House. "He's singing the Frank Sinatra song, 'I'll do it my way.'"

Ashley Parker, Seung Min Kim, and Philip Rucker, "Trump Chooses Impulse over Strategy as Crises Mount," *Washington Post*, **April 12, 2018**

Former White House staffers, demanding anonymity to avoid burning bridges to the administration, expressed relief that they no longer worked for Trump, recalling other tough moments in his tumultuous presidency.

"You just never knew what he was going to do, but usually it would make things worse," said one former aide.

Noah Bierman and Eli Stokols, "Trump's 'Everybody Does It' View of Politics Comes to Color His Conduct, and That of His Aides," *Los Angeles Times*, **August 22, 2018**

Inside the West Wing, a sense of numbness and dread has set in among senior advisers as they gird for what Trump will do next. "It's a return to the abyss," said one former official who's in frequent contact with the White House. *"This is back to being a one-man show, and everyone is on the outside looking in."*

Gabriel Sherman, "'Trump Is Nuts. This Time Really Feels Different': Trump Rejects 'War Council' Intervention, Goes It Alone." *Vanity Fair*, **August 27, 2018**

Less than two years into his term, the *New York Times* reported that "burned-out aides are eyeing the exits, as the mood in the White House is one of numbness and resignation that the President is growing only more emboldened to act on instinct alone."[21] Less than a year after John Kelly had been named Chief of Staff, he told visiting senators that the White House was "a miserable place to work."[22] The President had difficulties finding a replacement for Kelly. Trump's first choice, Nick Ayers, declined the offer and instead moved his family out of Washington, DC.

Unlike other toddlers, Trump will never actually mature. Also unlike other toddlers, Donald Trump has all of the constitutional and political prerogatives invested in the presidency. Crudely put, he has the power to say no to his caregivers. Without the disciplinary authority that parents and caregivers possess, White House staffers face limited options in keeping the Toddler in Chief out of trouble.[23] Over the span of Trump's first term, his staff have tried to use a variety of coping mechanisms. Some of them, such as encouraging the President's special interests, met with limited success. Most of the strategies, however, have failed and failed badly.

Morale inside the White House, never high to begin with, has turned particularly bleak, according to interviews with 10 former West Wing officials and Republicans close to the president. The issue is that many see Trump himself as the problem. "Trump is hated by everyone inside the White House," a former West Wing official told me. His shambolic management style, paranoia, and pattern of blaming staff for problems of his own making have left senior White House officials burned out and resentful, sources said. "It's total misery. People feel trapped," a former official said. "Trump always needs someone to blame," a second former official said. Sources said the leak of Trump's private schedules to Axios—which revealed how little work Trump actually does—was a signal of how disaffected his staff has become.

Gabriel Sherman, "'Trump Is Hated by Everyone Inside the White House': The State of the Union Left Trump Stoked—But Some of His Staff Are Miserable," *Vanity Fair*, **February 8, 2019**

Some current White House officials say they are exhausted amid the constant fighting and lack the energy to constrain a willful president bent on having his way. . . . A White House official described a "Who cares?" attitude creeping through the building under Mulvaney's hands-off management style.

Daniel Lippman, "Trump Veterans See a Presidency Veering off the Rails," *Politico*, **October 19, 2019**

Over time, Mr. Trump bridled and demanded the unstructured time he had so valued as an executive at Trump Tower. Mr. Priebus, who initially outsourced the details of Oval Office scheduling and paper flow to a deputy, has now taken over those tasks himself. He has reduced the pace of public events and, like a Montessori teacher, modulates structured work time with the slack periods Mr. Trump craves.

Glenn Thrush and Maggie Haberman, "Second Chance for 'Obamacare' Repeal. And for Reince Priebus." *New York Times*, **May 5, 2017**

The first and easiest staff response to the Toddler in Chief was simple accommodation to minor behavioral issues. For example, Trump likes to rip any piece of paper to shreds once he's done with it. That habit, however, is a violation of the Presidential Records Act, a law that requires all presidential documents to be preserved. Trump's staff failed to stop him from doing it. Instead, they assigned an entire department of records management analysts dedicated to taping Trump's papers back together.[24] This was not the best allocation of the federal government's human resources, but it likely saved the White House staff some agita.

There were other instances in which, right from his inauguration, Trump's senior staff would accommodate rather than constrain him. According to *Politico*'s Nahal Toosi, in some instances key staffers accepted and even dispersed what White House Counselor Kellyanne Conway called "alternative facts":

> In the days ahead of German Chancellor Angela Merkel's first visit to the White House during the Trump presidency, in March 2017, NSC [National Security Council] career staffers were told the president wanted to tell Merkel that other NATO countries owed the US money. Could they prepare a report on the topic? Career NSC staffers got to work and returned with the basics: that NATO countries don't owe the United States money because that's not how the military alliance works; that every NATO country is supposed to spend at least 2 percent of its GDP on defense, and that while many had fallen short of that commitment, others met it or were on track to do so. In short, no one 'owed' the United States anything.
>
> NSC career staffers presented this information to a senior administration official in the West Wing. Accord-

ing to one of them, the official replied: "The president is
going to say it anyway, so we need to help him. I mean, it's
not a legal document."[25]

Trump staffers also attempted to placate the President
through overindulgence. His subordinates took care to reassure the Toddler in Chief that he was doing a super-awesome
job as President. In one notorious June 2017 example, senior
Trump administration officials gathered for their first full
cabinet meeting. While television cameras filmed them,
cabinet members took turns in extoling the President for his
leadership and thanking Trump for the opportunity to serve
him. The *New York Times* explained that "the show of support for the President was in keeping with an intense effort
by the White House to boost Mr. Trump's mood" in the face
of lackluster poll numbers.[26] The strategy of fulsome praise
continued with a steady drumbeat of White House press
releases overflowing with cabinet members bestowing flattery
on Trump, a tactic that most prior administrations had not
used.[27] Allied leaders also attempted this gambit on several
occasions during Trump's first year as President.[28]

Another indulgence strategy was to provide Trump with
folders containing nothing but favorable press coverage.
Starting in his first few months in office, Trump was given
a folder twice a day "filled with screenshots of positive cable
news chyrons, admiring tweets, transcripts of fawning TV
interviews, praise-filled news stories, and sometimes just pictures of Trump on TV looking powerful," according to one
account.[29] When there was an insufficient number of positive
headlines, White House officials would ask the Republican
National Committee for flattering photos of the President.
Staffers would vie with each other for opportunity to deliver
the folder to Trump, because it put him in a better mood. One

former RNC official justified the practice by saying, "Maybe it's good for the country that the President is in a good mood in the morning."[30] This practice was fully institutionalized by 2018.[31]

The staff's habit of trying to feed him good news extended to polling data. According to *Politico*, "Aides in the White House often show Trump polls designed to make him feel good. . . . Usually they're the ones that focus just on voters who cast ballots for him in 2016 or are potential Trump supporters."[32] As the midterm elections approached, aides scheduled political rallies to boost Trump's mood.[33]

The indulgence strategy did not cause the President to stop acting like a toddler. Too many staffers had unrestricted access to the President, making it easy for them to distract or spin up the Toddler in Chief. Similarly, the tactic of providing the President with slanted or upbeat news stories had its downsides. One reason the President was slow to react during the family separation crisis on the southern border in June 2018 was that the public photos of crying children being separated from their families were not in keeping with the more positive photos Trump's aides showed him, which depicted the detained children smiling, playing video games, and exercising outdoors.[34] In trying to keep the President's spirits up, the Toddler in Chief's staff failed to warn him about brewing scandals until they received widespread media exposure.

None of the advice seemed to have any lasting effect on a president who views acting on his own impulses as a virtue. And these days, the staff has basically stopped trying: There is no character inhabiting the West Wing who is dispatched to counsel the president when he aims the powerful weapon of his Twitter feed at himself. . . .

Some Republicans have expressed concern that chief of staff John Kelly doesn't try to control the president's Twitter feed, which often distracts from enacting his legislative agenda. "Someone, I read the other day, said we all just react to the tweets," Kelly told reporters traveling with the president in Vietnam last week. "We don't. I don't. I don't allow the staff to. Believe it or not, I do not follow the tweets."

Annie Karni, "Aides Give Up on Trying to Control Trump's Tweets," *Politico***, November 17, 2017**

Inside the White House, aides over the past week have described an air of anxiety and volatility—with an uncontrollable commander in chief at its center.

These are the darkest days in at least half a year, they say, and they worry just how much further President Trump and his administration may plunge into unrest and malaise before they start to recover. As one official put it: 'We haven't bottomed out.'. . . .

Trump is testing the patience of his own staff, some of whom think he is not listening to their advice. White House counsel Donald McGahn and national economic council director Gary Cohn have been especially frustrated, according to other advisers.

The situation seems to be grating as well on White House chief of staff John F. Kelly, who had been on the ropes over his handling of domestic-abuse allegations against former staff secretary Rob Porter but who now appears on firmer footing. Talking last week about his move from being homeland security secretary to the West Wing, Kelly quipped, "God punished me."

Philip Rucker, Ashley Parker, and Josh Dawsey, "'Pure Madness': Dark Days inside the White House as Trump Shocks and Rages," *Washington Post***, March 3, 2018**

The brief rise and long descent of John Kelly's time as White House Chief of Staff perfectly encapsulates the arc of staffers who attempted to discipline Trump into not acting like a toddler. The fact that Trump wanted the former Marine general in the first place suggests that the President was aware on some level that he needed a more structured environment. When Kelly first came on board, press coverage stressed his desire to impose military discipline in the White House. Kelly ensured that all calls to and from the President went through the White House switchboard, so he could sign off on them. He acted as a veto point for any piece of information that could reach the Resolute Desk. He required that all staff members, including Trump's children, go through him to reach the President.[35] The *New York Times* reported that Kelly was "intent on cosseting Mr. Trump with bureaucratic competence and forcing staff members to keep to their lanes."[36] In that very same story, however, there were hints at the limits of Kelly's ability to constructively mold Trump's environment: "[Kelly] has told his new employees that he was hired to manage the staff, not the President. He will not try to change Mr. Trump's Twitter or TV-watching habits. . . . He has privately acknowledged that he cannot control the President and that his authority would be undermined if he tried and failed."[37]

On one level, former staffers acknowledge that ignoring the Twitter feed, however impossible that may be, might just save Kelly a losing battle. Since the campaign, aides have tried—and failed—to control the president's use of Twitter. Trump is familiar with the criticisms—he knows that his retweets and his commentary are "not presidential," he will tell aides, pre-empting the criticism he knows is coming. "The most success anyone has had, through numerous angles and schemes, has been to stop it momentarily, or to slow things down," said one former aide of Trump's tweets. "But it's just not possible to control it."

Annie Karni, "John Kelly's Losing Battle with Trump's Twitter Feed," *Politico***, November 29, 2017**

For months, aides were mostly able to redirect a neophyte president with warnings about the consequences of his actions, and mostly control his public behavior. . . .

Worried aides. . . . view the weekend's attacks on Mr. Mueller and the F.B.I. as a particularly disturbing taste of what they believe could come. They say privately that Mr. Trump does not understand the job the way he believes he does, and that they fear he will become even less inclined to take advice.

Maggie Haberman, "Newly Emboldened, Trump Says What He Really Feels," *New York Times*, **March 18, 2018**

Kelly's efforts to impose constraints on Trump had some initial success—and by initial, I mean a month at most. Less than three weeks after Kelly became Chief of Staff, Trump's "both sides" comments about Charlottesville highlighted the limits of his influence. One unofficial White House advisor explained to the *Washington Post*: "The Kelly era was a bright, shining interlude between failed attempts to right the Trump presidency and it has now come to a close after a short but glorious run. . . . Like all people who work for the president, he has since experienced the limits of the president's promises to cooperate in order to ensure the success of the enterprise."[38] Press reports soon appeared about Trump chafing at Kelly's restrictions.[39] By September 2017, whatever ability Kelly had to influence Trump's messaging had collapsed completely. He was unable to restrain the President from attacking NFL players in one breath and Kim Jong Un the next.[40]

Trump would face [a] crisis with deep demoralization and discord within his ranks, backed by advisers who consider him erratic, a national security adviser (H. R. McMaster) and economic adviser (Gary Cohn) who are both rumored to be eyeing the exits or being pushed that way by others, and a White House chief of staff in John Kelly, whose relationship with Trump is being frayed to near the breaking point.

All three of these men were once described as steadying forces for a president who likes to wing it on instinct. But all three are described by administration officials as wondering whether Trump is impervious to discipline.

John F. Harris and Andrew Restuccia, "Demoralized West Wing Stokes Fears over Trump's Capacity to Handle a Crisis," *Politico,* **March 2, 2018**

Mr. Kelly himself is also on thin ice, according to officials in the White House. He is said to have angered the president by privately saying "no" to the boss too often.

Michael D. Shear and Maggie Haberman, "'There Will Always Be Change,' Trump Says as More Personnel Shake-Ups Loom," *New York Times,* **March 15, 2018**

After more than 14 months in office, Trump is reshaping his administration, seeking people more likely to fall in line with his policies and tolerate his moods. The factionalism that defined the early days of his tenure has faded and he has lost some of the close aides who could manage his volatile impulses. To some, the White House is increasing taking on the feel of a squad of cheerleaders more than a team of rivals. . . .

The president believes that his recent decisions on tariffs and North Korea have breathed new life into his administration, and he is eager to take more "bold steps" that make his own mark. He has told confidants he wants to rid himself of staffers who hold him back. . . .

Trump has expressed frustration with aides [who] he believes try to "manage" him according to several current and former White House officials—and has grown tired of efforts by his staff to stall controversial actions they disagree with. Trump, the officials said, wants a lively discussion—he often talks about enjoying conflict among his aides— but has grown irritated that some try to undermine his decisions.

Zeke Miller, Jonathan Lemire, and Catherine Lucey, "Trump Jokes 'Who's Next?' as Tumult Engulfs His White House," Associated Press, March 16, 2018

Another source of tension was Trump's demand for unstructured time. During the first few months of Trump's presidency, early morning and breakfast meetings were on the schedule. The Toddler in Chief soon rebelled, however. When Kelly came on, he accommodated the President by instituting "Executive Time," long blocks of unscheduled time during which the 45th President could watch television, tweet, and call friends and cronies. According to White House schedules, on most days Trump would not arrive at the Oval Office until 11:00 a.m. His day would end at 6 p.m., earlier than for most of his predecessors. Subsequent staff efforts to cut back Executive Time and add more official meetings failed; one staffer acknowledged in June 2018 that "there's no going back."[41]

Unstructured playtime can be good for toddlers, but too much of it can be problematic—particularly if so much of the free time is devoted to watching television. The same appears to be true with Trump. According to Axios's Jonathan Swan, "Aides say Trump is always doing something—he's a whirl of activity and some aides wish he would sleep more—but his time in the residence is unstructured and undisciplined."[42] Trump associates have acknowledged that this unstructured time encourages all of Trump's worst toddler instincts. Barry Bennett, a 2016 Trump campaign advisor, told the *Los Angeles Times* that "you've got to give him suggestions because you've got to fill the vacuum."[43] Kelly attempted to do that with the creation of "Policy Time"—daily meetings in which advisors debated competing views over a specific issue, with Trump presiding.[44]

Those close to the president say that Trump has increasingly expressed fatigue at Kelly's attempts to shackle him and that while Trump is not ready to fire Kelly, he has begun gradually freezing out his top aide.

Trump recently told one confidant that he was "tired of being told no" by Kelly and has instead chosen to simply not tell Kelly things at all.

Jonathan Lemire and Catherine Lucey, "Inside a White House in Tumult, John Kelly's Clout Dwindles," Associated Press, April 5, 2018

As the fall of 2017 progressed, it seemed clear that Trump's staffers had decided not to fight Trump on the small examples of toddler behavior. The *Atlantic*'s David Graham noted, "As every parent knows, sometimes you just have to give in—let the kid have a victory on something less significant. Aides can try to prevent war with North Korea, and they can seek compromise on the Iran deal, and they can quietly kill the demand for more nukes, but they've got to let the president have his way on occasion. When Trump demands 'goddamned steam' to power catapults on aircraft carriers, aides shrug and let it go."[45] Trump staffers rationalized their service in the administration by arguing that they were preventing Trump's even crazier ideas from being implemented.[46]

One former senior administration official said the president's advisers tried the best they could to manage the president's discussions with world leaders, "but once he's up in the residence, we never know who he's speaking to."

At the start of his presidency, Mr. Trump's freewheeling conversations with world leaders prompted consternation among the president's senior aides, who took steps to keep him from making inappropriate comments or divulging sensitive information.

On more than one occasion, John Kelly, the White House's then-chief of staff, who was often in the room during calls with world leaders, briefly muted the line so he could caution Mr. Trump against continuing to talk about sensitive subjects, according to a person with knowledge of the matter. The small group of advisers in the room for the calls would also often pass the president notes offering guidance, the person said.

Vivian Salama, "Embarrassing Leaks Led to Clampdown on Trump's Phone Records," *Wall Street Journal*, **September 28, 2019**

Trump continued to rebel against Kelly's strictures in a variety of ways. As noted in chapter 7, his simplest gambit was to go to Mar-a-Lago. As the *Washington Post* reported in November 2017, "Trump feels especially liberated when he is at Mar-a-Lago. . . . There, Trump enjoys a less structured and disciplined environment than at the White House, where Kelly attempts to tightly control whom the President sees and what information he receives."[47] Indeed, Trump feels so relaxed at Mar-a-Lago that he has consented to impromptu interviews while there, flustering his staff.[48]

The President also took actions in the White House to bypass Kelly's paternalistic structures. He called aides to his residence in the evening and gave them assignments, along with instructions to keep them a secret from the Chief of Staff. Trump would also bypass the normal scheduling of White House phone calls so that he could talk to outside confidants without Kelly's knowledge.[49] After Kelly fumbled questions about his knowledge of White House Staff Secretary Rob Porter's history of domestic abuse, his ability to constrain Trump's toddler traits was weakened further.[50]

Kelly has done away with "meeting crashers," the West Wing aides who showed up for meetings uninvited, according to a White House aide, but he has not been able to curb Trump's practice of adding and subtracting advisers to meetings throughout the day or of turning scheduled gatherings into freewheeling discussions of subjects that suit his interests—including those suggested to him by his coterie of outside advisers, including Fox News host Sean Hannity.

"He comes down for the day, and whatever he saw on 'Fox and Friends,' he schedules meetings based on that," said one former White House official. "If it's Iran, it's 'Get John Bolton down here!' . . . If he's seen something on TV or [was] talking to Hannity the night before, he's got lots of flexibility to do whatever he wants to do."

Eliana Johnson, "How John Kelly Became 'Chief in Name Only,'" *Politico*, **July 29, 2018**

By March 2018, most of Kelly's strictures had been eviscerated. An exodus of Trump staffers began, led by Gary Cohn, H. R. McMaster, and Hope Hicks. Trump told friends that he wanted to be less reliant on his staff, because he believed they gave him bad advice.[51] Like any toddler free from adult supervision, Trump reveled in his newfound liberty, announcing tariffs and summits in a manner that surprised even his closest aides. He hired John Bolton as his third National Security Advisor against John Kelly's recommendation.[52] As one account put it, Trump was "acting as his own chief of staff, chief strategist, cable news producer, and communications director all rolled into one." Trump confidants described him as "'giddy'—a man who has finally fully indulged his itch to break free of John Kelly's restraints."[53] At the end of March 2018, Trump confidants were telling reporters: "This is now a president a little bit alone, isolated and without any moderating influences—and, if anything, a president who is being encouraged and goaded on by people around him. It really is a president unhinged."[54]

From the spring of 2018 onward, the press coverage suggests that White House staff have had to rely on more extreme carrots and sticks to get the President to do things expected of him. They scheduled a few days at Turnberry Country Club, Trump's golf resort in Scotland, to entice him to attend the July 2018 NATO Summit in Brussels.[55] John Bolton rushed to lock in the policy communiqué well before Trump arrived at the summit. This contravened usual practice but was done to ensure that Trump could not wreck the meeting once he arrived on the scene in the same manner that he did at the 2018 G-7 summit.[56] Even then, Trump continued to transgress in ways that embarrassed his staff. After his disgraceful performance at the Helsinki press conference, White House staff expressed shock and disappointment about the President's fawning over Russian President Vladimir Putin.[57]

The president's aides have begun to choose their battles or shape their advice to his approach. While the phrase "DO NOT CONGRATULATE" was written on Trump's briefing materials for his call with Putin last week . . . *the president's senior advisers also chose not to orally brief him on the talking point because they didn't think it would make a difference, officials said.*

"He'd say what he wants anyway," one official said.

Carol E. Lee, Courtney Kube, and Kristin Welker, "Trump Tells Aides Not to Talk Publicly about Russia Policy Moves," NBC News, March 29, 2018

His aides seem resigned to indulging the president's habits. White House staff tell Axios that rather than trying to force Trump to conform to the norms of presidential decorum and discretion, or to prevent him from spilling state secrets before dining-room guests—an effort reportedly spearheaded by John Kelly during his first few months as chief of staff—aides now mostly leave Trump alone, allowing him to do as he pleases. Besides his "working" lunches and dinners, Jonathan Swan reports, the president will be free to enjoy what White House officials describe as "Executive Time.". . . .

At first, Trump staffers tried to trick the president into doing his job, merging his professional duties with playtime—turning golf outings into political planning sessions, for instance, or scheduling working lunches with foreign leaders. *Yet after initially trying to adapt Trump to the presidency, they seem to have conceded that Trump has remade the office in his image....* These days, Trump's babysitters are more like chaperones, allowing the president to blow off steam on Twitter and do and say what he likes. The logic, perhaps, is that Trump has already demonstrated that nothing he does can hurt his popularity with his base, which has maintained its support of him through Charlottesville and Helsinki and the horror of family separation. At this point, his staffers seem to realize, they might as well let Trump be Trump.

Tina Nguyen, "White House Staff Have Given Up on Being Trump's Babysitter," *Vanity Fair*, August 6, 2018

After Helsinki, Kelly seemed to be increasingly checked out as Trump's minder. Press reports indicated he was coming in to the White House later, leaving earlier, and going to the gym in the middle of the day.[58] By the time Kelly formally departed in December 2018, he described the Chief of Staff position as a "bone-crushing hard job" or "worst job in the world." He also told associates that Mr. Trump was not up to role of President.[59] Kelly suggested to the *Los Angeles Times* that his greatest accomplishments as Chief of Staff had been invisible—it was the array of harebrained Trump schemes that he was able to veto.[60] His successor Mick Mulvaney said, "I don't think I'm telling any secrets—John hated the job."[61]

🗣

Trump has a pattern of catching his aides off guard with random policy announcements that are rooted more in his imagination and desires than any organized administration initiative.

Trump has sometimes issued directives publicly if he believes his subordinates are not executing his agenda forcefully enough or taking his wishes seriously. *"He thinks, 'Hey, if I say it on Twitter, then these guys will have to follow,'"* said one former White House official, who spoke on the condition of anonymity to candidly share the president's process.

Philip Rucker and Ashley Parker, "'In the Service of Whim': Officials Scramble to Make Trump's False Assertions Real," *Washington Post*, October 23, 2018

Despite his imposing military credentials, however, Mr. Kelly slowly realized the futility of trying to control the president, and ultimately resigned himself to a stalemate of coexistence, simply letting Trump be Trump and complaining to his colleagues about how miserable he was in the job. In the past year, he has often come to work late and left early, telling colleagues, "I'm leaving and I'm not coming back."

Annie Karni and Maggie Haberman, "John Kelly to Step Down as Trump, Facing New Perils, Shakes Up Staff," *New York Times*, December 8, 2018

By 2019, Trump's senior staff had reverted to an appeasement strategy. Approximately 60 percent of President Trump's schedule was devoted to unstructured "Executive Time."[62] Acting White House Chief of Staff Mick Mulvaney adopted a "let Trump be Trump" approach, loosening access to the President and enabling the Toddler in Chief's disruptive behavior.[63] Mulvaney made it clear to reporters that he enjoys the perquisites of power and is uninterested in attempting to constrain Trump's impulses.[64] He confirmed that Trump does not come down to the West Wing until around 11 a.m.; Trump's personal secretary complained that it was often later than that.[65] National Security Advisor John Bolton largely ended his predecessors' meetings of NSC principals, because they were disconnected from Trump's instincts. The result was "a national security process that, officials say, has shrunk

to little more than the instincts of an impulsive president"
according to the *New York Times*.[66] His new national security
team prevented Trump from acting on his most catastrophic
instincts, but only barely.[67] Indeed, Trump told reporters that
he constrained Bolton's bellicose impulses rather than vice
versa.[68]

For two years, they tried to tutor and confine him. They taught him
history, explained nuances and gamed out reverberations. They urged
careful deliberation, counseled restraint and prepared talking points
to try to sell mainstream actions to a restive conservative base hungry
for disruption. But in the end, they failed.

For President Trump, the era of containment is over.

One by one, the seasoned advisers seen as bulwarks against
Trump's most reckless impulses have been cast aside or, as Defense
Secretary Jim Mattis did Thursday, resigned in an extraordinary act
of protest. What Senate Foreign Relations Committee Chairman Bob
Corker (R-Tenn.) once dubbed an "adult day care center" has gone
out of business.

Philip Rucker, "'A Rogue Presidency': The Era of Containing Trump Is Over,
***Washington Post*, December 22, 2018**

For over a year, Mattis has been trying to reassure congressional leaders that he could help check some of Trump's impulses, in part by
intervening in the nuclear chain of command. In a break with normal
procedures, *Mattis reportedly told the commander of the Strategic
Command to keep him directly informed of any event that might lead
to a nuclear alert being sent to the president.* He even told the Strategic Command "not to put on a pot of coffee without letting him know."

Bruce Blair and Jon Wolfstahl, "Trump Can Launch Nuclear Weapons
Whenever He Wants, with or without Mattis," *Washington Post*, Decem-
ber 23, 2018

This surrender to the Toddler in Chief has extended to Trump's 2020 reelection campaign. According to the *Washington Post*, "Campaign advisers say they have come to trust Trump's political instincts, though they also recognize that he sometimes goes too far. Still, they say, they can only control what they can—and that often does not include the president."[69] As a Trump campaign aide described it, "He blows the hole and everyone else runs into the breach."[70] A former staffer explained, "The only way to preserve your sanity is to understand that wave after wave of people have tried to get [Trump] to do certain things and so you either sign up for who he is or get out while you can."[71]

By now the pattern for White House staffers under Trump has been locked in. They have admitted to reporters that they go through "a cycle of being enamored of Trump's larger-than-life persona, but then become frustrated by the environment he creates and allows, followed by anger at his self-destructive tendencies."[72] Similarly, the Toddler in Chief treats his staffers like new toys, enjoying them at the beginning, growing weary of them soon afterward, and eventually discarding them.[73] Former staffers have expressed concern to reporters that "after casting off advisers who displeased him at a record rate in his first two and a half years in office, Mr. Trump now has fewer aides around him willing or able to challenge him, much less restrain his more impulsive instincts."[74] According to former White House Communications Director Anthony Scaramucci, Trump's staff serves little purpose to him other than being "a prop in the back."[75]

What should have been a quiet weekend at home for President Trump—a small birthday gathering to celebrate his son, Barron, turning 13, and a Lenten service at the historic St. John's Episcopal

Church—instead mushroomed into a manic blur of frenzied, raging Twitter messages.

Trump tapped out 52 tweets in just 34 hours, marking his second-most prolific two-day stretch since becoming president—surpassed only by a 53-message flurry last fall focused largely on the arrival of Hurricane Florence. . . .

While Trump was pecking out angry nuggets, press secretary Sarah Sanders spent her weekend on vacation in West Virginia, and chief of staff Mick Mulvaney did the same in Las Vegas. White House officials made no real effort to intervene or rein Trump in, according to people familiar with how the president spent his days.

One Republican strategist in frequent touch with the White House said the staff had largely "given up" on trying to control their boss.

Ashley Parker, "Fifty-Two Tweets in 34 Hours: How a Trump Twitter Frenzy Defined a Weekend," *Washington Post***, March 24, 2019**

Trump's remaining staffers fall into one of three baskets: sycophants, Faustians, and rejects. The sycophants are the ones who excel at telling Trump that everything he does is great, even when what he has done is objectively awful. Dan Scavino epitomizes this group best, offering nothing but fulsome praise for the President. It is not a coincidence that the White House Director of Social Media started out as Trump's 16-year-old golf caddy.[76]

The Faustians include Mick Mulvaney, Economic Advisor Larry Kudlow, Secretary of State Mike Pompeo, and Attorney General Bill Barr. These individuals were not anyone's first-best or even second-best options for their positions. Trump hired them because he could not find anyone competent beyond those exiled to the Island of Misfit Wonks. These folks are Faustians because of the bargain they made with themselves to staff the Toddler in Chief. On the one hand, they must display fealty at every turn, endorsing policies and statements that they would have excoriated if they were out of power. On the other hand, Trump's short attention span enables them to pursue their own preferred policies so long as they do not publicly contradict the President. Pompeo will accede to Trump's wishes on North Korea provided he can be hawkish on arms control. Barr will preserve and defend Trump at all costs if it permits him the ability to extend executive power. Mulvaney will tolerate the Toddler in Chief in return for the freedom to run roughshod over Cabinet Secretaries to set regulatory policy. Because the President knows so little about policy, each of these subordinates can exercise considerable autonomy over their own policy bailiwicks.[77]

The final group are the rejects. As previously noted, Trump's first crop of staffers and administration officials were not the best people. As Trump's brand has become more tarnished, finding replacements for those exiting the administration has become ever more difficult. In numerous instances, the Toddler in Chief has resorted to hiring people whose reputations had already been tarnished. In 2018 Trump hired Bill Shine to be his Communications Director even though Shine had been forced out at Fox News for his poor handling of sexual harassment scandals. Ken Cuccinelli's immigration positions are too hardline to earn him Senate confirmation, but Trump tapped him to be the Acting Head of the US Citizenship and Immigration Services. Perhaps the best example is former Fox News commentator Monica Crowley. In early 2017 she withdrew her name from consideration for a National Security Council position after stories in CNN and *Politico* confirmed that she had plagiarized parts of both her PhD dissertation and her most recent book.[78] By 2019, however, Crowley had been hired to be a spokesperson for the Treasury Department.

Stepping back, the staffers who survive in the Trump administration tend to be those who tolerate and even emulate Trump's toddler-like traits. This raises a rather disturbing implication. The Mueller report's assessment of whether the President obstructed justice concluded, "The President's efforts to influence the investigation were mostly unsuccessful, but that is largely because the persons who surrounded the President declined to carry out orders or accede to his requests."[79] All of the officials who resisted Trump's entreaties—FBI Director James Comey, White House Counsel Don McGahn, Deputy White House Chief of Staff Rick Dearborn—are no longer in government. In their place, Trump appointed more pliant subordinates such as Barr, Kudlow, and Mulvaney. With each passing day, the only people eager to work for the Trump administration are those individuals who are willing to subordinate everything to the whims of the Toddler in Chief. These are staffers willing to prostrate themselves publicly by saying that the President did not have a temper tantrum, even if they were not in the room during the moment in question.[80]

Several White House officials expressed agreement during a staff meeting on Monday morning that the president's attacks [on U.S. Representative Elijah Cummings] were a bad move, according to people informed about the discussion, but they were uncertain who could intervene with him—or if anyone would even dare try.

Mr. Trump has told aides he sees his latest outbursts as smart strategy. The president has long been petrified of losing his base, and some aides believe he will need to maximize turnout from the voters who helped put him in the White House the first time given the highly partisan environment.

Several advisers said they were aghast that he was making such a target of Mr. Cummings. If anyone had tried to persuade the president of that, they were keeping it to themselves on Monday. But many advisers sounded defeated as they talked about a tweetstorm they hoped would end soon.

Peter Baker and Maggie Haberman, "Trump Widens War on Black Critics While Embracing 'Inner City Pastors,'" *New York Times*, July 29, 2019

This makes it easier to conceive of Trump being allowed, or even encouraged, to act on his worst instincts.[81] Former Speaker of the House Paul Ryan acknowledged this problem in 2019: "Those of us around him really helped to stop him from making bad decisions. *All the time.* It worked pretty well. . . . I think now . . . he sort of feels like he knows the job." Ryan added, "We helped him make much better decisions, which were contrary to kind of what his knee-jerk reaction was. Now, I think he's making some of those knee-jerk reactions."[82] Impeachment compounds these difficulties. It will make it even more difficult for the Trump White House to attract competent staff. Those remaining will have to devote extra time to preventing the Toddler in Chief from careening off the rails. One former White House aide acknowledged, "It may lead to less structured output from the White House."[83]

A senior administration official bemoaned how much of a gigantic pain impeachment proceedings would be for the White House staff to manage. The official said that is, in part, because being impeached would inevitably devastate Trump's focus, mood, actions, and agenda for the remainder of his first term.

Asawin Suebsaeng and Sam Stein, "Trump Ponders Violent Retribution as the White House Projects Impeachment Calm," *Daily Beast*, September 27, 2019

To take care of the Toddler in Chief three years into his term, the Trump administration has little choice but to scrape the bottom of the bottom of the barrel. This is fine. After all, what damage could a person with impulse control problems and the ability to launch nuclear weapons possibly do?

Will We All Live Happily Ever After?

Through your child, you will experience new heights of joy, love, pride, and excitement. You probably also will experience anxiety, anger and frustration. . . . The challenge is for you to accept and appreciate all the feelings with which your child expresses himself and arouses in you, and to use them in giving him steady guidance.

AMERICAN ACADEMY OF PEDIATRICS,
CARING FOR YOUR BABY AND YOUNG CHILD

Until recently, to understand America's political system, citizens would read classics like *Democracy in America*, *The American Political Tradition*, and *Profiles in Courage*. Then Donald J. Trump was elected President. Now Americans are reading *On Tyranny, How Democracies Die*, and the Mueller report. We are learning exactly how strong the country's institutions are in response to a President who displays the emotional maturity of a toddler. Unfortunately the answer appears to be, not very.

There is an abundance of evidence that Donald Trump, the 45th President of the United States, has the emotional and intellectual range of a misbehaving toddler. Outside observers, family members, and Trump biographers have all reached this conclusion. The primary data sources backing the claims made in this book have been the thousand-plus documented instances in which Trump's staff, subordinates, and loyal allies have described him in the press in ways that could be characterized as toddler-like. Across a range of behavioral and cognitive traits—temper tantrums, attention span, impulse control, oppositional behavior, and knowledge deficits—Trump has much more in common with small children than with the 43 men who preceded him. The reason his staff turnover is so high is the same reason turnover is so high at a daycare center: the pay is meager compared to what is demanded of employees.

If nothing else, readers of this book must conclude that the notion of Trump as a master political strategist is absurd. When Trump was running for President, and in his first few months in office, some observers argued that Trump's toddler traits were acts of cunning strategy. For example, in the first weeks of Trump's presidency, Paloma Sotelo argued in the *Huffington Post* that his toddler-like behavior was intentional: "Trump is not a child, [he] is an adult, who is—more or less—aware of his actions and their consequences. Even when sometimes it is hard to believe, behind each decision, declaration and tweet of the new Commander in Chief there is a political strategy. He is looking for a specific reaction among his supporters and detractors. What he does is a deliberated action, whether we like it or not."[1] Similarly, numerous pundits suggested that Trump's transgressive tweets were cleverly designed to distract the media from other negative stories.[2] His surprise 2016 victory convinced many pundits that Trump knew some core political truths that experts did not.

Those arguments have worn thin. One former Trump administration official told BuzzFeed that it is silly to think the 45th President is playing "three-dimensional chess." The official concluded, "More often than not he's just eating the

pieces."[3] Mark Krikorian, one of Trump's staunchest supporters on immigration, said, "There are both supporters and
detractors of his who imagine he's playing 40-dimensional
string theory chess, when in fact he's just operating from
his gut."[4] This book's simple thesis is that Donald Trump's
behavior demonstrates the opposite of strategy. He acts more
like the Toddler in Chief than the Commander in Chief. And
most of the guardrails designed to protect the country from
an out-of-control President have been worn down to the nub.

In these concluding pages, I first defend the Toddler in
Chief thesis against counterarguments. Second, I consider
the implications of having a President who thinks and acts
like a toddler—in particular, the paradox of a President who
some political scientists view as autocratic and others view
as spectacularly weak. Finally, I consider where the country
might go from here. How should the United States handle
the rest of its days living with a Toddler in Chief? Can the
guardrails that have been destroyed be rebuilt? How will our
long national nightmare of poorly run political daycare come
to an end?

In the process of curating the #ToddlerinChief thread on
Twitter, I have encountered two principal objections to it.
The first is that comparing Trump to a toddler is totally unfair
to toddlers. The second is that the toddler analogy does not
work as well as other analogies. Let's consider each objection
in turn.

Even as the connection was being made between Trump's
behavior and that of small children, some observers pushed
back against the Trump-as-toddler analogy. There are two
variants to this objection. The first is that comparing Trump
to a small child strips the President of his moral agency. *Chi-*

cago Tribune columnist Heidi Stevens argued that referring to Trump as the Toddler in Chief "implies a level of innocence and curiosity that's altogether absent from this president. It implies a work in progress. It's insulting to toddlers."[5]

At the same time, experts in child psychology make a slightly different argument: analogizing Trump to a small child underestimates the cognitive abilities of the latter. Psychology professor Alison Gopnik, for example, took to the pages of the *New York Times* to explain that four-year-olds do not act like Trump. According to her research, average four-year-olds "care deeply about the truth" and "can pay attention," possess "a strong moral sense," and "are sensitive to social norms."[6] Since Trump demonstrates none of these traits, he is clearly more cognitively impaired than a four-year-old.

The easiest response to Gopnik is to concede her point: Trump compares poorly to a four-year-old on every dimension that she listed. Indeed, the literature in developmental psychology has demonstrated that a neurotypical four-year-old possesses far more cognitive complexity and curiosity than is commonly understood.[7] However, the standard definition of a toddler is younger than age four. Indeed, the word "toddler" is a portmanteau of the Scottish words *todder* and *waddle*, referring to the awkward way in which a baby will first stand up and then stumble around.[8] In reviewing the American Academy of Pediatrics' guide for child care, the sections describing a two-year-old tracked far more closely to Trump's behavior than the sections for ages three, four, or older.[9]

What of the charge that comparing Trump to a toddler strips him of his moral agency? This objection seems a bit overwrought. To repeat myself from the introduction, this book's thesis is not that Trump *is* a toddler. Legally, he remains a mature man in full possession of his faculties. I am arguing that Trump's psychological makeup approximates a toddler and that this analogy is the best one to explain his behavior. To put it another way: even though Attorney General William Barr excused the President's attempts to obstruct justice during the Russia probe because he was "frustrated and angered,"[10] Trump's actual lawyers will be hard-pressed to rely on the toddler defense should he face prosecution for that or other crimes.

Perhaps this objection to the analogy has less to do with the Toddler in Chief and more to do with toddlers. No one interested in the toddler "brand" would want to be associated with Donald Trump. The toddler traits I have discussed in this book are all negative. Focusing on these dimensions gives this age demographic a bad rap. Toddlers are also intensely inquisitive human beings with boundless capacity for joy and love.

It should be noted that on occasion one can observe Trump displaying positive aspects of toddler behavior. His tendency to ask rapid-fire questions speaks to the occasional instances when he shares a positive toddler trait. His curiosity about space, space exploration, and a Space Force appear to be genuine and childlike.[11] Those moments, however, are far rarer than the episodes that wind up on the #ToddlerinChief thread. It is not just that Trump seems to act like a small boy; it is that he seems to act like an entitled, short-tempered small boy. It is little wonder that his older sister Maryanne told one biographer that Trump was "a brat" from the start, or that one of his elementary school teachers described him as "a little shit" to a different biographer.[12]

Finally, it should be acknowledged that analogizing Trump in this way omits the most important toddler trait of all: toddlers grow up. Trump clearly will not. In my #ToddlerinChief thread on Twitter, I write some variation of "I'll believe that Trump is growing into the presidency when his staff stops talking about him like a toddler."[13] After more than three years in office, Trump, unlike most preschoolers, shows no signs of maturing. By the time you read this, an infant who was born on Trump's inauguration day will demonstrate more emotionally maturity than the President of the United States.

●

Most of the sources cited in this book do not explicitly call Trump a toddler. Rather, they reference specific behavioral traits, such as a short attention span or a proclivity for temper tantrums. To make the case for the Toddler-in-Chief thesis, I have argued that because so many dimensions of Trump's behavior as President also appear in a toddler's developmental stage, the analogy is apt. To be fair, however, one could argue that these traits are present not only in small children. Teenagers could teach a masterclass in oppositional behavior. Adolescents are quite capable of developing an addiction to screens, as are other age demographics.

Many observers have argued that the 45th President more closely resembles a teenager than a toddler. Former GOP Senator Bob Corker explicitly compared Trump to a toddler, but he also compared him to a teenager. In September 2018 he told CNN, "Whining is pretty unbecoming of a 13 year-old. But it's very unbecoming of a 71 or 72 year-old."[14] In *Fear*, Bob Woodward writes, "Grievance was a big part of Trump's core, very much like a 14-year-old boy who felt he was being picked on unfairly. You couldn't talk to him in adult logic. Teenage logic was necessary."[15] Secretary of Defense James Mattis told colleagues that the President acted like a "fifth or sixth grader"—with the comprehension to match.[16] Masha Gessen, one of the more acute social observers of America in the Age of Trump, was even more explicit in making the teenager comparison:

[Trump] has often been compared to a toddler, but this comparison—as others have noted—seems unfair to toddlers, who generally recognize the authority of grownups to set rules and limits, and instinctively understand the need for them. Teenagers, on the other hand, sincerely don't see the point of grownups, even as they assert their right to act in a world created by them.[17]

Other observers have suggested that the way to think about Trump is as an entitled old man set in his ways. Former New Jersey governor Chris Christie, one of the earlier endorsers of Trump in the 2016 GOP primary, suggested on *ABC News Sunday* that one should think of Trump as that older, obdurate relative who comes for the holidays. "I want to ask everybody who's out in the audience today if they have a 72-year-old relative whose behavior they're attempting to change," he said, adding, "When people get older they become more and more convinced of the fact that what they're doing is the right thing, and it becomes harder to convince them otherwise."[18]

Some critics have gone further, suggesting that Trump is suffering from the cognitive decline that comes with old age. Psychology research does suggest that across several dimensions, the aging human brain reverts to a stage akin to small children.[19] MSNBC host Joe Scarborough, who has known Trump for quite some time, has suggested that the President is suffering from dementia.[20] Similarly, disgruntled White House staffers have made this accusation. Omarosa Maningault Newman has claimed the White House staff has kept Trump's deteriorating mental status a secret: "They continue to deceive this nation by how mentally declined he is. How difficult it is for him to process complex information. How he is not engaged in some of the most important decisions that impact our country."[21] Anthony Scaramucci told a reporter, "I think the guy is losing it, mentally. He has declining mental faculties; he's becoming more petulant; he's becoming more impetuous."[22] One peer-reviewed study concurred that Trump's impromptu speech showed signs of "linguistic decline."[23]

These counterarguments have some validity. Each can explain portions of Trump's behavior discussed in this book, but they cannot explain all of it as well as the toddler thesis. Adolescents and dotards usually possess some theory of mind. Toddlers do not. As developmental psychologists Stephanie Carlson and Louis Moses explain, "Younger preschoolers frequently state that beliefs and appearances always match reality, and that there can only be a single (realist) perspective on any state of affairs. Yet, by the time they are 5 years old, children have an appreciation of these matters that in core respects is recognizably adult-like."[24] Teenagers and old men might act like narcissists at times, but they normally possess the metacognition necessary to recognize it. Trump does not. As former US Representative Mark Sanford (R- SC) explained in 2018, "The tragedy of the Trump presidency is that he thinks it's about him. The president has taken those earnest beliefs by so many people across the country and has unfortunately fallen prey to thinking it's about him."[25] Trump's near-total lack of impulse control constrains his executive functioning far more severely than it would for an ordinary teenager or senior citizen.

Similarly, Trump's massive knowledge deficits make him closer to a toddler than a teenager or senior citizen. Both senior citizens and teenagers have developed some awareness of basic facts about how the world works. As chapter 5 demonstrates, however, Trump's acute ignorance of the world makes him function more like a toddler. Actually, it makes him worse than a toddler. Young children learn quickly to ask adults when they do not know something. Trump, on the other hand, loudly assumes that he knows everything.

Every behavioral trait discussed in this book is also discussed in the vast literature on parenting small children. Reasonable people can disagree about whether Trump acts more like a spoiled toddler, a moody teenager, or an old man returning soup at a deli. This might be the defining debate in the vast psychology literature that the Trump presidency will inevitably generate. How to adjudicate among these options is a question best left for future scholarship.[26] To paraphrase the Mueller report, if I had confidence after this thorough investigation of Donald Trump's behavior that the President clearly does not act like a toddler, I would so state. While this book does not conclude that the President behaves only like a toddler, it also does not exonerate him of that behavior.

In the introduction, I argued that Trump being a toddler was dangerous because of the deterioration of the guardrails that constrain the raw power of the presidency. But Trump's first few years in office raise an important question: can a Toddler in Chief really do *that* much damage?

Many political scientists argue that Trump is a fundamentally weak President, and they have a compelling case to make.[27] By conventional American politics standards, Trump's policy accomplishments have been meager. Despite having GOP control over both houses of Congress during the first two years of his presidency, he was only able to secure the passage of one significant piece of legislation: the tax bill. He failed in his efforts to get Congress to repeal Obamacare or provide appreciable funding for his border wall. Federal bureaucrats have resisted the President's ethically dubious orders through leaks, delays, memos, dissent channels, and official whistleblower complaints.[28] Even on policies where the Trump administration has been perceived as doing something, it has been feckless. His administration's push to shore up the coal industry, for example, has failed miserably.[29] Trump's deregulatory moves have frequently been halted in the courts due to violations of the Administrative Procedure Act. Most administrations win appeals against their regulatory changes 70 percent of the time. In the first two years of the Trump administration, its success rate was only 6 percent because the administration was so incompetent.[30]

In foreign affairs, Trump's biggest success has been the defeat of ISIS in Syria, but that was merely a continuation of a strategy mapped out in the Obama administration. Looking beyond that, Trump has failed to convert US leverage into appreciable gains in trade deals or arms control agreements. His trade wars have cost the US economy billions of dollars per month and have done nothing to fulfill his promise to shrink the US trade deficit—not that the trade deficit is a useful measure of anything.[31] None of his administration's "maximum pressure" campaigns have yielded any concessions to date.[32] His hardline policies on immigration have not stemmed the tide of Central American families seeking asylum by crossing the southern border. His one truly disruptive initiative, a series of summits with North Korea Leader Kim Jong Un, produced more symbolism than security. Given this record, it is unsurprising that the United Nations General Assembly laughed at Trump's 2018 suggestion that his administration had accomplished more than almost any prior administration.[33]

Trump's political instincts have also proven to be badly off the mark. He campaigned hard for Judge Roy Moore despite allegations of statutory rape, only to see a Democrat win a US

Senate seat in Alabama for the first time in a quarter-century. His party lost control of the House of Representatives in the midterm elections despite a booming economy in no small part because Trump chose to make the midterms all about the polarizing issue of immigration.[34] The President triggered the longest government shutdown in American history and in the end acquiesced to a deal worse than what was offered to him before it started. Despite an economy that by most standards looks rather robust throughout his tenure in office, he has had a historically high disapproval rating. After emerging from the Mueller probe without significant congressional reaction, the 45th president attempted to extort Ukraine's government for domestic political gain, triggering impeachment. Trump could be the first President in the history of Gallup polling to not have an approval rating of 50 percent or better at any time in his presidency.[35]

Trump has also failed to persuade the American people of the rightness of his policies. Polling about Trump's most high-profile policy moves confirm their unpopularity. Despite amped-up rhetoric from the administration about the threat posed by unchecked immigration, Gallup found "a record-high 75 percent of Americans, including majorities of all party groups, think immigration is a good thing for the US."[36] Despite the President's protectionist rhetoric, Gallup found public support for free trade at 74 percent in 2019, the highest level in the past 25 years.[37] Either pluralities or majorities oppose the tariffs implemented in 2018. Majorities disagree with Trump's tweeted claim that "trade wars are good, and easy to win."[38] CNN found that Americans preferred maintaining good relations with allies over imposing tariffs by 63 percent to 25 percent. And 65 percent of Americans believed that other world leaders do not respect Trump.[39] Opposition to Trump's policy of separating children of illegal immigrants from their families was even stronger. Despite Trump's prolific use of social media as a bully pulpit, he has alienated far more people than he has persuaded about the virtues of his approach to just about anything. If Richard Neustadt is correct than the chief power of the presidency is the ability to persuade, then Donald Trump has been a weak, ineffectual President.[40]

If one thinks of Trump as an overgrown two-year-old, his political performance begins to make more sense. An ongoing theme as his presidency has progressed is that fewer people fear him. As early as June 2017, the *Washington Post* reported that congressional Republicans were tuning out Donald Trump: "They have come to regard some of his threats as empty, concluding that crossing the president poses little danger."[41] Similarly, in March 2019 the *New York Times* reported that US-based companies had learned that Trump's threats were empty: "The president's scattershot attention span has diminished his power to persuade the business world to bend to his will. . . . Once fearsome tweetstorms have devolved into ephemeral annoyances."[42] Foreign diplomats have had the same reaction to Trump's threatening tweets; the best thing to do is ignore them because they do not amount to much.[43]

All of this is consistent with perceiving Trump as the Toddler in Chief. The President's myriad toddler traits have rendered him incapable of credibly committing to any bargaining position. This, in turn, has hampered his ability to negotiate with everyone ranging from Nancy Pelosi to Mitch McConnell to Angela Merkel to Xi Jinping. Threats of coercion are only effective if they are credible. Deals to settle disputes are unobtainable unless the President of the United States can follow through on pledges. Because other actors perceive Trump as possessing the constancy of a toddler, they see little reason to comply with his dictates.

Trump's own staffers have enabled this perception by

overindulging him. The pomp and circumstance of Trump's executive orders have been amplified, including Trump giving pens to key officials and attendees after the signing ceremony. But the executive orders reveal few significant policy shifts. One analysis concluded, "Generally the orders created committees or task forces, demanded reports or pressed for enforcement of existing laws."[44] It is almost as if Trump's staffers are pumping up the ceremonial aspect of these events to make the Toddler in Chief feel like he's actually governing, like a pretend President.

At the same time, however, this perspective underestimates the Toddler in Chief's damage to the United States polity in five important ways. The first is the carnage suffered by American foreign policy, the arena where the powers of the other government branches have receded the most. The President has used his authority to withdraw from a panoply of international treaties, ranging from the Trans-Pacific Partnership to the Iranian nuclear deal to the Intermediate Nuclear Forces treaty. He has threatened sanctions to coerce foreign governments such as Ukraine and China into investigating his domestic political opponents. On trade, the President has used his legal authorities to impose significant tariffs on a wide range of allies and adversaries. These tariffs—and the retaliatory moves by foreign countries—have exacted an escalating cost on the US economy.[45] His administration imposed an abhorrent travel ban from several Muslim-majority countries, an action that advanced neither American interests nor values. His administration has overhauled a welter of immigration and refugee policies to make them more restrictionist.[46] This included a policy to separate the children and parents of migrant families seeking asylum in the United

States. He declared a ban on transgender people serving in the military. In each of these cases, Congress has been unable to restrain the President, and the Supreme Court has sided with the Trump administration.

The immediate consequences of Trump's "America First" foreign policy have not been positive. Trump's toddler-like behavior has had significant effects on the global stage. At the end of his first year in office, Susan Glasser noted, "Seasoned diplomats who have seen Trump up close throw around words like 'catastrophic,' 'terrifying,' 'incompetent' and 'dangerous.'" She continued, "I listened to a group of sober policy wonks debate whether Trump was merely a 'laughingstock' or something more dangerous. Virtually all of those from whom I've heard this kind of ranting are leaders from close allies and partners of the United States."[47] Henry Kissinger, who praised Trump immediately after the 2016 election, was scathing in his assessment a few years later: "The entire foreign policy is based on a single unstable individual's reaction to perceptions of slights or flattery. If someone says something nice about him, they are our friend; if they say something unkind, if they don't kiss the ring, they are our enemy."[48] Unsurprisingly, whatever soft power the United States possessed at the end of the Obama era has evaporated under the Toddler in Chief.[49]

The Toddler in Chief's damage to America's standing in the world will last longer than is commonly appreciated. Presidents have the right to enact their foreign policies, but in absence of congressional buy-in, their only recourse is to do so through executive action. The current political polarization has eroded the notion that Presidents need to govern from the center. The combination of worn-down guardrails and Presidents emerging from the ends of the political spectrum could whipsaw US foreign policy between ultraconservative and ultraliberal approaches. In such a political climate, credible

US commitments cease to matter. Sustainable grand strategy becomes impossible.[50]

Second, Trump has essentially dared the courts to stop his executive power grabs, and in many cases the courts have blinked. In response to Democratic control of one of the chambers of Congress, Trump has reacted much as a toddler would to new forms of discipline—outright rejection. The slew of Congressional demands—particularly the House Ways and Means Committee request for Trump's tax returns—infuriated Trump. He has resisted congressional oversight on every level, repeatedly ordering executive agencies to rebuff legislative requests for documents and testimony.[51] Trump told ABC News that "Article II allows me to do whatever I want"; a few weeks later he told reporters, "Nobody ever mentions Article II. It gives me all of these rights at a level that nobody has ever seen before."[52] He is enamored of declaring a state of emergency because it affords him greater authority.[53] He did so along the southern border to justify an unprecedented reallocation of Defense Department funds to pay for construction of a wall. He even told a reporter that he was contemplating an executive order to end birthright citizenship.[54]

Trump has not followed through on that last idea, probably because the Supreme Court would declare it unconstitutional. Nonetheless, Trump was correct to view the judiciary as a weak constraint on an empowered presidency. It is unsurprising that the Trump administration has been so willing to go to court to defend its power grabs; their odds of success are decent. In these efforts, Trump has been aided by conservative lawyers who have advanced a strong version of unitary executive theory.[55] This theory argues that Presidents have the inherent constitutional authority to run all elements of the executive branch as they see fit. Particularly strong versions of unitary executive theory argue that the legislative and judicial branches have limited ability to interfere with presidential actions within the executive branch. Supreme Court rulings affirming the Trump administration on the travel ban and the transgender ban buttress this interpretation of the judiciary as a weak constraint.

Third, the Toddler in Chief has partially succeeded in deconstructing the federal bureaucracy, and those organizations will be hard to rebuild. In some agencies, Trump's political appointments have been so incompetent that they proved incapable of hampering the bureaucracy.[56] In other agencies, however, the neglect has been more malign. Trump's appointees at the Department of Agriculture, for example, had little respect for the scientific research performed by the department's scientists.[57] In 2018 Trump's Secretary of Agriculture centralized control over USDA researchers in an effort to limit the publication of any research critical of administration policies.[58] As a result the Department of Agriculture's best and brightest began to exit government service. By 2019, nonretirement departures from USDA research agencies had more than doubled compared to the previous three-year average.[59] A planned move of one research agency has caused more than two-thirds of its personnel to leave government service, which will lead to significant delays in the publication of vital research reports.[60] Similarly, the Department of Homeland Security has been battered from the President's obsession with slowing down migration across the southern border. With recalcitrant officials disinclined to violate the law to enact Trump's restrictionist policies, the result by mid-2019 was a constant upheaval of political appointees and low morale among the civil service. One former DHS official described the department as "gutted at all levels, from component heads to assistant secretaries to senior staff to counselors."[61]

The State Department is the cabinet agency that has suffered the most, however. The attacks on the Foreign Service have been unrelenting. In the first week of the Trump administration, the "Muslim travel ban" triggered a State Department dissent channel memo that garnered more than one thousand signatures. The dissent channel was established precisely to protect diplomats making an argument contrary to existing US foreign policy. Nonetheless, in response to this particular use, White House Press Secretary Sean Spicer said, "These career bureaucrats have a problem with it? I think they should either get with the program or they can go."[62] The White House quickly forced several senior career ambassadors out of their positions, a move that journalist Ronan Farrow labeled the "Mahogany Row massacre."[63]

One diplomat was told that a Trump appointee would oppose any Foreign Service Officers for leadership positions unless they passed the "Breitbart test," in reference to the online outlet that espouses populist nationalism.[64] The State Department's Inspector General has reported on political appointees taking punitive actions toward Foreign Service Officers deemed insufficiently loyal to Trump.[65] One stratagem was to assign suspect senior diplomats mundane tasks, such as the processing of routine Freedom of Information Act declassification requests.[66] One diplomat, resigning in protest in August 2019, poured cold water on the idea that bureaucrats were resisting the Toddler in Chief: "I have met neither the unsung hero nor the cunning villain of Deep State lore. If the resistance does exist, it should be clear by this point that it has failed."[67] Nancy McEldowney, the director of the Foreign Service Institute, stepped down in June 2017 despite her pre-Trump plan to stay in that position indefinitely. She described the State Department under Trump appointees as "a toxic, troubled environment and organization."[68] I have heard first-person accounts from high-ranking career officials at the Treasury Department and the Defense Department and within the intelligence community make similar characterizations of their own departments in the Age of Trump.

The effect of these attacks has been to erode the influence of career professionals in the Foreign Service.[69] In the first eight months of the Trump administration, approximately 12 percent of Foreign Affairs Officers left the State Department, an unusual drop in the first year of an administration. That reduction was concentrated in the upper tiers of the Foreign Service: the departures included 60 percent of Career Ambassadors (the diplomatic equivalent of a four-star general), 42 percent of Career Ministers (three-star general), and 17 percent of Minister Counselors (two-star general).[70] The self-imposed hiring freeze dropped the intake of new Foreign Service members from 366 in 2016 to approximately 100 in 2017. Applications to join the Foreign Service also plummeted by 26 percent in the first year of the Trump administration.[71] Given budget and staffing constraints, it is unsurprising that dissatisfaction among the diplomatic corps surged. The State Department dropped from fourth place in 2016 to eighth among 18 large agencies in the 2017 Partnership for Public Service survey of federal employees.[72] Even Trump appointees at State were forced to publicly acknowledge low staff morale.[73] However, when asked in the fall of 2017 about the dearth of State Department officials, Trump replied, "Let me tell you, the one that matters is me. I'm the only one that matters, because when it comes to it, that's what the policy is going to be."[74] *L'état, c'est* Toddler in Chief.

Fourth, Trump's rhetoric and actions have shredded norms that had previously regulated American political behavior. He fired James Comey despite a tradition of FBI Directors staying on from one administration to the next. He declined to reappoint Janet Yellen as Federal Reserve Chair and subsequently bashed his handpicked replacement for not lowering interest rates. He ordered the Department of Justice to investigate the origins of the FBI investigation into his 2016 campaign and continued to call for the prosecution of his political opponents.

On his first full day in office, Trump delivered what amounted to a campaign speech at CIA headquarters. He has repeatedly used uniformed military servicemen as political props. In his first week he issued an executive order without consulting any of the relevant cabinet departments. He fired his first Chief of Staff and Secretary of State via tweet. Trump has shown no compunction whatsoever with using social media to attack and insult Democrats, Republicans, athletes, and journalists. The formal press conference and daily White House briefings have been effectively discontinued; daily briefings at key cabinet departments have also been curtailed. He has refused to punish White House Counselor Kellyanne Conway for multiple violations of the Hatch Act despite a US Office of Special Counsel recommendation that she be fired.[75] Trump lies so frequently about so many things that the political class has become inured to his misstatements, racial slurs, and conspiracy theories.

Trump's defenders often like to say that what matters are Trump's actions, not his words.[76] This defense demonstrates a shallow grasp of the presidency as an institution. In both international relations and domestic politics, words matter greatly. A President's agenda-setting power comes as much from rhetoric as from executive action. President Trump's ability to set the political agenda has not waned; indeed, he has succeeded in dominating the political conversation since he was inaugurated in a way that exceeded his predecessors. The nature of his discourse—divisive, angry, infantile—has exacerbated pre-existing divisions within the country.[77] As political theorist Jacob T. Levy concludes, "Trump's speech, his especially outrageous and transparent lies, are words that have shaped the world: demonstrations of power, attempts to undermine the existence of shared belief in truth and facts."[78] Trump's rhetoric has not only eviscerated existing norms about political discourse, it has salted the earth. Attempts to discredit any outlet that criticizes Trump as the "enemy of the people" makes it that much harder for citizens across the political aisle to agree on basic facts.

The bully pulpit is one of the vital "informal institutions" that make up the modern presidency.[79] During moments of crisis, the expectation has always been that the President will employ rhetoric to unify rather than divide. Trump has shattered this norm. Most of Trump's rhetoric, untethered to anything resembling a structured speech, is at the mercy of his impulses. As President, he has declared the entire main-stream media to be the "enemy of the people" and labeled his political opponents as "treasonous" on multiple occasions. As Peter Baker concluded in the *New York Times*, "The old-fashioned idea that a president, once reaching office, should at least pretend to be the leader of all the people these days seems so, well, old-fashioned. Mr. Trump does not bother with the pretense. He is speaking to his people, not the people."[80] Levy notes that Trump's rhetoric is devoid of any sense of higher purpose:

> Trump's apologists are now reduced to saying that his speech has been worse than his actions so far, the reverse of this usual pattern. The effect is the reverse, too. When he tells us that there are "very fine people on both sides" as between the Klan and their critics, he turns the moral compass of American public discourse upside-down. . . . A norm that was built up through speech, persuasion, and

belief can be undermined the same way. Trump's own racism, his embrace of white nationalist discourse, and his encouragement of the alt-right over the past two years have, through words, made a start on that transformation.[81]

As President, Trump has paid almost no political price for these breaches of political decorum. Indeed, as *Vox*'s Ezra Klein pointed out during the 2016 campaign, Trump's lack of shame was a political asset: "He has the reality television star's ability to operate entirely without shame, and that permits him to operate entirely without restraint. It is the single scariest facet of his personality. It is the one that allows him to go where others won't, to say what others can't, to do what others wouldn't."[82] US Representative Justin Amash said the exact same thing after Trump was inaugurated: "Most people feel shame when they do or say something wrong, especially when it's so public. The president feels comfortable saying two things that are completely contradictory in one sentence. . . . It gives him this superpower that other people don't have."[83] In other words, Trump's toddler traits have helped him to act in an unconstrained manner.

Fifth, the reason Trump has paid such a small political price for his multiple transgressions, is that he maintains the rabid support of GOP partisans. In a polarized age, Donald Trump's immaturity has barely affected his standing with Republicans; indeed, his toddler-like style of tantrums and unchecked impulses is now embraced by Republicans as simply "unorthodox." He has consistently polled close to 90 percent approval among Republican voters. One March 2019 survey revealed that 78 percent of Fox News viewers believed that Trump has been the most successful President in American history.[84] The midterm elections forced out many of the moderate GOP members of Congress, such as US Representatives Mark Sanford and Mike Coffman, who were willing to speak out against him. Others, such as Senators Bob Corker and Jeff Flake, declined to run again. Approximately 40 percent of the GOP members of Congress in office at the time of Trump's inauguration will be leaving through a combination of retirements and electoral defeats by the start of 2020.[85] What remains is the Trump rump. In preparing for 2020, Trump has fused the Republican National Committee within his own reelection campaign to an unprecedented degree.[86]

Other pillars of GOP power have fallen in line behind the Toddler in Chief. Fox News has adjusted its guest commentators to avoid individuals who would upset the 45th President.[87] Self-proclaimed "institutionalists" such as Senate Majority Leader Mitch McConnell, went along with Trump's March 2019 decision to declare a state of emergency at the southern border—even though that move undercut the authority of the legislative branch. As *Politico* reporter Tim Alberta concluded, "If the first year of Donald Trump's term witnessed a president adapting to the philosophies of his party, the second year saw a party bending to the will, and the whims, of its president."[88] As the impeachment votes demonstrated, for as long as he is President, the GOP is Trump's party. And as long as the GOP remains under Trump's thumb, he will be able to act like a toddler with little fear of serious political retribution.

Even though Trump's actions to date have not triggered global catastrophes, he has exasperated his staff to the point where his current advisors have all adopted the "Let Trump Be Trump" mantra. One of his stoutest defenders, former White House legislative director Marc Short, acknowledged in 2018 that Trump "does function as his own chief of staff in a lot of ways. He may not even know what all [his current staffers] do."[89] In this environment, his staff no longer serves as a significant constraint. Instead, they are enablers, reverse engineering policies and justifications for Trump's worst impulses. Trump's Acting Chief of Staff Mick Mulvaney justified a White House advance staffer's request to keep the *USS John McCain* hidden from Trump's view during a May 2019 visit to Japan as "not an unreasonable ask" given how Trump "feels" about McCain.[90] Indeed, as previously noted, Trump's staffers and supporters have subtly shifted their defense of Trump. In his first year in office, they would note that he was an unorthodox President learning on the job. Now they merely say that he is an unorthodox President. To paraphrase former White House Press Secretary Sarah Huckabee Sanders, the President's behavior speaks for itself.

In some ways, Trump's presidency helps to explain the debate among American politics scholars about the relative power of the presidency. His inability to get much done through traditional means bolsters the traditional argument for the presidency as a weak institution that relies primarily on persuasion. On the other hand, Trump's foreign policy tantrums, power grabs, destruction of government organizations, evisceration of political norms, and cowing of the GOP establishment illuminate the awesome scope of the modern President's powers. If the goal is to destroy rather than create, then even a Toddler in Chief exercises considerable power.

The degradation of Trump's presidency does not just distort America's moral compass; it also puts the country at risk. Precisely because Trump seems to act and talk like a toddler, it is easy to not take him seriously. As early as the first week of Trump's presidency, foreign leaders were discounting his tantrums as something the Toddler in Chief needed to get out of his system.[91] Every time Trump issues an empty threat, his political rivals learn to discount his words even further.

Trump does follow through on his pledges on occasion, however. He has launched trade wars. He shut the government down, even though it made no logical sense. A vital part of international relations is the ability to credibly signal intent to others. If Trump's threats and promises are not taken seriously, his ability to deter and coerce become compromised. Gérard Araud, the former French ambassador to the United States, told the *Washington Post* that under Trump, "The chain of command, of information up and down, is basically broken. So it's quite difficult to pick up information or transmit messages" from the administration.[92] The likelihood of the United States stumbling accidentally into a conflict increases considerably. This is particularly true given the ultrahawkish nature of Trump's national security team.[93]

The country is at the mercy of Trump's impulses and those have not been promising to date. In one briefing, he wanted to expand the nuclear arsenal tenfold.[94] In a meeting with Latin American leaders, he expressed interest in invading Venezuela. In response to a sarin gas attack in Syria, Trump told his Secretary of Defense to assassinate Syrian dictator Bashar Al-Assad. He has inquired about using nuclear weapons to stop hurricanes from reaching the United States.[95] He told his staff that along the Southern border he wanted an electrified wall "with spikes on top that could pierce human flesh" along with a moat "stocked with snakes or alligators." He also wanted soldiers to "shoot migrants in the legs to slow them down."[96]

In each of these instances, his staff talked him out of taking such rash actions. The problem is not what the Toddler in Chief has done to date. His actions, while disturbing, have not been catastrophic. The problem is that he is untethered and unsupervised. Before he departed, former Chief of Staff John Kelly warned Trump that if he only appointed yes men to his staff, he would be impeached. When news of Kelly's warning came out, the White House Press Secretary claimed that the former Chief of Staff "was totally unequipped to handle the genius of our current President."[97]

In many ways Trump has been a remarkably lucky President; he has not faced an acute foreign policy emergency while in office. His handling of smaller crises does not inspire confidence, however. His policies have exacerbated conditions along the southern border, and he had no real response to the Saudi murder of a US permanent resident and *Washington Post* columnist in Turkey. In his brinksmanship with North Korea and Iran, Trump has followed a pattern of issuing hyperbolic threats only to back down at the last moment. Indeed, like a scared child, he has gone so far as to pretend that genuinely provocative actions by both of those countries have not happened. Based on Trump's behavior as cataloged in this book, the idea of Trump coping with a true crisis—a terrorist attack, a global pandemic, a great power clash with China—is truly frightening.

The history of modern states being ruled by actual toddlers is scant and scary. The most obvious case is Emperor Pu Yi of China's Manchu Dynasty. He ascended to the throne in 1908 at the age of two. According to his autobiography, Pu Yi responded to his ascension by throwing a temper tantrum and refusing to go to the Forbidden City for his coronation. In the end, he only agreed to go if his wet nurse carried him. During the ceremony, he threw candy at the Empress Dowager. His father, attempting to placate him, cooed, "It will soon be over."[98] For the courtiers in the Forbidden City, this was a bad omen. As it turned out their foreboding was prescient. Pu Yi acknowledged that while Emperor he was "without any real awareness of the political situation." He was the last Emperor of China, abdicating from his post at the age of five "with a similar lack of comprehension of the true situation."[99]

Other modern leaders have possessed traits akin to the Toddler in Chief. Kaiser Wilhelm II resembles Donald Trump on several dimensions. Born into privilege, Wilhelm also believed in the power of personal diplomacy and took care to cater to his country's nationalist right wing.[100] The parallels to the Toddler in Chief are even stronger than that, however. German admiral Alfred von Tirpitz quickly surmised that the Kaiser did not "live in the real world" and learned how to rile him up sufficiently to secure backing for Germany's naval expansion.[101] Negotiations with the Kaiser were difficult because he was constantly changing his mind and misinterpreted what his interlocutors told him. The Kaiser was also a speechmaker who could not stick to his prepared text. Wilhelm's entourage treated him in ways akin to Trump's White House staff. According to one mentor, the Kaiser did little but read news reports about himself.[102] He exasperated even the most obsequious of his aides. One of them, Bernhard von Bülow, praised Wilhelm constantly, but also complained to a friend, "You cannot have the faintest idea what I have prevented, and how much of my time I must devote to restoring order where our All Highest Master has created chaos."[103] Wilhelm's record of achievement also sets a concerning example. He let an alliance with Russia expire in 1890 because he believed he could extract a better deal. He could not. Misreading the situation badly, the Kaiser unwittingly enabled the formation of the Triple Entente. Oh, and he subsequently helped Europe blunder into the First World War.

The end of a centuries-old dynasty and start of a world war are not encouraging as predictors for Trump's legacy. Looking to the future, how should the United States handle the current Toddler in Chief? Are there ways to prevent future Toddlers in Chief from being a constant source of chaos muppets in our lives?[104]

The rise of the Toddler in Chief serves as an important cautionary tale for citizens and political scientists alike. For far too long, Americans took our institutions for granted and underestimated the importance of political leadership. To be fair, this error is not confined to ordinary Americans. The dirty secret about much of political science is that individual leaders are not presumed to matter. Political scientists have long privileged structural and institutional factors over the importance of individual leaders. Most international relations theories argue that the international system imposes powerful structural constraints on the behavior of individual foreign policy leaders.[105] At the dawn of the century, the structural grip on international relations scholarship was so strong that scholars lamented the deficit of work on individual decision makers.[106]

This has been equally true for the study of American politics. Ezra Klein correctly observed a few years ago, "Political scientists traffic in structural explanations for American politics."[107] The discipline forgot that individual leaders can make a huge difference in governance outcomes. As Arthur Schlesinger observed, historically "each President's distinctive temperament and character, his values, standards, style, his habits, expectations, idiosyncrasies, compulsions, phobias recast the White House and pervaded the entire government."[108] Presidents are not just dependent variables; they are significant independent variables as well. This is consistent with a growing literature on the importance of individual leaders.[109] A President's psychological makeup matters more than ever.

The most important thing to do is also the most difficult:

stop defining the presidency down. The original claim from Trump's supporters that he would mature into the presidency has been replaced by the explanation that he is an unorthodox President. According to this line of argument, he has redefined the meaning of "presidential." Or, as Trump put it to his staffers, his behavior is "modern-day presidential."[110] Some observers have seized upon Trump's transgressions to argue that the modern presidency was an impractical institution that needs to be overhauled.[111]

Others have resisted the notion that this time is different and have seized on the flimsiest of signs to argue that everything is fine. They argue that the guardrails have not worn down that much. To do this, they have had to define "adults in the room" down. John Kelly was perceived to be one, even though his political judgment and volcanic temper are almost as bad as Trump's.[112] The situation among his staff deteriorated so sadly that, according to a *Politico* profile of John Bolton, "a man once seen by Washington's foreign policy elites as a dangerous enabler of the President's worse impulses had taken on a surprising new identity: the adult in the room."[113] Claiming that John Bolton represented an anchor of maturity in the West Wing was grasping at the thinnest of reeds. Trump explicitly stated that he constrained Bolton far more than the reverse. For other observers, it took only the slightest hint of maturity from Trump for them to persuade themselves that, this time, he is really going to grow into the office.[114]

The desire to normalize Trump's behavior is strong, even among his critics. That is because living through the chaos of the Toddler in Chief has turned most Americans into the mental equivalent of exhausted parents. According to Gallup, in 2018 more Americans were stressed, worried, and angry than at any point in the past 12 years.[115] That is extraordinary when you consider what transpired during that stretch. American stress levels are among the highest in the world, matching or exceeding stress levels of Iranians, Rwandans, and Venezuelans. One could attribute this stress to the Toddler in Chief. Pew, for example, asked to describe how Trump's comments and statements made them feel. The top seven responses were: concerned, confused, embarrassed, exhausted, angry, insulted, and frightened.[116] Those track closely to the emotional state of the parents of toddlers behaving badly in public.

Given the state of national exhaustion, it is understandable that many Americans, particularly those who pay close attention to politics, ache for normalcy. Rationalizing Trump is one way to respond. Even among political scientists, there is a tendency to commit what Georgetown professor Daniel Nexon has called "analytical normalization": the act of explaining and assessing Trump's presidency as if one were considering a typical President and a typical administration.[117] As this book has hopefully demonstrated, this impulse should be resisted. Some limited comparisons can be made between Trump's traits and those of his predecessors. Andrew Jackson and Andrew Johnson shared Trump's temper. Johnson and Warren Harding also demonstrated knowledge deficits. Lyndon Johnson and Richard Nixon were inveterate TV-watchers. None of Trump's predecessors, however, shared all these traits. In that sense, we are in terra incognita.[118] Donald Trump is unlike all other Presidents; far more than his predecessors, Trump acts like more like the Toddler in Chief than the Commander in Chief. As long as he is President, his staff, the courts, Congress, and the rest of the country should treat him the way they would treat a spoiled toddler in need of discipline. The Toddler in Chief needs to be swaddled with constraints before he harms himself and those around him.

The American presidency needs to be child-proofed. This means rebuilding as many guardrails as possible. This will not necessarily be the popular thing to do. Child-proofing sounds great right up until the moment one is faced with opening a child-proofed bottle of aspirin while nursing a hangover. To their credit, leading 2020 Democrats have called for greater checks on the presidency.[119] Parties out of power advocate for presidential constraints until the moment they control the Oval Office, however. Champions of the strong version of unitary executive theory will blanch at checks on the presidency. Asking staffers or career professionals to do their job, however, is garden-variety bureaucratic politics.[120] They are, furthermore, the kind of constraints than an experienced leader can easily surmount.[121]

To properly rebuild the guardrails, Congress will have to play a greater role, and therein lies the rub. As noted in the introduction, the legislative branch ceded power to the executive due to the paralysis of polarization. This does not mean that Congress lacks the tools to constrain the Toddler in Chief, however. As political scientist Josh Chafetz has argued, the legislative branch has powerful tools at its disposal, including the power of the purse, the contempt power, and freedom of speech and debate.[122] True institutionalists will have a bipartisan interest in ensuring Congress plays a greater public role in checking and balancing against presidential prerogatives.

In the end, the most important check on the Toddler in Chief will have to come from the American people. The United States is a comparatively young country, but political theorists and political leaders have been calling on Americans to grow the hell up for quite some time. Max Weber, in his famous 1919 "Politics as a Vocation" lecture, warned, "America cannot continue to be ruled by amateurs."[123] In his first inaugural address, Barack Obama said, "We remain a young nation. But in the words of Scripture, the time has come to set aside childish things."

Those who agree with Weber and Obama are likely disappointed by the state of the American body politic. Multiple conservative commentators have acknowledged that Trump's ability to capture the GOP nomination reflected the dumbing down of Republican party politics into empty slogans aimed at the base.[124] US Representative Tom Reed epitomized this trend when he told *The Hill*, "The power of President Trump is that he's a disrupter. . . . And I'm a big fan of a disrupter in this town."[125] Only in the United States could the word "disrupter" morph from a description of badly behaved toddlers into a favorable description of business titans and political leaders. Historian Jeremi Suri correctly notes, "Disruption . . . is not a long-term strategy. It is an anti-strategy."[126] There is a very fine line between a disrupter and a powerful man simply having tantrum after tantrum. As Alan Wolfe noted recently in *The Politics of Petulance*, Trump has tapped into a "deep strain of political immaturity in American political life."[127]

Wolfe asks in his conclusion if "the American people will become ready to act like adults."[128] Based on public opinion surveys, the tentative answer is, yes. Despite a booming economy, President Trump's approval percentage continues to bounce between the high 30s and low 40s. Furthermore, a majority of the American people seem to share the opinion that Trump possesses many toddler-like traits. According to the Pew Research Center, an overwhelming majority of Americans believe that Trump has a bad temper. Just 28 percent of Americans believed that Trump was even-tempered. Even a plurality of Republican respondents agreed that Trump's temper was a problem. Similarly, 61 percent of Americans believe that Trump is "too impulsive" in making decisions.[129]

In other words, a solid majority of Americans believe that Trump possesses toddler-like traits.

Whether that majority will translate into a rejection of the Toddler in Chief remains an open question. Trump did not receive a plurality of votes in 2016, so it is difficult to blame the American people for his Electoral College victory. That excuse will be harder to maintain if he wins reelection in 2020. And there are decent reasons to believe that he is favored to win. Trump is the incumbent, and the economy as of this writing is in solid shape. Political polarization has helped to lock in support from multinational corporations and high net-worth individuals, giving the 45th President a decided financial advantage.[130] Most Republicans who are still Republicans appear to be willing to live with Trump's immaturity in return for tax cuts, conservative judges, and owning the libs.

Donald Trump is never going to grow up. Expecting him to mature is indulging in make-believe. It will be up to the American people, and not the Toddler in Chief, to set aside childish things. If voters re-elect Trump in 2020, then he is no longer the most immature American. The American electorate would be just as developmentally delayed as the 45th President. The true Toddlers in Chief would be us.

ACKNOWLEDGMENTS

As a regular contributor to the *Washington Post* since 2014, I have had to write about Donald Trump many, many, many times. As an international relations scholar, I have had to analyze the foreign policy of Donald Trump from every possible angle. Over the years, I have discovered a basic conundrum in this exercise. Any honest assessment of Trump's performance as President inevitably inspires two contrasting responses.

One response is despair. The Trump White House has succeeded in destroying an awful lot of existing structures. It has withdrawn from a bevy of international agreements, worsening the global governance of climate change and nuclear nonproliferation. It has launched multiple trade wars at a high cost with little to show for it in the way of trade concessions. The administration has prosecuted a draconian policy on immigration without slowing down flows of migrants. Trump has undercut almost every pillar of the liberal international order. The administration has pushed through bloated budgets and massive tax cuts that have temporarily goosed the economy at the expense of any whiff of fiscal probity; booming economies are not supposed to be running trillion-dollar deficits. It has ignored and stonewalled congressional oversight. The President has demonized his political opponents and repeatedly impugned the mainstream media as "the enemy of the people." Oh, and it seems quite clear that

Trump has obstructed justice and violated the foreign emoluments clause of the Constitution.

The other response, however, is laughter. The Trump White House has beclowned itself so frequently, across such a wide variety of issues, that it is difficult not to chuckle at the buffoonery on display. Policy announcements are rolled out without any advance planning. Senior cabinet officials are left out of the loop on decisions in their bailiwick; Trump sometimes contradicts or argues with senior cabinet officials in real time while on camera. White House press releases are littered with typos and misspellings. High-ranking appointments are announced without any vetting. Sebastian Gorka was employed at the White House—Sebastian Gorka! The most powerful subordinate in the West Wing remains Trump's hopelessly unqualified son-in-law Jared Kushner. The President tweets incessantly. His communications team is forced to defend his myriad misstatements and malapropisms, while his policy team is forced to reverse-engineer doctrines from tweets. On the policy side, Trump's team has been so incompetent that "Infrastructure Week" is now an inside joke among the cognoscenti about this administration's haplessness. On the political side, Trump's party lost a Senate race in deep-red Alabama and got walloped in the 2018 midterms despite a healthy economy.

The question is how a political observer can reconcile these two reactions to President Trump. My answer is this book. Donald Trump possesses all the behavioral traits of a toddler except the incontinence. The more one pictures Trump as an overgrown toddler, the easier it becomes to understand both sides of his presidency.

I am grateful to many people for their assistance during the crafting of this book. At University of Chicago Press, my editor Chuck Myers proved to be his usual excellent guide, tweaking the manuscript in a hundred little ways to make it better. Jenni Fry polished my prose. At the *Washington Post*, Mike Madden, Adam Kushner, and Marty Baron encouraged me to see how far the toddler analogy could hold up in my Spoiler Alerts columns—the answer is "pretty far!" I am grateful to Bethany Albertson, Jim Goldgeier, Jack Goldsmith, Meg Guliford, James Joyner, Dara Lind, Laura McKenna, Amrita Narlikar, Elizabeth Saunders, Ayanna Thomas, and Benjamin Wittes for feedback on rough drafts. I thank the anonymous reveiwers for the University of Chicago Press as well for their thoughtful comments and suggestions. The core of the book is the data gathered from my #ToddlerinChief Twitter thread, and I thank all those on Twitter who steered me toward examples of immature presidential behavior that I might have otherwise missed. My family—Erika, Sam, Lauren, and Mimi—were extremely supportive during the intense writing phases.

Finally, I am most grateful to the bevy of journalists who reported on Trump during his presidency. This book required very little original research. I functioned more like a curator, collating the original reporting of others. In doing so I leaned heavily on others who observe Trump more assiduously than myself. I thank Daniel Dale, Matthew Gertz, and Glenn Kessler in particular for their idiosyncratic niches of Trump coverage. The *Atlantic*, Axios, CNN, the *Daily Beast*, *Politico*, the *New Yorker*, the *New York Times*, the *Wall Street Journal*, the *Washington Post*, and other news outlets provided outstanding coverage of the Trump White House despite unrelenting administration attacks on the fourth estate. I found myself constantly amazed at the capacity of Tim Alberta, Peter Baker, Robert Costa, Josh Dawsey, Maggie Haberman, Eliana Johnson, Annie Karni, Jonathan Lemire, Carol Leonnig, Lachlan Markay, Seung Min Kim, Peter Nicholas, Damian Paletta,

Ashley Parker, Andrew Restuccia, Philip Rucker, Asawin Suebsaeng, and Jonathan Swan to report with such accuracy and astringency on this administration's dysfunction. I have never met any of these reporters in person, but this book would not have been possible without them.

As a close reader of political journalism during the Age of Trump, I am all too aware that it has been the best of times and the worst of times for reporters. Thanks to all the journalists cited in this book for their copy. I hope I put it to good use.

Daniel W. Drezner
DECEMBER 13, 2019

NOTES

INTRODUCTION

1 While Trump is the 45th president, he is only the 44th man to occupy the office; Grover Cleveland is counted twice because of his
nonconsecutive terms. So for those of you who thought I counted
wrong, please allow me this toddler-like response: nyah nyah
nyah!!

2 Chuck Schumer, quoted in Ben Kamisar, "Schumer: Trump's
'Temper Tantrum' over Wall Funding Is Leading to Shutdown,"
NBC News, December 16, 2018; Sally Yates (@SallyQYates),
Twitter, January 5, 2019, 10:11 a.m., https://twitter.com
/SallyQYates/status/1081583896217694209; Nancy Pelosi, quot-
ed in Paul Kane, Philip Rucker, and Josh Dawsey, "'She Wields
the Knife': Pelosi Moves to Belittle and Undercut Trump in Shut-
down Fight," *Washington Post*, January 16, 2019.

3 Glenn Thrush, "Pelosi Warns Democrats: Stay in the Center or
Trump May Contest Election Results," *New York Times*, May 4,
2019.

4 See, for example, Caitlin Oprysko, "Bullock: 'We're Expecting
More from Preschoolers' Than Trump," *Politico*, May 15, 2019.

5 Jack Shafer, "Donald Trump Is a 2-Year-Old: It's Time for the
Press to Treat Him Like One," *Politico*, June 1, 2016.

6 Mark Wilson, "Data Proves It: Trump Has the Emotional Maturity of a Toddler," *Fast Company*, January 20, 2017.

7 Trevor Noah, *The Daily Show*, November 30, 2016, segment
accessed on YouTube at https://www.youtube.com/watch?v
=9P1IVQJdVvE.

8 David Brooks, "When the World Is Led by a Child," *New York*

Times, May 15, 2017; Ross Douthat, "The 25th Amendment Solution for Removing Trump," *New York Times*, May 16, 2017.

9 David A. Graham, "The Infantilization of the President," *Atlantic*, October 11, 2017.

10 Dana Milbank, "President Trump Is Entering His Terrible Twos," *Washington Post*, January 7, 2019.

11 Adam Serwer, "Trump the Toddler," *Atlantic*, January 10, 2019.

12 Tony Schwartz, quoted in Jane Mayer, "Donald Trump's Ghostwriter Tells All," *New Yorker*, July 18, 2016.

13 Donald J. Trump and Tony Schwartz, *The Art of the Deal* (New York: Random House, 1987), 176.

14 The triggering story was Alexander Burns and Maggie Haberman, "Inside the Failing Mission to Tame Donald Trump's Tongue," *New York Times*, August 13, 2016.

15 Joshua Green, *Devil's Bargain* (New York: Penguin, 2017), 201. See also Bob Woodward, *Fear: Trump in the White House* (New York: Simon & Schuster, 2018), 14.

16 Woodward, *Fear*, 37.

17 Trump also told Stahl, "I'm President and You're Not." *60 Minutes*, October 14, 2018, transcript available at https://www.cbsnews.com/news/donald-trump-full-interview-60-minutes-transcript-lesley-stahl-2018-10-14/.

18 Mary Papenfuss, "Jim Acosta: Trump 'Hates' Mattis Letter—And News Stories That He Needs Adult Supervision," *Huffington Post*, December 21, 2018; See also Josh Wagner, Josh Dawsey, and Robert Costa, "Trump Pushes Back on Chief of Staff's Claims That Border Wall Pledges Are 'Uninformed,'" *Washington Post*, January 18, 2018; Michael C. Bender, "Trump Gets White House Witnesses to Attest to His 'Very Calm' Demeanor," *Wall Street Journal*, May 23, 2019.

19 Michael D'Antonio, *Never Enough: Donald Trump and the Pursuit of Success* (New York: Thomas Dunne, 2015), 40.

20 Trump and Schwartz, *Art of the Deal*, 70–71.

21 Paul Schwartzman and Michael E. Miller, "Confident. Incorrigible. Bully: Little Donny Was a Lot like Candidate Donald Trump," *Washington Post*, June 22, 2016.

22 Tim O'Brien, quoted in Michael Kruse, "'He Was Surprised as Anyone,'" *Politico*, November 11, 2016.

23 Jason Kurtz, "Van Jones on Trump: 'He Became President of the United States in That Moment, Period,'" CNN, March 1, 2017.

24 Mark Hensch, "CNN Host: 'Donald Trump Became President' Last Night," *The Hill*, April 7, 2017.

25 Ashley Parker and Robert Costa, "'Everyone Tunes In': Inside Trump's Obsession with Cable TV," *Washington Post*, April 23, 2017. Throughout this book, unless otherwise indicated, all emphases are mine and not in the original text.

26 Daniel W. Drezner (@dandrezner), Twitter, April 25, 2017, 9:23 a.m., https://twitter.com/dandrezner/status/856876322001432581. This tweet begins a thread of more than a thousand tweets, but its functionality on Twitter is far from perfect.

27 Josh Dawsey, Shane Goldmacher, and Alex Isenstadt, "The Education of Donald Trump," *Politico*, April 27, 2017.

28 Robbie Gramer, "NATO Frantically Tries to Trump-Proof President's First Visit," *Foreign Policy*, May 15, 2017.

29 Hunter Walker, "Even Some in White House Are Frustrated by the Stonewalling on Donald Jr.'s Meeting," Yahoo News, July 12, 2017.

30 Katie Walsh, quoted in Michael Wolff, "Donald Trump Didn't Want to Be President," *New York*, January 3, 2018.

31 Erick Erickson, "The Problem for the GOP," *Maven*, January 23, 2018. Erickson subsequently deleted that portion of his blog entry, but not before I captured it here: Daniel W. Drezner (@dandrezner), Twitter, January 23, 2018, 7:35 a.m., https://twitter.com/dandrezner/status/955796157095084033.

32 Sonam Sheth, "'He's Losing His S---': Trump's Advisers Are Increasingly Worried about His Mental State following Days of Erratic Behavior," *Business Insider*, September 6, 2019; Karen DeYoung, Dan Lamothe, Missy Ryan, and Michael Birnbaum, "Trump Decided to Leave Troops in Syria after Conversations about Oil, Officials Say," *Washington Post*, October 25, 2019.

33 On Mattis, see Patrick Radden Keefe, "McMaster and Commander," *New Yorker*, April 23, 2018; on Kelly, see Tara Palmeri (@

tarapalmeri), Twitter, September 4, 2018, 8:26 p.m., https://
twitter.com/tarapalmeri/status/1037150064391737344.

34 Vivian Salama and Jill Colvin, "Kelly Wins Praise across the Aisle,
but Will Trump Change?" Associated Press, August 1, 2017.

35 Quotes from, respectively, Josh Dawsey, "Trump's Dizzying Day
of Interviews," *Politico*, May 1 2017; Dawsey, Eliana Johnson, and
Josh Meyer, "Trump's Handling of Classified Info Brings New
Chaos to White House," *Politico*, May 15, 2017; and Eli Stokols, Re-
becca Ballhaus, and Louise Radnofsky, "Fired FBI Director James
Comey to Testify in Public," *Wall Street Journal*, May 20, 2017.

36 On the importance of same-party cues on partisans, see Tim
Groeling and Matthew Baum, "Crossing the Water's Edge: Elite
Rhetoric, Media Coverage, and the Rally-Round-the-Flag Phe-
nomenon," *Journal of Politics* 70 (October 2008): 1065–85.

37 "I Am Part of the Resistance inside the Trump Administration,"
New York Times, September 5, 2018.

38 Jake Tapper (@JakeTapper), Twitter, August 2, 2019, 4:08 p.m.,
https://twitter.com/jaketapper/status/1157397870724702208.

39 Gabriella Munoz, "Trump Goes after Anonymous Sources, Says
Stories That Use Them Are 'Fiction,'" *Washington Times*, August
28, 2018.

40 Indeed, the odds are excellent that Lewandowski is one of
those anonymous sources. Corey Lewandowski, quoted in Marc
Leibovich, "On the Trump-Mood Beat—But Why?" *New York
Times Magazine*, November 30, 2018. The story makes clear that
Lewandowski has offered anonymous quotes to reporters in the
past.

41 Newt Gingrich, quoted in Ashley Parker and Robert Costa,
"Trump's Lack of Discipline Leaves New Chief of Staff Frustrated
and Dismayed," *Washington Post*, August 16, 2017.

42 CNN State of the Union (@CNNSotu), Twitter, February 11, 2018, 8:34 a.m., https://twitter.com/CNNSotu/sta-
tus/962696451024355335.

43 Bob Corker (@SenBobCorker), Twitter, October 8, 2017,
10:13 a.m., https://twitter.com/SenBobCorker/status/
917045348820049920.

44 Karl Rove, "Political Death by 1,000 Tweets," *Wall Street Journal*, June 7, 2017.

45 Christopher Ruddy, quoted in Ashley Parker, Philip Rucker, Tom Hamburger, Robert Costa, and Matt Zapotosky, "'Buckle Up': As Mueller Probe Enters Second Year, Trump and Allies Go on War Footing," *Washington Post*, May 13, 2018.

46 Urs Gehriger, "Tucker Carlson: Trump Is Not Capable," *Die Weltwoche*, December 7, 2018, https://www.weltwoche.ch/ausgaben/2018–49/artikel/trump-is-not-capable-die-weltwoche-ausgabe-49–2018.html.

47 Aaron Blake, "Rex Tillerson on Trump: 'Undisciplined, Doesn't Like to Read' and Tries to Do Illegal Things," *Washington Post*, December 7, 2018.

48 Ryan Costello (@RyanCostello), Twitter, December 21, 2018, 1:28 p.m., https://twitter.com/ryancostello/status/1076197684401373184.

49 Rachel Frazin, "Graham: Trump 'Can Be a Handful,'" *The Hill*, February 7, 2019.

50 Adam Kinzinger (@RepKinzinger), Twitter, August 2, 2019, 11:12 a.m., https://twitter.com/repkinzinger/status/1157323336139137024?lang=en.

51 Tim Alberta, *American Carnage: On the Front Lines of the Republican Civil War and the Rise of President Trump* (New York: Harper Collins, 2019), 489.

52 Chris Christie, *Let Me Finish* (New York: Hachette, 2019), 5.

53 Robert S. Mueller III, *Report on the Investigation into Russian Interference in the 2016 Presidential Election*, March 2019, 2:32n155.

54 Mueller, *Report*, 2:39, 2:81, 2:85.

55 Mueller, *Report*, 2:51, 2:54, 2:57, 2:79.

56 See Dana Milbank, "The United States Is Being Run by a Toddler," *Washington Post*, November 8, 2019.

57 Isabel Oakeshott, "Britain's Man in the US Says Trump Is 'Inept,'" *Daily Mail*, July 7, 2019.

58 David E. Sanger, "'It Could Have Been Any of Us': Disdain for Trump Runs among Ambassadors," *New York Times*, July 10, 2019.

59 Siobhán O'Grady and Claire Parker, "U.K. Ambassador Kim Dar-roch's Private Cables Were Frank. Trump's Public Response Was a 'Nasty Diplomatic Step,'" *Washington Post*, July 10, 2019.

60 To qualify for inclusion, a respected media outlet had to source the toddler-like descriptions of the president from individuals who had a vested interest in Trump succeeding as president.

61 Michael Scherer and Zeke Miller, "Donald Trump after Hours," *Time*, May 11, 2017.

62 Felicia Sonmez, Anne Gearan, and Damian Paletta, "Trump Post-pones Denmark Trip after Prime Minister Declines to Sell Him Greenland," *Washington Post*, August 21, 2019.

63 Woodward, *Fear*; Omarosa Maningault-Newman, *Unhinged: An Insider's Account of the Trump White House* (New York: Gallery, 2018); Howard Kurtz, *Media Madness: Donald Trump, the Press, and the War over the Truth* (New York: Regnery, 2018); Cliff Sims, *Team of Vipers: My 500 Extraordinary Days in the Trump White House* (New York: Thomas Dunne Books, 2019).

64 Josh Chafetz, *Congress's Constitution: Legislative Authority and the Separation of Powers* (New Haven: Yale University Press, 2017). It is true that, compared to the Articles of Confederation, the Constitution created a stronger executive. This does not viti-ate the point that the framers wanted an executive who was less powerful than the King of England who inspired the American Revolution. See Jill Lepore, *These Truths: A History of the United States* (New York: W. W. Norton, 2018), chap. 4.

65 Alexander Hamilton, James Madison, and John Jay, *The Federal-ist Papers* (New York: Bantam, 1982), 263.

66 Hamilton, Madison, and Jay, *Federalist Papers*, Federalist no. 69 (Hamilton), 348–54.

67 Daniel Carpenter, *The Forging of Bureaucratic Autonomy: Rep-utations, Networks, and Policy Innovation in Executive Agen-cies, 1862–1928* (Princeton: Princeton University Press, 2001); Karen Orren and Stephen Skowronek, "Pathways to the Present: Political Development in America," In *The Oxford Handbook of American Political Development*, ed. Brian Glenn and Steven Teles (New York: Oxford University Press, 2016); Philip Rocco, "The Anti-Analytic Presidency Revisited," *Forum* 15 (July 2017).

68 Christopher Condon, "Here's a Timeline of All Trump's Key Quotes on Powell and the Fed," *Bloomberg*, July 22, 2019.

69 Jimmy Carter, quoted in Ronald Randall, "Presidential Power versus Bureaucratic Intransigence: The Influence of the Nixon Administration on Welfare Policy," *American Political Science Review* 73 (September 1979), 795.

70 Gretchen Helmke and Steven Levitsky, "Informal Institutions and Comparative Politics: A Research Agenda," *Perspectives on Politics* 2 (December 2004), 727.

71 Julia Azari and Jennifer Smith, "Unwritten Rules: Informal Institutions in Established Democracies," *Perspectives on Politics* 10 (March 2012), 49.

72 Peter Haas, "Introduction: Epistemic Communities and International Policy Coordination," *International Organization* 46 (Winter 1992): 1–35.

73 Barack Obama, quoted in Yoni Appelbaum, "Memo to Trump: This Is Why You're Losing," *Atlantic*, June 15, 2017.

74 Richard Neustadt, *Presidential Power and the Modern Presidents* (New York: Free Press, 1990), 7.

75 William Howell and Terry Moe, *Relic: How Our Constitution Undermines Effective Government—And Why We Need a More Powerful Presidency* (New York: Basic Books, 2016), xvii.

76 Yashar Ali, "What George W. Bush Really Thought of Donald Trump's Inauguration," *New York*, March 29, 2017.

77 See, for example, Eric Posner, "Are There Limits to Trump's Power?" *New York Times*, November 10, 2016; Jack Goldsmith, "Libertarian Panic, Unlawful Action, and the Trump Presidency," *Lawfare*, November 22, 2016; Daron Acemoglu, "We Are the Last Defense against Trump," *Foreign Policy*, January 18, 2017.

78 On the history of bad Presidential behavior, see James M. Banner, ed., *Presidential Misconduct: From George Washington to Today* (New York: New Press, 2019).

79 Arthur Schlesinger Jr., *The Imperial Presidency*, 3rd ed. (Boston: Houghton Mifflin, 2004), x.

80 Philip J. Cooper, *By Order of the President: The Use and Abuse of Executive Direct Action* (Lawrence: University Press of Kansas, 2002), 2. See also William Howell, *Power without Persuasion:*

The Politics of Direct Presidential Action (Princeton: Princeton University Press, 2003).

81 Howell, *Power without Persuasion,* 7.

82 Julia Azari, "The Constitution Doesn't Say Enough about Limiting Executive Power," *Vox,* April 11, 2019, https://www.vox .com/mischiefs-of-faction/2019/4/11/18306412/constitution -executive-power-limits.

83 Schlesinger Jr., *Imperial Presidency,* 208.

84 For a full list, see Barbara Salazar Torreon and Sofia Plagakis, "Instances of Use of United States Armed Forces Abroad, 1798– 2019," Congressional Research Service Report 7-5700, July 17, 2019.

85 See, on this point, James Goldgeier and Elizabeth Saunders, "The Unconstrained Presidency," *Foreign Affairs* 97 (September/October 2018): 144–56.

86 Mira Rapp-Hooper and Mathew Waxman, "Presidential Alliance Powers," *Washington Quarterly* 42 (Summer 2019): 67–83.

87 See Douglas Irwin, *Clashing over Commerce: A History of U.S. Trade Policy* (Chicago: University of Chicago Press, 2017), chap. 9.

88 Linda Fowler, *Watchdogs on the Hill: The Decline of Congressional Oversight of U.S. Foreign Relations* (Princeton: Princeton University Press, 2015).

89 Helen Milner and Dustin Tingley, *Sailing the Water's Edge: The Domestic Politics of American Foreign Policy* (Princeton: Princeton University Press, 2015).

90 Howell, *Power without Persuasion,* 134.

91 Jacob Hacker and Paul Pierson, *Off Center: The Republican Revolution and the Erosion of American Democracy* (New Haven: Yale University Press, 2005); Charles A. Kupchan and Peter L. Trubowitz. "Dead Center: The Demise of Liberal Internationalism in the United States," *International Security* 32 (Fall 2007): 7–44; Thomas Mann and Norman Ornstein, *It's Even Worse Than It Looks: How the American Constitutional System Collided with the New Politics of Extremism* (New York: Basic Books, 2012); Pew Research Center, "Political Polarization in

the American Public," June 12, 2014, http://www.people-press
.org/2014/06/12/political-polarization-in-the-american-public/;
Kenneth Schultz, "Perils of Polarization for U.S. Foreign Policy,"
Washington Quarterly 40 (Winter 2018): 7–28.

92 See, for example, Christopher Hare and Keith Poole, "The Polarization of Contemporary American Politics," *Polity* 46 (July
2014): 411–29; Mann and Ornstein, *It's Even Worse.*

93 Andrew Rudalevige, *The New Imperial Presidency* (Ann Arbor:
University of Michigan Press, 2005), 15. See also Howell, *Power
without Persuasion,* 176–77.

94 Christopher Ingraham, "Six Times Trump Said Executive Orders
Were Bad before He Decided They Were Actually Good," *Washington Post,* April 25, 2017.

95 Howell, *Power without Persuasion,* chap. 6.

96 Hedrick Smith, *The Power Game: How Washington Works* (New
York: Ballantine, 1988).

97 Randall, "Presidential Power"; Andrew Nathan, *The Administra-
tive Presidency* (New York: John Wiley and Sons, 1983); Andrew
Rudalevige, "Bureaucratic Control and the Future of Presidential
Power," *White House Studies* 10 (February 2010): 51–68; Gary
Hollibaugh, Gabriel Horton, and David Lewis. "Presidents and
Patronage," *American Journal of Political Science* 58 (October
2014): 1024–42.

98 Danny Vinik, "America's Government Is Getting Old," *Politico,*
September 27, 2017.

99 See Michael Lewis, *The Fifth Risk* (New York: W. W. Norton, 2018).

100 Philip Rucker and Robert Costa, "Bannon Vows a Daily Fight for
'Deconstruction of the Administrative State.'" *Washington Post,*
February 23, 2017.

101 See Tom Nichols, *The Death of Expertise* (New York: Oxford University Press, 2017), and Daniel W. Drezner, *The Ideas Industry*
(New York: Oxford University Press, 2017), chap. 2, from which
this paragraph is drawn.

102 Gallup, "75% in U.S. See Widespread Government Corruption,"
September 19, 2015, http://www.gallup.com/poll/185759
/widespread-government-corruption.aspx.

103 Gallup, "Honesty/Ethics in Professions," http://www.gallup.com /poll/1654/honesty-ethics-professions.aspx.

104 Tom W. Smith and Jaesok Son, "Trends in Public Attitudes about Confidence in Institutions," National Opinion Research Center, University of Chicago, May 2013, http://www.norc.org/PDFs /GSS%20Reports/Trends%20in%20Confidence%20Institutions _Final.pdf.

105 Scott Detrow, "Show's Over? Trump Pledges to Be 'So Presidential You Will Be So Bored,'" NPR, April 21, 2016.

106 Jonathan Martin, Maggie Haberman, and Alexander Burns, "Trump Pressed Top Republicans to End Senate Russia Inquiry," *New York Times*, November 30, 2017.

107 Kimberly Dozier, "New Power Center in Trumpland: The 'Axis of Adults,'" *Daily Beast*, April 16, 2017; Ilan Goldenberg, "Here's How Trump's 'Axis of Adults' Weathered the First 100 Days," *Foreign Policy*, April 28, 2017; Annie Karni, "Tillerson's Stock Rises in the White House," *Politico*, April 15, 2017; Tara Palmeri, "Trump Learning to Love Bush Aides," *Politico*, April 17, 2017; James Mann, "The Adults in the Room, " *New York Review of Books*, October 26, 2017.

108 See, for example, Elizabeth Saunders, "Leaders, Advisers, and the Political Origins of Elite Support for War," *Journal of Conflict Resolution* 62 (October 2018): 2118–49.

109 Woodward, *Fear*, 73–74.

110 Matthew Lee and Josh Lederman, "Trump Wants Out of Syria, but Don't Say 'Timeline,'" Associated Press, April 5, 2018.

111 Helene Cooper, Peter Baker, Eric Schmitt, and Mitchel Ferman, "Two Years In, Trump Struggles to Master Role of Military Commander," *New York Times*, November 16, 2018.

112 Richard Spencer, "I Was Fired as Navy Secretary. Here's What I've Learned Because of It," *Washington Post*, November 27, 2019.

113 Barbara Starr, "Trump Is Fraying Nerves inside the Pentagon," CNN, January 17, 2019.

114 Quoted in Jonathan Martin and Mark Landler, "Bob Corker Says Trump's Recklessness Threatens 'World War III,'" *New York Times*, October 8, 2017.

115 Eliana Johnson, "How John Kelly Became 'Chief in Name Only,'" *Politico*, July 29, 2018.

116 Nancy Cook, "Trump Bulldozes across the Presidency's Red Lines," *Politico*, April 12, 2019.

117 Karen DeYoung and Greg Jaffe, "For Some Foreign Diplomats, the Trump White House Is a Troubling Enigma," *Washington Post*, October 9, 2017.

118 Karen DeYoung and Josh Dawsey, "France Tries to Orchestrate a No-Drama G-7 Summit, but Trump Is the X Factor," *Washington Post*, August 22, 2019.

119 Woodward, *Fear*, 225–26; VandeHei and Allen, "Trump's State of Mind"; Peter Baker and Maggie Haberman, "Trump, Defending His Mental Fitness, Says He's a 'Very Stable Genius,'" *New York Times*, January 6, 2018.

120 Cook, "Trump Bulldozes."

121 Alexi McCammond and Jonathan Swan, "Insider Leaks Trump's 'Executive Time'–Filled Private Schedules," Axios, February 3, 2019.

CHAPTER ONE

1   Marc Leibovich, "On the Trump-Mood Beat—But Why?" *New York Times Magazine*, November 30, 2018. Leibovich also noted about the anonymous sources, "To state the obvious, any on-the-record source inside the White House willing to discuss the president with any meaningful level of candor would almost certainly not keep her or his job."

2   See Daniel W. Drezner, "The Angry Populist as Foreign Policy Leader: Real Change or Just Hot Air?" *Fletcher Forum of World Affairs* 41 (Spring 2017): 23–43.

3   Steven Webster, "Anger and Declining Trust in Government in the American Electorate," *Political Behavior* 40 (December 2018): 933–64; Ethan C. Busby, Joshua R. Gubler, and Kirk A. Hawkins, "Framing and Blame Attribution in Populist Rhetoric," *Journal of Politics* 81 (April 2019): 616–30.

4   Curt Mills, "Trump: 'I Will Gladly Accept the Mantle of Anger,'" *Washington Examiner*, January 14, 2016.

5   Albert Hirschman, *The Passions and the Interests* (Princeton: Princeton University Press, 1977); Steven Pinker, *The Better Angels of Our Nature* (New York: Viking, 2011); Andrew Linklatter, "Anger and World Politics: How Collective Emotions Shift over Time," *International Theory* 6 (November 2014): 574–78.

6   Neta Crawford, "Institutionalizing Passion in World Politics: Fear and Empathy," *International Theory* 6 (November 2014), 540. See also Leonie Huddy, Stanley Feldman, and Erin Cassese, "On the Distinct Political Effects of Anxiety and Anger," In *The Affect Effect: Dynamics of Emotion in Political Thinking and Behavior*, ed. Russell W. Neuman, George E. Marcus, Ann N. Crigler, and Michael MacKuen (Chicago: University of Chicago Press, 2007), 202–30; and Todd Hall, "On Provocation: Outrage, International Relations, and the Franco-Prussian War," *Security Studies* 26 (January 2017): 1–29.

7   Daniel W. Drezner, "Why Do Populists Get Lost in Translation?" *Washington Post*, February 23, 2017.

8   Michael Hirsh, "How Trump Practices 'Escalation Dominance,'" *Foreign Policy*, April 19, 2019.

9   James Fearon, "Domestic Political Audiences and the Escalation of International Disputes," *American Political Science Review* 88 (September 1994): 577–92.

10   Hall, "On Provocation."

11   Asawin Suebsaeng and Lachlan Markay, "John Kelly Pushing Out Omarosa for 'Triggering' Trump," *Daily Beast*, September 2, 2017.

12   On Miller, see McKay Coppins, "Trump's Right-Hand Troll," *Atlantic*, May 28, 2018. On Navarro, see Bob Woodward, *Fear: Trump in the White House* (New York: Simon & Schuster, 2018), 277.

13   Daniel Lippman, "The Print Reader in Chief: Inside Trump's Retro Media Diet," *Politico*, July 29, 2019.

14   Lippman, "Print Reader in Chief." On Kelly's temporary success, see Jonathan Swan, "Trump's New World," Axios, September 15, 2017.

15   Glenn Thrush and Maggie Haberman, "Forceful Chief of Staff Grates on Trump, and the Feeling Is Mutual," *New York Times*, September 1, 2017.

16 Michael S. Schmidt and Maggie Haberman, "Trump Humiliated Jeff Sessions after Mueller Appointment," *New York Times*, September 14, 2017.

17 Zack Beauchamp, "'Toxic on a Day-to-Day Level': How Trump Is Mismanaging the White House," *Vox*, October 5, 2017.

18 See, for example, Mark Landler and Maggie Haberman, "Trump Urges Unity, but Puerto Rico and Las Vegas Visits Could Test His Words," *New York Times*, October 2, 2017; Josh Dawsey, "White House Aides Lean on Delays and Distraction to Manage Trump," *Politico*, October 9, 2017; Andrew Restuccia and Nancy Cook, "White House Puts Mueller on Notice after Raids," *Politico*, April 10, 2018.

19 See Kathryn Dunn Tempas, "Record-Setting White House Staff Turnover Continues with News of Counsel's Departure," Brookings Institution, https://www.brookings.edu/blog/fix-gov/2018/10/19/record-setting-white-house-staff-turnover-continues-with-news-of-counsels-departure/, October 28, 2018; Denise Lu and Karen Yourish, "The Turnover at the Top of the Trump Administration Is Unprecedented," *New York Times*, March 29, 2019.

20 "Several senior officials say televised briefings stopped because of worry TV watcher-in-chief, President Trump, would get angry if he saw something he didn't like," Barbara Starr on CNN's Reliable Sources. Transcript accessed at http://transcripts.cnn.com/TRANSCRIPTS/1906/02/rs.01.html.

21 Michael S. Schmidt, "White House Asked McGahn to Declare Trump Never Obstructed Justice," *New York Times*, May 10, 2019.

22 Jonathan Swan and Alayna Treene, "Former White House Counsel Don McGahn off the Record," Axios, April 7, 2019.

CHAPTER TWO

1   Richard Neustadt, *Presidential Power and the Modern Presidents* (New York: Free Press, 1990).

2   Alberto Nardelli, "This Is What European Diplomats Really Think about Donald Trump," BuzzFeed, August 9, 2017.

3   Colby Itkowitz and Mike DeBonis, "Former Bush Official Puts Trump on the Couch: A '10 Out of 10 Narcissist,'" *Washington Post*, May 15, 2019.

4   Barrett quoted in Michael Kruse, "'He Was Surprised as Anyone,'" *Politico*, November 11, 2016.

5   Tim O'Brien, quoted in Toluse Olorunnipa, "'It'll Happen Fast': Trump Creates Problems and Then Rushes in to Solve Them," *Washington Post*, March 29, 2019.

6   Tony Schwartz, quoted in Jane Mayer, "Donald Trump's Ghost-writer Tells All," *New Yorker*, July 18, 2016.

7   Comey's memo can be accessed at https://www.documentcloud.org/documents/4442900-Ex-FBI-Director-James-Comey-s -memos.html.

8   Bob Woodward, *Fear: Trump in the White House* (New York: Simon & Schuster, 2018), 83.

9   Damian Paletta, Erica Werner, and Taylor Telford, "GOP Senators Raise Alarms, Criticize Trump as U.S.-China Trade War Heats Up," *Washington Post*, May 14, 2019.

10 Woodward, *Fear*, 271.

11 Woodward, *Fear*, 230–31.

12 Rebecca Ballhaus and Byron Tau, "Trump Meets Rosenstein about Democratic Surveillance Memo," *Wall Street Journal*, February 6, 2018.

13 See chapter 5 for more on this aspect of the Toddler in Chief.

14 Ashley Parker and Greg Jaffe, "Inside the 'Adult Day-Care Center': How Aides Try to Control and Coerce Trump," *Washington Post*, October 16, 2017. See also Peter Nicholas and Rebecca Ballhaus, "Talking to Trump: A How-to Guide," *Wall Street Journal*, January 18, 2018.

15 Elaina Plott, "Ignoring Trump's Orders, Hoping He'll Forget," *Atlantic*, May 15, 2019.

16 Katie Benner, "Inside the Government, Addressing Domestic Terrorism Has Been Fraught," *New York Times*, August 11, 2019.

17 Julian E. Barnes and Helene Cooper, "Trump Discussed Pulling U.S. from NATO, Aides Say Amid New Concerns over Russia," *New York Times*, January 14, 2019.

CHAPTER THREE

1   Kellyanne Conway, quoted in Philip Rucker and Robert Costa, "'It's a Hard Problem': Inside Trump's Decision to Send More Troops to Afghanistan," *Washington Post*, August 21, 2017.

2   David Nakamura and Damian Paletta, "Trump Unrestrained: Recent Moves Show President Listening to His Gut More Than Advisers," *Washington Post*, March 13, 2018.

3   Tim O'Brien, quoted in Michael Kruse, "'He Was Surprised as Anyone,'" *Politico*, November 11, 2016.

4   Rick Wilson, *Everything Trump Touches Dies* (New York: Free Press, 2018), 89.

5   Philip Rucker, Josh Dawsey, and Damian Paletta, "Trump Slams Fed Chair, Questions Climate Change and Threatens to Cancel Putin Meeting in Wide-Ranging Interview with the *Post*," *Washington Post*, November 27, 2018.

6   Unnamed Trump advisor, quoted in Jonathan Swan, "Trump's Strategic Planning Inspiration: Mike Tyson," Axios, January 16, 2019.

7   Trump's decision to stay in Afghanistan would be the best example of this; unsurprisingly, it also represents the apex of Trump's advisors' influence and a decision that Trump subsequently regretted. See Bob Woodward, *Fear: Trump in the White House* (New York: Simon & Schuster, 2018), 254–60. In many of the other examples that come to mind—his choices for the judiciary, for example—Trump's role has been minimal.

8   Michael Hirsh, "How Trump Practices 'Escalation Dominance,'" *Foreign Policy*, April 19, 2019.

9   Juhani E. Lehto, Petri Juujärvi, Libbe Kooistra and Lea Pulkkinen, "Dimensions of Executive Functioning: Evidence from Children," *British Journal of Developmental Psychology* 21 (March 2003): 59–80.

10 Akira Miyake et al., "The Unity and Diversity of Executive Functions and Their Contributions to Complex 'Frontal Lobe' Tasks: A Latent Variable Analysis," *Cognitive Psychology* 41 (August 2000): 49–100.

11 Stephanie Carlson, Louis Moses, and Hollie Rix, "The Role of Inhibitory Processes in Young Children's Difficulties with Deception and False Belief," *Child Development* 69 (June 1998): 672–91.

12 Stephanie Carlson and Louis Moses, "Individual Differences in Inhibitory Control and Children's Theory of Mind," *Child Development* 72 (August 2001): 1032–53; Stephanie Carlson, Dorothy Maskill, and Luke Williams, "Executive Function and Theory of Mind: Stability and Prediction from Ages 2 to 3," *Developmental Psychology* 40 (November 2004): 1105–22.

13 See Lou Cannon, *President Reagan: The Role of a Lifetime* (New York: PublicAffairs, 2008), 539–40; Robert McFarlane, *Special Trust* (New York: Cadell & Davies, 1994), 21.

14 Wesley Morgan, "How Trump Trips Up His Own Afghan Peace Efforts," *Politico*, August 16, 2019; Sami Yousafzai, Erin Banco, and Christopher Dickey, "The Taliban Scoff at Trump's Afghan Peace Talks Bluff," *Daily Beast*, September 4, 2019.

15 Susan Glasser, "Mike Pompeo, the Secretary of Trump," *New Yorker*, August 19, 2019.

16 Nishant Kishore et al., "Mortality in Puerto Rico after Hurricane Maria," *New England Journal of Medicine* 379 (July 12, 2018): 162–70.

17 On Trump's attempted denials, see Zack Beauchamp, "Trump's Puerto Rico Tweets Are the Purest Expression of His Presidency," *Vox*, September 13, 2018. On Trump's allies distancing themselves from him, see Alex Isenstadt and Marc Caputo, "Trump Rails on Top Florida Ally over Hurricane Maria Flap," *Politico*, September 18, 2018.

18 Tracy Jan, Arelis R. Hernández, Josh Dawsey, and Damian Paletta, "After Butting Heads with Trump Administration, Top HUD Official Departs Agency," *Washington Post*, January 25, 2019.

19 Peter Baker and Maggie Haberman, "Trump Widens War on Black Critics While Embracing 'Inner City Pastors,'" *New York Times*, July 29, 2019.

20 Tim Alberta, *American Carnage: On the Front Lines of the Republican Civil War and the Rise of President Trump* (New York: Harper Collins, 2019), 561–62.

21 Jim Newell, "The Administration Is Handing Its Enemies Tools to Topple Trump the Usual Way," *Slate*, March 28, 2019.

22 Asawin Suebsaeng and Andrew Desiderio, "'Clean-Up on Aisle Trump': President Reverses Course on Neo-Nazis, Slams the 'Alt-Left,'" *Daily Beast*, August 15, 2017.

23 Anne Sartori, *Deterrence by Diplomacy* (Princeton: Princeton University Press, 2007); John Mearsheimer, *Why Leaders Lie: The Truth about Lying in International Politics* (New York: Oxford University Press, 2011).

24 Karen DeYoung and Josh Dawsey, "For Inured Foreign Officials, the Sting of Trump's Tweets Has Begun to Dull," *Washington Post*, April 30, 2019.

25 Julie Pace and Alan Fram, "Trump's Impulses Put White House Credibility on the Line," Associated Press, March 24, 2018.

26 John Cornyn, quoted in David Nakamura and Seung Min Kim, "'He's a Gut Politician': Trump's Go-to Negotiating Tactics Aren't Working in the Shutdown Standoff," *Washington Post*, January 9, 2019.

27 John Bresnehan and Burgess Everett, "Trump's Credibility on Capitol Hill Is Shot," *Politico*, January 17, 2018.

28 Wilson, *Everything Trump Touches* Dies, 46.

29 See, for example, Woodward, *Fear*, 205.

30 Woodward, *Fear*, 206.

31 See, for example, Woodward, *Fear*, 234–35.

32 Nick Miroff, "ICE Raids Targeting Migrant Families Slated to Start Sunday in Major U.S. Cities," *Washington Post*, June 21, 2019.

33 Janet Hook, Kristina Peterson, and Michael C. Bender, "Alabama Defeat Stokes Divisions among Republicans," *Wall Street Journal*, December 13, 2017.

34 Peter Baker, "Riding an Untamed Horse: Priebus Opens Up on Serving Trump," *New York Times*, February 14, 2018.

35 Marist College Institute for Public Opinion, "Trump at Lowest Point with 35% Job Approval Rating . . . Crack at the Base," August 16, 2017, http://maristpoll.marist.edu/wp-content/misc/usapolls/us170809/Complete%20Survey%20Findings

_Marist%20Poll_USA_President%20Trump_August%20 2017_FINAL.pdf; Quinnipiac University, "U.S. Voters Feel Good about Economy, but Not Trump, Quinnipiac University National Poll Finds; Voters Take a Knee for Both Trump and NFL Players," October 11, 2017, https://poll.qu.edu/images/polling/us/ us10112017_Uhj87ke.pdf/; Eli Yokley, "Almost 3 in 4 Americans Say Trump Uses Twitter Too Much," Morning Consult, May 31, 2018, https://morningconsult.com/2018/05/31/almost-3-in-4-americans-say-trump-uses-twitter-too-much/.

36 Ben Leubsdorf and Nick Timiraos, "Trump Tweeted about Jobs Report before Release," *Wall Street Journal*, June 1, 2018.

37 Jeremy Diamond and Kevin Liptak, "Trump's Man with the Singapore Plan: Joe Hagin," CNN, June 4, 2018.

CHAPTER FOUR

1 Howard Kurtz, *Media Madness: Donald Trump, the Press, and the War over the Truth* (New York: Regnery, 2018), chap. 6.

2 Maggie Haberman (@maggieNYT), Twitter, June 5, 2017, 11:51 p.m., https://twitter.com/maggieNYT/status /871771530707050497.

3 Frances Gardner and Daniel Shaw, "Behavioral Problems of Infancy and Preschool Children (0–5)," in *Rutter's Child and Adolescent Psychiatry*, 5th ed., ed. M. Rutter (New York: Blackwell, 2008).

4 Sandy Jones, *The Toddler Years* (New York: Sterling, 2011), 76.

5 Trevor Noah, *The Daily Show*, November 30, 2016, accessed at https://www.youtube.com/watch?v=9P1IVQJdVvE.

6 D'Antonio quoted in Philip Rucker, Robert Costa, and Josh Dawsey, "Trump Creates Political Storm with False Claim on Puerto Rico Hurricane Death Toll," *Washington Post*, September 13, 2018.

7 Bob Woodward, *Fear: Trump in the White House* (New York: Simon & Schuster, 2018), 176.

8 See Irving Janis, *Groupthink: Psychological Studies of Policy Decisions and Fiascoes* (Boston: Houghton Mifflin, 1982).

9   "Transcript: Donald Trump Foreign Policy Speech," *New York Times*, April 27, 2016, https://www.nytimes.com/2016/04/28/us/politics/transcript-trump-foreign-policy.html.

10 For more examples, see Chris Cillizza, "A Running List of Donald Trump's Conspiracy Theories," CNN, September 13, 2018.

11 Maggie Haberman and Jonathan Martin, "Trump Once Said the 'Access Hollywood' Tape Was Real: Now He's Not Sure," *New York Times*, November 28, 2017.

12 Jonathan Swan, "Trump Lied to RNC Donors about 'Tim Apple' Video," Axios, March 16, 2019.

13 Jake Sherman and Anna Palmer, *The Hill to Die On* (New York: Crown Books, 2019), 265.

14 See, for example, Gabriel Sherman, "'I've Got Another Nut Job Here Who Thinks He's Running Things': Are Trump and Kelly Headed for Divorce?" *Vanity Fair*, January 22, 2018.

15 Glenn Kessler, Salvador Rizzo, and Meg Kelly, "President Trump Has Made More than 10,000 False or Misleading Claims," *Washington Post*, April 29, 2019; Daniel Dale, "Every False Claim Donald Trump Has Made as President," *Toronto Star*, http://projects.thestar.com/donald-trump-fact-check/.

16 Jonathan Swan, "White House Perjury Panic," Axios, January 28, 2018.

17 Peter Baker and Linda Qiu, "Inside What Even an Ally Calls Trump's 'Reality Distortion Field,'" *New York Times*, October 31, 2018.

18 Betsy Woodruff and Asawin Suebsaeng, "White House Abruptly Canceled Trump's Meeting with Intel Chiefs," *Daily Beast*, January 31, 2019.

19 John Walcott, "'Willful Ignorance': Inside President Trump's Troubled Intelligence Briefings," *Time*, February 5, 2019; Julian E. Barnes and Michael S. Schmidt, "To Woo a Skeptical Trump, Intelligence Chiefs Talk Economics Instead of Spies," *New York Times*, March 3, 2019.

20 Barbara Starr, Zachary Cohen, Elise Labott, Kaitlan Collins, and Jamie Gangel, "McMaster Could Leave WH after Months of Tension with Trump," CNN, February 22, 2018.

21 Nancy Cook, "Trump Is Tiring of Mulvaney," *Politico*, June 25, 2019.

22 Asawin Suebsaeng, "Trump and Omarosa Had a 'F*cking Weird' Fight with Vietnam Vets," *Daily Beast*, August 17, 2018.

23 On Charlottesville, see Woodward, *Fear*, 241–44; on McCain, see "Katie Rogers, Nicholas Fandos, and Maggie Haberman, "Trump Relents under Pressure, Offering 'Respect' to McCain," *New York Times*, August 27, 2018; on his tweets about the "Squad," see Michael Scherer, Josh Dawsey, Ashley Parker, and Seung Min Kim, "'He Always Doubles Down': Inside the Political Crisis Caused by Trump's Racist Tweets," *Washington Post*, July 20, 2019.

24 Nancy Cook, "The Short Arc of a Sharpie Captures the Long Arc of Trump," *Politico*, September 5, 2019; Andrew Freedman, Colby Itkowitz, and Jason Samenow, "NOAA Staff Warned in Sept. 1 Directive against Contradicting Trump," *Washington Post*, September 7, 2019; Daniel W. Drezner, "The Perfect Synecdoche for the Trump Presidency," *Washington Post*, September 10, 2019; Peter Baker, Lisa Friedman, and Christopher Flavelle, "Trump Pressed Top Aide to Have Weather Service 'Clarify' Forecast That Contradicted Trump," *New York Times*, September 11, 2019.

25 Caroline Mortimer, "Donald Trump's Staff Get Him to Agree to Policies by Saying 'Obama Wouldn't Have Done It,'" *Independent*, February 7, 2017.

CHAPTER FIVE

1 Sandy Jones, *The Toddler Years* (New York: Sterling, 2011), 38.

2 Kathleen Stassen Berger, *The Developing Person through Childhood and Adolescence*, 2nd ed. (New York; Worth Publishers, 1986).

3 Stephanie Carlson, Louis Moses, and Hollie Rix, "The Role of Inhibitory Processes in Young Children's Difficulties with Deception and False Belief," *Child Development* 69 (June 1998): 672–91.

4 Tony Schwartz, quoted in Jane Mayer, "Donald Trump's Ghostwriter Tells All," *New Yorker*, July 18, 2016.

5 Michael D'Antonio, quoted in Michael Kruse, "'He Was Surprised as Anyone,'" *Politico*, November 11, 2016.

6   Jake Sherman and Anna Palmer, *The Hill to Die On* (New York: Crown Books, 2019), 73.

7   Nancy Cook and Ben White, "'They Are Riding a Rubber Ducky into Alligator-Infested Waters,'" *Politico*, September 4, 2019.

8   Glenn Kessler, Salvador Rizzo, and Meg Kelly, "President Trump Has Made 13,435 False or Misleading Claims over 993 Days," *Washington Post*, October 13, 2019. To be fair, the journalist Daniel Dale engaged in a similar fact-checking exercise and counted approximately half the number of false claims during the same time period. See Daniel Dale, "Every False Claim Donald Trump Has Made as President," *Toronto Star*, http://projects.thestar.com/donald-trump-fact-check/.

9   See Harry Frankfurt, *On Bullshit* (Princeton: Princeton University Press, 2005). No, really, go read it.

10 Daniel Dale (ddale8), Twitter, August 8, 2019, 6:28 a.m. https://twitter.com/ddale8/status/1159426229449232386.

11 Chris Cillizza, "'We'll See What Happens': An Investigation into Donald Trump's Favorite Phrase," CNN, May 13, 2019.

12 Melissa Chan, "5 Things President Trump Says America Doesn't Know," *Time*, March 24, 2017.

13 Jenna Johnson, "'People Don't Realize': Trump and the Historical Facts He Wants You to Know," *Washington Post*, April 18, 2018.

14 See, for example, Tim Alberta, *American Carnage: On the Front Lines of the Republican Civil War and the Rise of President Trump* (New York: Harper Collins, 2019), 449.

15 Bob Woodward, *Fear: Trump in the White House* (New York: Simon & Schuster, 2018), 262.

16 Woodward, *Fear*, 263 and 287.

17 Rebecca Morin, "'Idiot,' 'Dope,' 'Moron': How Trump's Aides Have Insulted the Boss," *Politico*, September 4, 2018.

18 Philip Rucker, Josh Dawsey, and Damian Paletta, "'Am I Out of Touch?': Trump Administration Struggles to Show Empathy for Workers," *Washington Post*, January 24, 2019.

19 Steve Eder, "Did a Queens Podiatrist Help Donald Trump Avoid Vietnam?" *New York Times*, December 26, 2018.

20 Steve Bannon, quoted in Woodward, *Fear*, 75.

21 "A Transcript of Donald Trump's Meeting with the *Washington Post* Editorial Board," *Washington Post*, March 21, 2016; Maggie Haberman and David Sanger, "Transcript: Donald Trump Expounds on His Foreign Policy Views," *New York Times*, March 26, 2016; Bob Woodward and Robert Costa, "Transcript: Donald Trump Interview with Bob Woodward and Robert Costa," *Washington Post*, April 2, 2016; Maggie Haberman and David Sanger, "Transcript: Donald Trump on NATO, Turkey's Coup Attempt and the World," *New York Times*, July 21, 2016.

22 Maggie Haberman and David Sanger, "Donald Trump's Trial Balloons Are Catching Up with Him," *New York Times*, April 9, 2016.

23 Glenn Thrush and Maggie Haberman, "Trump and Staff Rethink Tactics after Stumbles," *New York Times*, February 5, 2017; Damian Paletta and Rob Taylor, "Trump Slams Australia Refugee Deal as 'Dumb,' Hints at Possible Pullout," *Wall Street Journal*, February 1, 2017; Jonathan Landay and David Rohde, "In Call with Putin, Trump Denounced Obama-Era Nuclear Arms Treaty," Reuters, February 9, 2017.

24 Mattathias Schwartz, "Mike Pompeo's Mission: Clean Up Trump's Messes," *New York Times Magazine*, February 26, 2019.

25 "Transcript, May 21, 2019, Interview with Secretary Tillerson," US House of Representatives Committee on Foreign Affairs website, https://foreignaffairs.house.gov/_cache/files/e/7/e7bd0ed2 -cf98-4f6d-a473-0406b0c50cde /23A0BEE4DF2B55E9D91259F04A3B22FA.tillerson-transcript -interview-5-21-19.pdf.

26 Josh Dawsey, Robert Costa, and Ashley Parker, "Inside the Tense, Profane White House Meeting on Immigration," *Washington Post*, January 15, 2018.

27 Sam Stein and Asawin Suebsaeng, "Team Trump's Goal for the Next Three Weeks: Keep Him 'the Hell Away' from Chuck Schumer," *Daily Beast*, January 23, 2018.

28 Marc Fisher, "Donald Trump Doesn't Read Much: Being President Probably Wouldn't Change That," *Washington Post*, July 17, 2016.

29 Trump's poor theory of mind also helps to explain why his lies are

so bald-faced. Some interpret his obvious lies as a demonstration of power, and there is likely some truth in that. It might also be the case, however, that Trump is simply incapable of recognizing how his utterances will appear to others.

30 Eliza Collins, "Trump: I Consult Myself on Foreign Policy," *Politico*, March 16, 2016.

31 Amy Harder and Jonathan Swan, "Trump's Manic Energy Policy," Axios, July 29, 2018; Toluse Olorunnipa and Josh Dawsey, "Trump Disparages Boeing 737s in Private before Grounding the Plane after Deadly Crash," *Washington Post*, March 13, 2019; Jonathan Swan and Joann Muller, "Trump Hates "Crazy" Driverless Cars," Axios, March 17, 2019.

32 Andrew Restuccia, "Trump Fixates on IQ as a Measure of Self-Worth," *Politico*, May 30, 2019.

33 Sheryl Gay Stolberg, Maggie Haberman, and Peter Baker, "Trump Was Repeatedly Warned That Ukraine Conspiracy Theory Was 'Completely Debunked'," *New York Times*, September 29, 2019.

34 Philip Rucker, Damian Paletta, and Josh Dawsey, "Trump, Banking on Strong Economy to Win Reelection, Frets over a Possible Downturn," *Washington Post*, August 15, 2019. See also Josh Boak and Jonathan Lemire, "Signs of Recession Worry Trump Ahead of 2020," Associated Press, August 17, 2019.

35 Peter Nicholas, "The Art of Flattering the President," *Atlantic*, June 8, 2019.

36 Josh Dawsey, Philip Rucker, ad Ashley Parker, "Trump Complains about Traveling to Canada ahead of Singapore Summit with Kim," *Washington Post*, June 6, 2018; Ben Riley-Smith, "Donald Trump 'Tired of Theresa May's School Mistress Tone' and Will Not Hold Talks with Her at G7," *Daily Telegraph*, June 8, 2018.

37 Kevin Liptak, Michelle Kosinski, and Jeremy Diamond, "Trump to Skip Climate Portion of G7 after Twitter Spat with Macron and Trudeau," CNN, June 8, 2018.

38 Greg Jaffe, Josh Dawsey, and Carol Leonnig, "Ahead of NATO and Putin Summits, Trump's Unorthodox Diplomacy Rattles Allies," *Washington Post*, July 6, 2018. See also Woodward, *Fear*, 231–32.

39   Elizabeth Saunders, "No Substitute for Experience: Presidents, Advisers, and Information in Group Decision-Making," *International Organization* 71 (April 2017): S219–47.

40   Saunders, "No Substitute for Experience," S224.

41   "Interview with Secretary Tillerson," 111–12.

42   Peter Baker, "As Trump Swerves on Trade War, It's Whiplash for the Rest of the World," *New York Times*, August 26, 2019.

CHAPTER SIX

1   American Academy of Pediatrics, *Caring for Your Baby and Young Child* (New York: Bantam, 2014), 814–16.

2   World Health Organization, "To Grow Up Healthy, Children Need to Sit Less and Play More," April 24, 2019, https://www.who.int/news-room/detail/24-04-2019-to-grow-up-healthy-children-need-to-sit-less-and-play-more.

3   Unless otherwise noted, the claims in this paragraph are found in American Academy of Pediatrics, *Caring for Your Baby and Young Child*, 813–17.

4   Linda S. Pagani, Caroline Fitzpatrick, and Traci A. Barnett, "Early Childhood Television Viewing and Kindergarten Entry Readiness," *Pediatric Research* 77 (September 2013): 350–55.

5   American Academy of Pediatrics, *Caring for Your Baby and Young Child*, 814.

6   Braydon Carter, "Trump: I Don't Watch Much Television 'Primarily Because of Documents,'" *The Hill*, November 11, 2017.

7   Maggie Haberman, Glenn Thrush, and Peter Baker, "Inside Trump's Hour-by-Hour Battle for Self-Preservation," *New York Times*, December 9, 2017.

8   On Pence, see Peter Nicholas, "A Survival Guide for the Trump White House," *Atlantic*, April 14, 2019. On Ryan, see Cliff Sims, *Team of Vipers: My 500 Extraordinary Days in the Trump White House* (New York: Thomas Dunne, 2019), 115–16.

9   Anna Altman, "Matt Gertz Tracks How Fox News Manipulates Trump," *Columbia Journalism Review*, February 13, 2019.

10 Jane Mayer, "Donald Trump's Ghostwriter Tells All," *New Yorker*,
    July 18, 2016.

11 Philip Elliott, "Inside Donald Trump's Twitter-Fueled Weekend
    Meltdown," *Time*, February 20, 2018.

12 Winneke A. van der Schuur et al., "The Consequences of Media
    Multitasking for Youth: A Review," *Computers in Human Behav-
    ior* 53 (December 2015): 204–15.

13 Brandon C. W. Ralph, David R. Thomson, James Allan Cheyne,
    and Daniel Smilek, "Media Multitasking and Failures of Atten-
    tion in Everyday Life," *Psychological Research* 78 (September
    2014): 661–69.

14 Bob Woodward, *Fear: Trump in the White House* (New York:
    Simon & Schuster, 2018), 102.

15 Monica Hesse, "I Tried to Watch as Much 'Fox & Friends' as the
    President: Here's What I Learned," *Washington Post*, March 16,
    2017. See also Andrew Marantz, "How 'Fox & Friends' Rewrites
    Trump's Reality," *New Yorker*, January 8, 2018.

16 For example, see John Koblin and Nick Corasaniti, "One Nation,
    under Fox: 18 Hours with a Network That Shapes America," *New
    York Times*, March 25, 2017.

17 Unnamed White House official, quoted in Olivia Nuzzi, "Donald
    Trump and Sean Hannity Like to Talk before Bedtime," *New York*,
    May 14, 2018.

18 Jake Sherman and Anna Palmer, *The Hill to Die On* (New York:
    Crown Books, 2019), 192.

19 Sherman and Palmer, *Hill to Die On*, 216, 372–81.

20 Jonathan Swan, "Trump Considered Declaring State of Emergen-
    cy in Baltimore," Axios, August 4, 2019.

21 Asawin Suebsaeng, "After Mass Shootings, Trump Veers Quickly
    from Horror to Score Settling," *Daily Beast*, August 5, 2019.

22 Rocque Planas, "How Fox News Anointed Trump's New Border
    Chief," *Huffington Post*, May 15, 2019.

23 Matthew Gertz, "A Comprehensive Review of the Revolving Door
    between Fox and the Trump Administration," Media Matters for
    America, July 22, 2019.

24 Manuel Roig-Franzia, "Hard-Line Views Made Lou Dobbs a Fox

Powerhouse: Now He's Shaping Trump's Border Policy," *Washington Post*, April 27, 2019; Maxwell Tani, Betsy Woodruff, and Asawin Suebsaeng, "Tucker Carlson Tells Trump in Private: No War with Iran," *Daily Beast*, June 20, 2019.

25 Kate Nocera et al., "Sean Spicer Has Resigned," BuzzFeed, July 21, 2017.

26 Jim Acosta (@Acosta), Twitter, August 2, 2019, 3:49 p.m. https://twitter.com/Acosta/status/1157392890089357317.

27 Tim Alberta, *American Carnage: On the Front Lines of the Republican Civil War and the Rise of President Trump* (New York: Harper Collins, 2019), 461–62.

28 Alberta, *American Carnage*, 462, and Woodward, *Fear*, 195.

29 Josh Dawsey, "Trump's Must-See TV: Judge Jeanine's Show and Her Positive Take on the President," *Washington Post*, April 5, 2018.

30 John Wagner and Josh Dawsey, "With One Tweet, Trump Inserts Himself into Florida's GOP Gubernatorial Primary," *Washington Post*, December 22, 2017.

31 Nuzzi, "Donald Trump and Sean Hannity."

CHAPTER SEVEN

1 "President Trump in Fire Truck," C-SPAN, July 17, 2017, https://www.youtube.com/watch?v=N-TSHiOF-UA.

2 Farah Stockman and Keith Bradsher, "Donald Trump Soured on a Deal, and Hong Kong Partners Became Litigants," *New York Times*, May 30, 2016.

3 David Bossie and Corey Lewandowski, *Let Trump Be Trump: The Inside Story of His Rise to the Presidency* (New York: Center Street, 2017), 89–90.

4 Julie Pace, "Worldwide Effort Set to Keep Trump Happy on 1st Trip Abroad," Associated Press, May 17, 2017.

5 Maya Oppenheim, "Donald Trump Shuns Japanese Food for American Burger at Golf Club near Tokyo," *Independent*, November 6, 2017.

6   Kaitlin Collins and Kevin Liptak, "Inside Trump's Air Force One: 'It's Like Being Held Captive,'" CNN, May 25, 2019.

7   Jennifer Steinhauer, "Trump Kicks Away Obama Traditions Even at the Dinner Table," *New York Times*, December 14, 2018.

8   Eliza Relman, "Trump's Former Bodyguard Went on McDonald's Runs for Him Because the White House Kitchen Couldn't Satisfy His Cravings for a Quarter Pounder," *Business Insider*, November 7, 2017; Sam Gillette, "President Trump's Love Affair with Fast Food: A Brief (and Salty) History," *People*, February 26, 2019.

9   Collins and Liptak, "Inside Trump's Air Force One."

10   Peggy McGlone, "What Happened When Trump Visited the African American History Museum, According to Its Founding Director," *Washington Post*, August 31, 2019.

11   Eliana Johnson and Daniel Lippman, "Trump's 'Truly Bizarre' Visit to Mt. Vernon," *Politico*, April 10, 2019.

12   American Academy of Pediatrics, *Caring for Your Baby and Young Child* (New York: Bantam, 2014), 387.

13   Vivian Salama, "Trump in Paris: The Curious Case of His Friend Jim," Associated Press, July 12, 2017.

14   Toluse Olorunnipa, "Trump's Speeches Feature Mystery Men the White House Won't Name," Bloomberg, August 16, 2018.

15   Maggie Haberman and Glenn Thrush, "New White House Chief of Staff Has an Enforcer," *New York Times*, September 8, 2017.

16   Robert S. Mueller III, *Report on the Investigation into Russian Interference in the 2016 Presidential Election*, March 2019, 2:32n155.

17   Bob Woodward, *Fear: Trump in the White House* (New York: Simon and Schuster, 2018), 251.

18   American Academy of Pediatrics, *Caring for Your Baby and Young Child.*

19   Daniel Lippman, Andrew Restuccia, and Eliana Johnson, "Trump's New Nickname for Pete Buttigieg: 'Alfred E. Neuman,'" *Politico*, May 10, 2019.

20   Sandy Jones, *The Toddler Years* (New York: Sterling, 2011), 104.

21   Jake Sherman and Anna Palmer, *The Hill to Die On* (New York: Crown Books, 2019), 152–53.

22 Matthew Dallek, "In the Weeds," *Washington Post*, September 13, 2019.

CHAPTER EIGHT

1   Marcy Whitebook and Laura Sakai, "Turnover Begets Turnover: An Examination of Job and Occupational Instability among Child Care Center Staff," *Early Childhood Research Quarterly* 18 (Autumn 2003): 273–93.

2   Daniel W. Drezner, *The Ideas Industry: How Pessimists, Partisans, and Plutocrats are Transforming the Marketplace of Ideas* (New York: Oxford University Press, 2017).

3   Philip Bump, "Donald Trump Only Hires the Best People (at Generating Unhelpful Headlines)," *Washington Post*, August 30, 2016.

4   David Lewis, "Trump's Slow Pace of Appointments Is Hurting Government—and His Own Agenda," *Washington Post*, August 3, 2017.

5   Heather Ba and Terry Sullivan, "Why Does It Take So Long to Confirm Trump's Appointments?" *Washington Post*, April 24, 2019.

6   Kathryn Dunn Tempas, "Tracking Turnover in the Trump Administration," Brookings Institution, July 2019.

7   See Denise Lu and Karen Yourish, "The Turnover at the Top of the Trump Administration," *New York Times*, April 12, 2019.

8   Eliana Johnson, "Kelly Knew before Abuse Reports That Porter Would Be Denied Security Clearance," *Politico*, February 8, 2018.

9   Jason Silverstein and Nicole Hensley, "The Running List of Typos from President Trump's White House," *New York Daily News*, May 20, 2018.

10 Monmouth University, "Few Say Trump Hires 'Best People,'" August 20, 2018, https://www.monmouth.edu/polling-institute/reports/monmouthpoll_US_082018/.

11 Chris Christie, *Let Me Finish* (New York: Hachette, 2019), 5–6.

12 Christie, *Let Me Finish*, 5–6. See also Michael Lewis, *The Fifth Risk* (New York: W. W. Norton, 2018), 28–32.

13 Jonathan Swan, Juliet Bartz, Alayna Treene, and Orion Rummler,

"Exclusive: Leaked Trump Vetting Docs," *Axios*, June 23, 2019.

14 Sebastian Murdock, "Trump Attacks, Then Says He Relies on Press to Vet Nominees," *Huffington Post*, August 2, 2019.

15 "Open Letter on Donald Trump from GOP National Security Leaders," *War on the Rocks*, March 2, 2016, http://warontherocks .com/2016/03/open-letter-on-donald-trump-from-gop-national -security-leaders/; "A Letter From G.O.P. National Security Officials Opposing Donald Trump," *New York Times*, August 8, 2018, https://www.nytimes.com/interactive/2016/08/08/us/politics /national-security-letter-trump.html. Full disclosure: I was one of the signatories to the March letter.

16 "Transcript, May 21, 2019, Interview with Secretary Tillerson," US House of Representatives Committee on Foreign Affairs website, 24, https://foreignaffairs.house.gov/_cache/files/e/7 /e7bd0ed2-cf98-4f6d-a473-0406b0c50cde /23A0BEE4DF2B55E9D91259F04A3B22FA.tillerson-transcript -interview-5-21-19.pdf.

17 Bill Faries and Mira Rojanasakul, "At Trump's State Department, Eight of Ten Top Jobs Are Empty," Bloomberg, March 13, 2018.

18 Annie Linskey, "Putting 'White House' on the Resume Is Less of a Boost," *Boston Globe*, May 15, 2018.

19 Tarini Parti, "Trapped in the White House: Many Trump Aides Are Too "Toxic" to Get Jobs," BuzzFeed, April 13, 2018.

20 Tim Alberta, *American Carnage: On the Front Lines of the Republican Civil War and the Rise of President Trump* (New York: Harper Collins, 2019), 412.

21 Maggie Haberman and Katie Rogers, "'Drama, Action, Emotional Power': As Exhausted Aides Eye the Exits, Trump Is Reenergized," *New York Times*, June 10, 2018.

22 Haberman and Rogers, "'Drama, Action, Emotional Power.'"

23 In Trump's first few months in office, Melania Trump had yet to move into the White House, and it was initially hoped by some staffers that the First Lady would constrain Trump's worst impulses. This did not come to pass.

24 Annie Karni, "Meet the Guys Who Tape Trump's Papers Back Together," *Politico*, June 10, 2018.

25 Nahal Toosi, "Inside the Chaotic Early Days of Trump's Foreign Policy," *Politico*, March 1, 2019.

26 Julia Hirschfield Davis, "Trump's Cabinet, with a Prod, Extols the 'Blessing' of Serving Him," *New York Times*, June 12, 2017.

27 Ashley Parker and Greg Jaffe, "Inside the 'Adult Day-Care Center': How Aides Try to Control and Coerce Trump," *Washington Post*, October 16, 2017.

28 Matthew Nussbaum, "Foreign Leaders Who Embraced Trump Now Feel Burned," *Politico*, June 7, 2018.

29 Alex Thompson, "Trump Gets a Folder Full of Positive News about Himself Twice a Day," Vice News, https://news.vice.com /en_ca/article/zmygpe/trump-folder-positive-news-white-house, August 9, 2017.

30 Alex Thompson, "Trump Gets a Folder of Positive News."

31 Mike Allen, "Trump's Bedtime Story: 'The Book,'" Axios, June 8, 2018.

32 Josh Dawsey and Steven Shepard, "Trump Still Loves Polls," *Politico*, November 18, 2017.

33 Clare Foran and Kevin Liptak, "Trump's Lawyers Updated Him on the Mueller Investigation: Then Trump Tweeted," CNN, August 1, 2018.

34 Philip Rucker, Josh Dawsey, and Seung Min Kim, "Trump Defiant as Crisis Grows over Family Separation at the Border," *Washington Post*, June 18, 2018.

35 Ashley Parker and Robert Costa, "Trump's Lack of Discipline Leaves New Chief of Staff Frustrated and Dismayed," *Washington Post*, August 16, 2017.

36 Glenn Thrush, Michael D. Shear, and Maggie Haberman, "John Kelly Quickly Moves to Impose Military Discipline on White House," *New York Times*, August 3, 2017.

37 Thrush, Shear, and Haberman, "Kelly Quickly Moves to Impose Military Discipline."

38 Thrush, Shear, and Haberman, "Kelly Quickly Moves to Impose Military Discipline."

39 Philip Rucker and Ashley Parker, "During a Summer of Crisis, Trump Chafes against Criticism and New Controls," *Washington Post*, Au-

gust 31, 2017. Some of Trump's friends nicknamed Kelly "The Church Lady" because of his schoolmarmish management style.

40 Julie Hirschfield Davis, "Is Trump All Talk on North Korea? The Uncertainty Sends a Shiver," *New York Times*, September 24, 2017.

41 Allen, "Trump's Bedtime Story."

42 Jonathan Swan, "Trump's Secret, Shrinking Schedule," Axios, January 8, 2018.

43 Noah Bierman, Cathleen Decker, and Brian Bennett, "Trump Unleashes Himself from Would-Be Handlers, Lashing Out Mornings, Nights and Weekends," *Los Angeles Times*, October 10, 2017. See also Eliana Johnson and Daniel Lippman, "9 hours of 'Executive Time': Trump's Unstructured Days Define His Presidency," *Politico*, October 29, 2018.

44 Ashley Parker, Josh Dawsey, and Philip Rucker, "'When You Lose That Power': How John Kelly Faded as White House Disciplinarian," *Washington Post*, April 7, 2018.

45 David Graham, "The Infantilization of the President," *Atlantic*, October 11, 2017. To understand the "goddamned steam reference, see J. D. Simkins, "Navy Should Return to 'Goddamned Steam' on Carrier, Trump Says," *Navy Times*, May 11, 2017.

46 Mike Allen, "Why Top White House Officials Won't Quit Trump," Axios, August 20, 2017.

47 Ashley Parker and Philip Rucker, "Trump Veers Past Guardrails, Feeling Impervious to the Uproar He Causes," *Washington Post*, November 29, 2017.

48 Ashley Parker and Josh Dawsey, "Time at Mar-a-Lago Is a Respite for Trump—and a Headache for His Staff," *Washington Post*, December 30, 2017.

49 Michael C. Bender, "Trump Finds Loopholes in Chief of Staff's New Regime," *Wall Street Journal*, December 5, 2019.

50 Philip Rucker, "John Kelly's Credibility Is at Risk after Defending Aide Accused of Domestic Violence," *Washington Post*, February 8, 2018.

51 Catherine Lucey and Jonathan Lemire, "Trump Flies Solo More, Is Said to Want to Rely Less on Staff," Associated Press, March 10, 2018.

52 Jonathan Lemire and Catherine Lucey, "Inside a White House in Tumult, John Kelly's Clout Dwindles," Associated Press, April 5, 2018.

53 Jonathan Swan, "Trump's Giddy Spree," Axios, March 11, 2018.

54 Philip Ricker and Robert Costa, "'Tired of the Wait Game': White House Stabilizers Gone, Trump Calling His Own Shots," *Washington Post*, March 31, 2018.

55 Annie Karni, "Trump's Turnberry Getaway: A Little Golf, a Lot of Promoting," *Politico*, July 14, 2018.

56 Helene Cooper and Julian E. Barnes, "U.S. Officials Scrambled behind the Scenes to Shield NATO Deal from Trump," *New York Times*, August 9, 2018.

57 Jonathan Swan and Mike Allen, "Trump's Helsinki Humiliation," Axios, July 15, 2018; Julie Hirschfield Davis, "Trump, at Putin's Side, Questions U.S. Intelligence on 2016 Election," *New York Times*, July 16, 2018.

58 Eliana Johnson, "How John Kelly Became 'Chief in Name Only,'" *Politico*, July 29, 2018.

59 Maggie Haberman, "Kelly, on His Way Out, Says Administration Long Ago Abandoned Idea of Concrete Wall," *New York Times*, December 30, 2018.

60 Molly O'Toole, "John F. Kelly Says His Tenure as Trump's Chief of Staff Is Best Measured by What the President Did Not Do," *Los Angeles Times*, December 30, 2018.

61 Elaina Plott and Peter Nicholas, "Trump's Chief of Staff Says He's Having a Ball," *Atlantic*, April 25, 2019.

62 Alexi McCammond and Jonathan Swan, "Insider Leaks Trump's 'Executive Time'-Filled Private Schedules," Axios, February 3, 2019.

63 Peter Baker and Maggie Haberman, "Mick Mulvaney Tries Letting Trump Be Trump," *New York Times*, April 10, 2019.

64 Plott and Nicholas, "Trump's Chief of Staff Says He's Having a Ball."

65 Plott and Nicholas, "Trump's Chief of Staff Says He's Having a Ball."; Katie Rogers, Annie Karni, and Maggie Haberman, "Trump's Personal Assistant, Madeleine Westerhout, Shared Inti-

mate Details of First Family," *New York Times*, August 30, 2019.

66 Mark Landler and Helene Cooper, "Bolton Walked Back Syria Statement: His Disdain for Debate Helped Produce It," *New York Times*, January 7, 2019.

67 See Julian E. Barnes and Helene Cooper, "Trump Discussed Pulling U.S. from NATO, Aides Say amid New Concerns over Russia," *New York Times*, January 14, 2019.

68 Peter Baker and Maggie Haberman, "Trump Undercuts Bolton on North Korea and Iran," *New York Times*, May 28, 2019.

69 Ashley Parker and Toluse Olorunnipa, "Trump Seeks to Campaign on Problems He Promised to Fix," *Washington Post*, April 8, 2019.

70 Brian Bennett, "'My Whole Life Is a Bet': Inside President Trump's Gamble on an Untested Re-election Strategy," *Time*, June 20, 2019.

71 Unnamed former White House staffer, quoted in Gabby Orr, "How Trump Aides Rushed to Repackage the 'Go Back' Tweets," *Politico*, July 15, 2019.

72 Jim VendeHei and Mike Allen, "Trump Creep: Bad Habits Spread Fast," Axios, February 14, 2018.

73 See, for example, Nancy Cook, "Trump Is Tiring of Mulvaney," *Politico*, June 25, 2019; Jennifer Jacobs and Justin Sink, "Trump's Trade Chief Lectures His Boss and Gets an Earful in Return," Bloomberg, February 22, 2019.

74 Peter Baker and Maggie Haberman, "Trump's Interest in Buying Greenland Seemed Like a Joke. Then It Got Ugly." *New York Times*, August 21, 2019. See also Nancy Cook, "An Unshackled Trump Finally Gets the Presidency He Always Wanted," *Politico*, September 19, 2019.

75 Ashley Parker and Philip Rucker, "'You're a Prop in the Back': Advisers Struggle to Obey Trump's Kafkaesque Rules," *Washington Post*, September 11, 2019.

76 Andrew Restuccia, Daniel Lippman, and Eliana Johnson, "'Get Scavino in Here': Trump's Twitter Guru Is the Ultimate Insider," *Politico*, May 16, 2019.

77 On Bolton, see Dexter Filkins, "John Bolton on the Warpath," *New*

Yorker, April 29, 2019. On Pompeo, see Daniel W. Drezner, "Mike Pompeo's Faustian Bargain," *Washington Post*, November 29, 2018. On Barr, see Adam Serwer, "The Dangerous Ideas of Bill Barr," *Atlantic*, May 2, 2019. On Mulvaney, see Seung Min Kim, Lisa Rein, Josh Dawsey, and Erica Werner, "'His Own': Mulvaney Builds 'an Empire for the Right Wing' as Trump's Chief of Staff," *Washington Post*, July 15, 2019.

78   Andrew Kaczynski, "Trump National Security Pick Monica Crowley Plagiarized Multiple Sources in 2012 Book," CNN, January 7, 2017; Alex Caton and Grace Watkins, "Trump Pick Monica Crowley Plagiarized Parts of Her Ph.D. Dissertation," *Politico*, January 9, 2017. These were not the first instances of plagiarism for Crowley. See also Timothy Noah, "Nixon's Monica Stonewalls about Plagiarism!" *Slate*, August 23, 1999.

79   Mueller, *Report*, 2:158.

80   See Deputy Press Secretary Hogan Gidley's comments quoted in Michael C. Bender, "Trump Gets White House Witnesses to Attest to His 'Very Calm' Demeanor," *Wall Street Journal*, May 23, 2019.

81   Peter Nicholas and Elaina Plott, "Trump's Guardrails Are Gone," *Atlantic*, April 19, 2019.

82   Paul Ryan, quoted in Alberta, *American Carnage*, 556.

83   Ashley Parker, Philip Rucker, and Josh Dawsey, "Seven days: Inside Trump's frenetic response to the whistleblower complaint and the battle over impeachment," *Washington Post*, September 25, 2019.

CONCLUSION

1   Paloma Sotelo, "Let's Stop Comparing Donald Trump to Babies and Kids," *Huffington Post*, February 6, 2017.

2   See, for example, Jonathan Chait, "Donald Trump Wants You to Burn the Flag While He Burns the Constitution," *New York*, November 29, 2016.

3   Tarini Parti and Chris Geidner, "Trump Allies Don't See 'Three-Dimensional Chess' in Dinesh D'Souza's Pardon," BuzzFeed, May

31, 2018. See also Mark Landler and Julie Hirschfield Davis, "After Another Week of Chaos, Trump Repairs to Palm Beach: No One Knows What Comes Next," *New York Times*, March 23, 2018.

4 Krikorian quoted in Nahal Toosi, "Trump's Use of Immigration as 2020 Wedge Could Backfire on Other Policies," *Politico*, August 11, 2019.

5 Heidi Stevens, "Stop Comparing President Trump to a Toddler," *Chicago Tribune*, June 13, 2018.

6 Alison Gopnik, "4-Year-Olds Don't Act like Trump," *New York Times*, May 20, 2017.

7 Stephanie Carlson and Louis Moses, "Individual Differences in Inhibitory Control and Children's Theory of Mind," *Child Development* 72 (August 2001): 1032–53.

8 Sandy Jones, *The Toddler Years* (New York: Sterling, 2011), vii.

9 American Academy of Pediatrics, *Caring for Your Baby and Young Child*, 6th ed. (New York: Bantam, 2014).

10 Stephen Dinan, "William Barr: Donald Trump Was Right to Be 'Frustrated' by Russia Narrative," *Washington Times*, April 18, 2019.

11 See Cliff Sims, *Team of Vipers: My 500 Extraordinary Days in the Trump White House* (New York: Thomas Dunne Books, 2019), 84–90.

12 Maryanne Trump quoted in Tim O'Brien, *TrumpNation: The Art of Being the Donald* (New York: Business Plus, 2005), p. 49; Trump's teacher quoted in Michael Kranish and Marc Fisher, *Trump Revealed: An American Journey of Ambition, Ego, Money, and Power* (New York: Scribner, 2016), p.35. See, more generally, Michael Kruse, "If He's Not in a Fight, He Looks for One,'" *Politico*, September 23, 2019.

13 Daniel W. Drezner (@dandrezner), Twitter, April 25, 2017, 9:23 a.m., https://twitter.com/dandrezner/status/856876322001432581.

14 Manu Raju, "GOP Sen. Bob Corker to Trump: Stop 'Whining' about Sessions," CNN, September 4, 2018.

15 Bob Woodward, *Fear: Trump in the White House* (New York: Simon and Schuster, 2018), 299. See also Jonathan Chait, "The

President as Adolescent Bully," *New York*, April 1, 2019.

16 Woodward, *Fear*, 308.

17 Masha Gessen, "Trump Doesn't Govern like a Toddler, He Governs like a Teenager," *New Yorker*, October 16, 2017.

18 Full clip posted by ABC News Politics (@ABCPolitics), Twitter, December 23, 2018, 10:04 a.m., https://twitter.com/ABCPolitics/status/1076871248917889025.

19 Philip Zelazo, Fergus Craik, and Laura Booth, "Executive Function across the Life Span," *Acta Psychologica* 115 (February 2004): 167–83.

20 Rebecca Savransky, "Scarborough: Trump Allies Told Me He Has Dementia," *The Hill*, November 30, 2017.

21 Omarosa Maningault-Newman, quoted in NBC News (@NBCNews), Twitter, August 12, 2018, 9:20 a.m., https://twitter.com/NBCNews/status/1028647323172306946.

22 William D. Cohan, "Oh My God, This Jackass': The Mooch Explains Why He Thinks Trump Is 'Crazy,' 'Narcissistic,' and a 'Paper Tiger' Who Will Drop Out By March 2020," *Vanity Fair*, August 16, 2019.

23 Marc Coutanche and John Paulus, "An Empirical Analysis of Popular Press Claims regarding Linguistic Change in President Donald J. Trump," *Frontiers in Psychology* 9 (November 2018): 1–5.

24 Carlson and Moses, "Individual Differences in Inhibitory Control."

25 Josh Dawsey, "'Nasty Guy': Trump Attacks Critic, Touts Accomplishments in House GOP Meeting on Immigration," *Washington Post*, June 19, 2018.

26 An excellent test will be President Trump's reaction to this book upon publication. Trump-as-teenager would likely respond by studiously ignoring it. Trump-as-dotard would likely forget being angry if he heard about the book. The Toddler in Chief, however, would not let go, and tweet at least once about "Dopey Dan Drezner, whom I have never met. . . ."

27 See, for example, Matthew Glassman, "Donald Trump Is a Dangerously Weak President," *Vox*, December 27, 2017; David Lewis, Patrick Bernhard, and Emily You, "President Trump as Manager:

Reflections on the First Year," *Presidential Studies Quarterly* 48 (September 2018): 480–501; Corey Robin, "Why Has It Taken Us So Long to See Trump's Weakness?" *New York*, February 20, 2019.

28 Juliet Elperin, Lisa Rein, and Marc Fisher, "Resistance from Within: Federal Workers Push Back against Trump," *Washington Post*, January 31, 2017; Yoni Appelbaum, "Memo to Trump: This Is Why You're Losing," *Atlantic*, June 15, 2017.

29 Jonathan Chait, "Trump Has Lost His War on the War on Coal," *New York*, February 18, 2019.

30 Fred Barbash and Deanna Paul, "The Real Reason the Trump Administration Is Constantly Losing in Court," *Washington Post*, March 19, 2019.

31 Mary Amiti, Stephen Redding, and David Weinstein, "The Impact of the 2018 Trade War on US Prices and Welfare," National Bureau of Economic Research Working Paper no. 25672, March 2019.

32 Daniel W. Drezner, "Economic Statecraft in the Age of Trump," *Washington Quarterly* 42, (Fall 2019): 7–24.

33 Daniel W. Drezner, "The World Is Laughing at President Trump," *Washington Post*, September 26, 2018.

34 Tim Alberta, *American Carnage: On the Front Lines of the Republican Civil War and the Rise of President Trump* (New York: Harper Collins, 2019), 529–48.

35 The Gallup data can be accessed at https://news.gallup.com /poll/203198/presidential-approval-ratings-donald-trump.aspx.

36 Megan Brennan, "Record-High 75% of Americans Say Immigration Is Good Thing," Gallup, https://news.gallup.com /poll/235793/record-high-americans-say-immigration-good-thing.aspx, June 21, 2018.

37 Jeffrey M. Jones, "Slim Majority in U.S. See Trade as Benefiting American Workers," Gallup, https://news.gallup.com /poll/247970/slim-majority-trade-benefitting-workers.aspx, March 21, 2019.

38 Daniel W. Drezner, "The Economic Case for Free Trade Is Stronger Than Ever," *Reason*, June 2018.

39 CNN poll, http://cdn.cnn.com/cnn/2018/images/06/20/rel6e.-.economy,.trade.pdf.

40 Richard Neustadt, *Presidential Power and the Modern President* (New York: Free Press, 1990).

41 Philip Rucker, Robert Costa, and Ashley Parker, "Who's Afraid of Trump? Not Enough Republicans—at Least for Now," *Washington Post*, June 27, 2017.

42 Alan Rappeport, "How Companies Learned to Stop Fearing Trump's Twitter Wrath," *New York Times*, March 20, 2019.

43 Karen DeYoung and Josh Dawsey, "For Inured Foreign Officials, the Sting of Trump's Tweets Has Begun to Dull," *Washington Post*, April 30, 2019.

44 Noah Bierman, "What's behind All Those Executive Orders Trump Loves to Sign? Not Much," *Los Angeles Times*, March 27, 2019.

45 Amiti, Redding, and Weinstein, "The Impact of the 2018 Trade War on US Prices and Welfare."

46 Perry Bacon Jr., "Trump Hasn't Needed the Wall to Remake U.S. Immigration Policy," FiveThirtyEight, December 6, 2018.

47 Susan Glasser, "Donald Trump's Year of Living Dangerously," *Politico*, January/February 2018.

48 Henry Kissinger, quoted in Michael Wolff, *Siege: Trump under Fire* (New York: Henry Holt, 2019), 253.

49 Daniel W. Drezner, "The World Hates President Trump," *Washington Post*, January 22, 2018.

50 Daniel W. Drezner, "This Time Is Different: Why U.S. Foreign Policy Will Never Recover," *Foreign Affairs* 98 (May/June 2019): 10–17.

51 Burgess Everett and Josh Dawsey, "White House Orders Agencies to Ignore Democrats' Oversight Requests," *Politico*, June 2, 2017; Tom Hamburger, Karoun Demirjian, Josh Dawsey, and Rachael Bade, "Trump Moves to Resist House Inquiries, Setting Up Fight over Congressional Subpoena Powers," *Washington Post*, April 16, 2019; Charlie Savage, "Trump Vows Stonewall of 'All' House Subpoenas, Setting Up Fight over Powers," *New York Times*, April 24, 2019.

52 Jason Lemon, "Trump Insists That the Constitution's Article II
    'Allows Me to Do Whatever I Want,'" *Newsweek*, June 16, 2019;
    Donald J. Trump, remarks before Marine One departure, July 12,
    2019, https://www.whitehouse.gov/briefings-statements
    /remarks-president-trump-marine-one-departure-52/.

53 Elizabeth Goitein, "The Alarming Scope of the President's Emer-
    gency Powers," *Atlantic*, January/February 2019.

54 Jonathan Swan and Stef Knight, "Exclusive: Trump Targeting
    Birthright Citizenship with Executive Order," Axios, October 30,
    2018.

55 See Attorney General William Barr's lecture to the Federalist
    Society, November 15, 2019, http://www.justice.gov/opa/speech
    /attorney-general-william-p-barr-delivers-19th-annual-barbara
    -k-olson-memorial-lecture.

56 As one Department of Housing and Urban Development official
    explained about Trump's political appointees, "They're honestly
    some of the nicest people I've ever worked with, but they're totally
    incompetent. It's not that they don't have the right answers. They
    don't even know the questions. . . . This isn't the EPA or the State
    Department where the leadership is actively trying to undermine
    the workforce. It feels like we just have benign neglect." Quoted
    in Rachel Cohen, "'I Fully Intend to Outlast These People': 18
    Federal Workers on What It's Really Like to Work for the Trump
    Administration," *Washingtonian*, April 7, 2019.

57 See Lewis, *Fifth Risk*, chap. 2.

58 Ryan McCrimmon, "Economists Flee Agriculture Dept. after
    Feeling Punished under Trump," *Politico*, May 7, 2019; Helena
    Bottemiller Evich, "Agriculture Department Buries Studies Show-
    ing Dangers of Climate Change," June 29, 2019; Helena Botte-
    miller Evich, "Trump's USDA Buried Sweeping Climate Change
    Response Plan," *Politico*, July 18, 2019.

59 McCrimmon, "Economists Flee Agriculture Dept. after Feeling
    Punished under Trump."

60 Liz Crampton, "USDA Expects 'Significant Delays' in Economic
    Research Reports," *Politico*, September 24, 2019.

61 Unnamed former DHS official, quoted in Jason Zengerle, "Inside

Trump's Border Wars," *New York Times Magazine*, July 16, 2019; see also Garrett Graff, "The Border Patrol Hits a Breaking Point," *Politico*, July 15, 2019.

62 Nahal Toosi, "White House Slap at Dissenting Diplomats Sparks Fear of Reprisal," *Politico*, January 30, 2017.

63 Ronan Farrow, *War on Peace: The End of Diplomacy and the Decline of American Influence* (New York: W. W. Norton 2018), ix.

64 Ursa Zeya, "Trump Is Making American Diplomacy White Again," *Politico*, September 17, 2018.

65 Colum Lynch and Robbie Gramer, "Federal Watchdogs Target Bullying, Retaliation at State Department," *Foreign Policy*, September 7, 2018. See also Robbie Gramer and Amy Mackinnon, "U.S. Ambassador to Ukraine Recalled in 'Political Hit Job,' Lawmakers Say," *Foreign Policy*, May 7, 2019; Department of State Office of the Inspector General, "Review of Allegations of Politicized and Other Improper Personnel Practices in the Bureau of International Organization Affairs," ESP-19-05, August 2019.

66 Farrow, *War on Peace*; Jason Zengerle, "Rex Tillerson and the Unraveling of the State Department," *New York Times Magazine*, October 17, 2017.

67 Chuck Park, "I Can No Longer Justify Being a Part of Trump's 'Complacent State.' So I'm Resigning." *Washington Post*, August 8, 2019. See, more generally, Jeet Heer, "The Myth of Resistance inside the Trump Administration," *The Nation*, August 9, 2019.

68 Nancy McEldowney, quoted in Roger Cohen, "The Desperation of Our Diplomats," *New York Times*, July 28, 2017.

69 Daniel W. Drezner, "Present at the Destruction: The Trump Administration and the Foreign Policy Bureaucracy," *Journal of Politics* 81 (April 2019): 723–30.

70 Barbara Stephenson, "Time to Ask Why," *Foreign Service Journal*, December 2017.

71 Daniel Lippman and Nahal Toosi, "Interest in U.S. Diplomatic Corps Tumbles in Early Months of Trump," *Politico*, August 12, 2017; Ronan Farrow, *War on Peace*, 274.

72 Drezner, "Present at the Destruction," 727–28.

73 Matthew Lee, "State Department Admits Low Morale, as It De-
fends Reorganization," *Associated Press*, November 18, 2017.

74 Elliot Hannon, "Trump on Core State Department Vacancies:
"I'm the Only One That Matters," *Slate*, November 3, 2017.

75 John Wagner and Michelle Ye Hee Lee, "Trump Says He Won't
Fire Kellyanne Conway over Hatch Act Violations," *Washington
Post*, June 14, 2019.

76 This is in some ways an update of Salena Zito's claim during the
2016 campaign that Trump should be taken seriously but not
literally. See Salena Zito, "Taking Trump Seriously, Not Literally,"
Atlantic, September 23, 2016.

77 Ezra Klein, "Trump Is Winning," *Vox*, January 29, 2018.

78 Jacob T. Levy, "The Weight of the Words," Niskanen Center
website, February 7, 2018, https://www.niskanencenter.org/the
-weight-of-the-words/.

79 Julia Azari and Jennifer Smith, "Unwritten Rules: Informal Institutions in Established Democracies," *Perspectives on Politics* 10
(March 2012): 37–55.

80 Peter Baker, "A President of the People or a President of His People?" *New York Times*, April 16, 2019.

81 Levy, "Weight of the Words."

82 Ezra Klein, "The Rise of Donald Trump Is a Terrifying Moment in
American Politics," *Vox*, February 10, 2016.

83 Justin Amash, quoted in Alberta, *American Carnage*, 505.

84 Maxwell Tani, "Poll: 78% of GOP Fox News Viewers Say Trump Is
Best President Ever," *Daily Beast*, March 21, 2019.

85 Rachel Bade, "Trump's Takeover of GOP Forces Many House
Republicans to Head for the Exits," *Washington Post*, September
22, 2019.

86 Alex Isenstadt, "Trump Launches Unprecedented Reelection
Machine," *Politico*, December 18, 2018.

87 Asawin Suebsaeng and Andrew Kirell, "Former Trump Aide
David Bossie Has Disappeared from Fox after Pissing Off Trump,"
Daily Beast, June 4, 2019.

88 Alberta, *American Carnage*, 495.

89 Ashley Parker, Josh Dawsey, and Philip Rucker, "Trump Adminis-

tration Prepares for Massive Shake-up after Midterms," *Washington Post*, November 5, 2018.

90 Rebecca Klar, "Mulvaney: Attempt to Move USS John McCain during Trump Visit 'Not Unreasonable,'" *The Hill*, June 2, 2019.

91 Daniel W. Drezner, "How Much Weight Will Trump's Words Carry on the World Stage?" *Washington Post*, February 3, 2017.

92 Karen DeYoung, "Departing French Ambassador Reflects on a Turbulent Time in Washington," *Washington Post*, April 19, 2019.

93 Jonathan Swan, "Why Trump Keeps Bolton," Axios, July 21, 2019. On the general ability of advisors to freelance with an inexperienced president, see Elizabeth Saunders, "No Substitute for Experience: Presidents, Advisers, and Information in Group Decision-Making," *International Organization* 71 (April 2017): S219–47.

94 Courtney Kube, Kristen Welker, Carol E. Lee, and Savannah Guthrie, "Trump Wanted Tenfold Increase in Nuclear Arsenal, Surprising Military," NBC News, October 11, 2017.

95 Jonathan Swan and Margaret Talev, "Trump Suggested Nuking Hurricanes to Stop Them from Hitting U.S." Axios, August 25, 2019.

96 Michael D. Shear and Julie Hirschfield Davis, "Shoot Migrants' Legs, Build Alligator Moat: Behind Trump's Ideas for Border," *New York Times*, October 1, 2019.

97 David M. Drucker, "'I Feel Bad That I Left': John Kelly Warned Trump He Would be Impeached, *Washington Examiner*, October 26, 2019.

98 Henry Pu Yi, *The Last Manchu: The Autobiography of Henry Pu Yi, Last Emperor of China* (New York: Skyhorse, 2010), 5.

99 Pu Yi, *Last Manchu*, 6.

100 To be fair to the Kaiser, he had a more persuasive case to make than Trump, given that he was a blood relative to most of the royal courts in Europe at the time.

101 Miranda Carter, *George, Nicholas and Wilhelm: Three Royal Cousins and the Road to World War I* (New York: Knopf, 2010), 207. See also François Heisbourg, "The Emperor vs the Adults: Donald Trump and Wilhelm II," *Survival* 59 (April-May 2017); 7–12.

102 Carter, *George, Nicholas and Wilhelm*, 132.

103 Carter, *George, Nicholas and Wilhelm*, 213.

104 On the very important concept of chaos muppets, see Dahlia Lithwick, "Chaos Theory: A Unified Theory of Muppet Types," *Slate*, June 8, 2012.

105 See Daniel W. Drezner, *The Ideas Industry: How Pessimists, Partisans, and Plutocrats Are Transforming the Marketplace of Ideas* (New York: Oxford University Press), chap. 4.

106 Daniel Byman and Kenneth Pollack, "Let Us Now Praise Great Men: Bringing the Statesman Back In," *International Security* 25 (Spring 2001): 107–46.

107 Ezra Klein, "How Political Science Conquered Washington," *Vox*, September 2, 2014.

108 Arthur Schlesinger Jr., *The Imperial Presidency*, 3rd ed. (Boston: Houghton Mifflin, 2004), 212.

109 Rose McDermott, *Political Psychology in International Relations* (Ann Arbor: University of Michigan Press, 2004); Joseph Nye, *Presidential Leadership and the Creation of the American Era* (Princeton: Princeton University Press, 2013); Elizabeth Saunders, *Leaders at War: How Presidents Shape Military Interventions* (Ithaca: Cornell University Press, 2011); Michael Horowitz, Allan Stam, and Cali Ellis, *Why Leaders Fight* (New York: Cambridge University Press, 2015).

110 Sims, *Team of Vipers*, 148.

111 See, for example, Jack Shafer, "How Baby Donald Slew the Imperial Presidency," *Politico*, March 10, 2017, and John Dickerson, "The Hardest Job in the World," *Atlantic*, May 2018.

112 See Woodward, *Fear*, 240.

113 Elise Labott, "John Bolton Is Living His Dream," *Politico*, February 4, 2019.

114 See, for examples, Asawin Suebsaeng and Lachlan Markay, "Trump Manages to Not Screw Up for a Day, Stunning His Aides," *Daily Beast*, June 9, 2017; or Jonathan Allen, "What's Driving the Toned-Down Trump?" NBC News, December 4, 2018.

115 Julie Ray, "Americans' Stress, Worry and Anger Intensified in 2018," Gallup, April 25, 2019. Accessed at https://news

.gallup.com/poll/249098/americans-stress-worry-anger
-intensified-2018.aspx.

116 Pew Research Center, "Public Highly Critical of State of Political Discourse in the U.S.," June 2019.

117 Daniel Nexon, "Normalizing Trump," *Lawyers, Guns, and Money* (blog), April 9, 2018, http://www.lawyersgunsmoneyblog .com/2018/04/normalizing-trump.

118 Also, it is interesting that most of the presidents mentioned in this paragraph are judged poorly by historians.

119 Charlie Savage, "Presidential Power Must Be Curbed after Trump, 2020 Candidates Say," *New York Times*, September 12, 2019.

120 See, on this point, Naunihal Singh, "Steven Bannon Is Wrong: The White House 'Resistance' Is the Opposite of a Coup," *Washington Post*, September 11, 2018; Jonathan Bernstein, "Thwarting Trump from Within Isn't Anti-Democratic," Bloomberg, September 13, 2018; Josh Chafetz, "Constitutional Maturity, or Reading Weber in the Age of Trump," *Constitutional Commentary* 34 (2019): 17–41.

121 Elizabeth Saunders, "No Substitute for Experience: Presidents, Advisers, and Information in Group Decision-Making," *International Organization* 71 (April 2017): S219–47.

122 Josh Chafetz, *Congress's Constitution: Legislative Authority and the Separation of Powers* (New Haven: Yale University Press, 2017).

123 Max Weber, quoted in Chafetz, "Constitutional Maturity, or Reading Weber in the Age of Trump," 18.

124 Matt K. Lewis, *Too Dumb to Fail* (New York: Hachette, 2016); Charles Sykes, *How the Right Lost Its Mind* (New York: St. Martin's Press, 2017); Rick Wilson, *Everything Trump Touches Dies* (New York: Free Press, 2018); Alberta, *American Carnage*.

125 Juliegrace Brufke, "House Republicans Dismissive of Paul Ryan's Take on Trump," *The Hill*, July 12, 2019.

126 Jeremi Suri, *The Impossible Presidency* (New York: Basic Books, 2019), p. 290.

127 Alan Wolfe, *The Politics of Petulance: America in an Age of Immaturity* (Chicago: University of Chicago Press, 2018), 15.

128 Wolfe, *Politics of Petulance*, 164.

129 "Majority Says Trump Has Done 'Too Little' to Distance Himself from White Nationalists," Pew Research Center website, March 28, 2019, https://www.people-press.org/2019/03/28/majority-says-trump-has-done-too-little-to-distance-himself-from-white-nationalists/.

130 See Daniel W. Drezner, "Political Economy of Secular Stagnation: Why Capital in the United States Swipes Right," in *Facing Up to Low Productivity Growth*, ed. Adam Posen and Jeromin Zettelmeyer (Washington: Peterson Institute for International Economics, 2019).

SELECTED BIBLIOGRAPHY

The bulk of this book's sources come from the daily and long-form press coverage of the Trump administration. Where more in-depth research was required, I relied primarily on the following publications.

AMERICAN POLITICAL DEVELOPMENT

Azari, Julia, and Jennifer Smith. "Unwritten Rules: Informal Institutions in Established Democracies," *Perspectives on Politics* 10 (March 2012): 37–55.

Banner, James M., ed. *Presidential Misconduct: From George Washington to Today.* New York: New Press, 2019.

Calabresi, Steven G., and Kevin H. Rhodes. "The Structural Constitution: Unitary Executive, Plural Judiciary." *Harvard Law Review* 105 (April 1992): 1153–216.

Carpenter, Daniel. *The Forging of Bureaucratic Autonomy: Reputations, Networks, and Policy Innovation in Executive Agencies, 1862–1928.* Princeton: Princeton University Press, 2001.

Chafetz, Josh. *Congress's Constitution: Legislative Authority and the Separation of Powers.* New Haven: Yale University Press, 2002.

Cooper, Philip J. *By Order of the President: The Use and Abuse of Executive Direct Action.* Lawrence: University Press of Kansas, 2002.

Drezner, Daniel W. *The Ideas Industry: How Pessimists, Partisans, and Plutocrats Are Transforming the Marketplace of Ideas.* New York: Oxford University Press, 2017.

Drezner, Daniel W. "Political Economy of Secular Stagnation: Why

Capital in the United States Swipes Right." In *Facing Up to Low Productivity Growth*, edited by Adam Posen and Jeromin Zettelmeyer. Washington: Peterson Institute for International Economics, 2019.

Drezner, Daniel W. "Present at the Destruction: The Trump Administration and the Foreign Policy Bureaucracy." *Journal of Politics* 81 (April 2019): 723–30.

Fowler, Linda. *Watchdogs on the Hill: The Decline of Congressional Oversight of U.S. Foreign Relations*. Princeton: Princeton University Press, 2015.

Hacker, Jacob, and Paul Pierson. *Off Center: The Republican Revolution and the Erosion of American Democracy*. New Haven: Yale University Press, 2005.

Hamilton, Alexander, James Madison, and John Jay. *The Federalist Papers*. New York: Bantam, 1982.

Hare, Christopher, and Keith Poole. "The Polarization of Contemporary American Politics." *Polity* 46 (July 2014): 411–29.

Hollibaugh, Gary, Gabriel Horton, and David Lewis. "Presidents and Patronage." *American Journal of Political Science* 58 (October 2014): 1024–42.

Howell, William. *Power without Persuasion: The Politics of Direct Presidential Action*. Princeton: Princeton University Press, 2003.

Howell, William, and Terry Moe. *Relic: How Our Constitution Undermines Effective Government—And Why We Need a More Powerful Presidency*. New York: Basic Books, 2016.

Irwin, Douglas. *Clashing over Commerce: A History of U.S. Trade Policy*. Chicago: University of Chicago Press, 2017.

Lepore, Jill. *These Truths: A History of the United States*. New York: W. W. Norton, 2018.

Mann, Thomas, and Norman Ornstein. *It's Even Worse Than It Looks: How the American Constitutional System Collided with the New Politics of Extremism*. New York: Basic Books, 2012.

Nathan, Andrew. *The Administrative Presidency*. New York: John Wiley and Sons, 1983.

Neustadt, Richard. *Presidential Power and the Modern Presidents*. New York: Free Press, 1990.

Nye, Joseph. *Presidential Leadership and the Creation of the American Era*. Princeton: Princeton University Press, 2013.

Orren, Karen, and Stephen Skowronek. "Pathways to the Present: Political Development in America." In *The Oxford Handbook of American Political Development*, edited by Brian Glenn and Steven Teles. New York: Oxford University Press, 2016.

Randall, Ronald. "Presidential Power versus Bureaucratic Intransigence: The Influence of the Nixon Administration on Welfare Policy." *American Political Science Review* 73 (September 1979): 795–810.

Rocco, Philip. "The Anti-Analytic Presidency Revisited." *Forum* 15 (July 2017).

Rudalevige, Andrew. *The New Imperial Presidency*. Ann Arbor: University of Michigan Press, 2005.

Rudalevige, Andrew. "Bureaucratic Control and the Future of Presidential Power." *White House Studies* 10 (February 2010): 51–68.

Schlesinger, Arthur. *The Imperial Presidency*, 3rd ed. Boston: Houghton Mifflin, 2004.

Smith, Hedrick. *The Power Game: How Washington Works*. New York: Ballantine, 1988.

AMERICAN FOREIGN POLICY

Byman Daniel, and Kenneth Pollack. "Let Us Now Praise Great Men: Bringing the Statesman Back In." *International Security* 25 (Spring 2001): 107–46.

Crawford, Neta. "Institutionalizing Passion in World Politics: Fear and Empathy," *International Theory* 6 (November 2014): 535–57.

Drezner, Daniel W. "The Angry Populist as Foreign Policy Leader: Real Change or Just Hot Air?" *Fletcher Forum of World Affairs* 41 (Spring 2017): 23–43.

Drezner, Daniel W. "This Time Is Different: Why U.S. Foreign Policy Will Never Recover." *Foreign Affairs* 98 (May/June 2019): 10–17.

Fearon. James. "Domestic Political Audiences and the Escalation of International Disputes," *American Political Science Review* 88 (September 1994): 577–92.

Goldgeier, James, and Elizabeth Saunders. "The Unconstrained Presidency." *Foreign Affairs* 97 (September/October 2018): 144–56.

Haas, Peter. "Introduction: Epistemic Communities and International Policy Coordination." *International Organization* 46 (Winter 1992): 1–35.

Hall, Todd. "On Provocation: Outrage, International Relations, and the Franco-Prussian War," *Security Studies* 26 (January 2017): 1–29.

Janis, Irving. *Groupthink: Psychological Studies of Policy Decisions and Fiascoes*. Boston: Houghton Mifflin, 1982.

Kupchan, Charles A., and Peter L. Trubowitz. "Dead Center: The Demise of Liberal Internationalism in the United States." *International Security* 32 (Fall 2007): 7–44.

Linklatter, Andrew. "Anger and World Politics: How Collective Emotions Shift over Time." *International Theory* 6 (November 2014): 574–78.

McDermott, Rose. *Political Psychology in International Relations*. Ann Arbor: University of Michigan Press, 2004.

Mearsheimer, John. *Why Leaders Lie: The Truth about Lying in International Politics*. New York: Oxford University Press, 2011.

Milner, Helen, and Dustin Tingley. *Sailing the Water's Edge: The Domestic Politics of American Foreign Policy*. Princeton: Princeton University Press, 2015.

Rapp-Hooper, Mira, and Mathew Waxman. "Presidential Alliance Powers." *Washington Quarterly* 42 (Summer 2019): 67–83.

Sartori, Anne. *Deterrence by Diplomacy*. Princeton: Princeton University Press, 2007.

Saunders, Elizabeth. *Leaders at War: How Presidents Shape Military Interventions*. Ithaca: Cornell University Press, 2011.

Saunders, Elizabeth. "No Substitute for Experience: Presidents, Advisers, and Information in Group Decision-Making." *International Organization* 71 (April 2017): S219–47.

Saunders, Elizabeth. "Leaders, Advisers, and the Political Origins of Elite Support for War." *Journal of Conflict Resolution* 62 (October 2018): 2118–49.

Schultz, Kenneth. "Perils of Polarization for U.S. Foreign Policy." *Washington Quarterly* 40 (Winter 2018): 7–28.

DEVELOPMENTAL PSYCHOLOGY

American Academy of Pediatrics. *Caring for Your Baby and Young Child*. New York: Bantam, 2014.

Berger, Kathleen Stassen. *The Developing Person through Childhood and Adolescence*, 2nd ed. New York; Worth Publishers, 1986.

Carlson, Stephanie, Dorothy Maskill, and Luke Williams. "Executive Function and Theory of Mind: Stability and Prediction from Ages 2 to 3." *Developmental Psychology* 40 (November 2004): 1105–22.

Carlson, Stephanie, and Louis Moses. "Individual Differences in Inhibitory Control and Children's Theory of Mind." *Child Development* 72 (August 2001): 1032–53.

Carlson, Stephanie, Louis Moses, and Hollie Rix. "The Role of Inhibitory Processes in Young Children's Difficulties with Deception and False Belief," *Child Development* 69 (June 1998): 672–91.

Gardner, Frances, and Daniel Shaw. "Behavioral Problems of Infancy and Preschool Children (0–5)." In *Rutter's Child and Adolescent Psychiatry*, 5th ed., M. Rutter, ed. New York: Blackwell, 2008.

Jones, Sandy. *The Toddler Years*. New York: Sterling, 2011.

Lehto, Juhani E., Petri Juujärvi, Libbe Kooistra, and Lea Pulkkinen. "Dimensions of Executive Functioning: Evidence from Children." *British Journal of Developmental Psychology* 21 (March 2003): 59–80.

Miyake, Akira, et al. "The Unity and Diversity of Executive Functions and Their Contributions to Complex 'Frontal Lobe' Tasks: A Latent Variable Analysis." *Cognitive Psychology* 41 (August 2000): 49–100.

Pagani, Linda S., Caroline Fitzpatrick, and Traci A. Barnett. "Early Childhood Television Viewing and Kindergarten Entry Readiness," *Pediatric Research* 77 (September 2013): 350–55.

van der Schuur, Winneke A., et al. "The Consequences of Media Multitasking for Youth: A Review." *Computers in Human Behavior* 53 (December 2015): 204–15.

Whitebook, Marcy, and Laura Sakai. "Turnover Begets Turnover: An Examination of Job and Occupational Instability among Child Care Center Staff." *Early Childhood Research Quarterly* 18 (Autumn 2003): 273–93.

Zelazo, Philip, Fergus Craik, and Laura Booth. "Executive Function across the Life Span." *Acta Psychologica* 115 (February 2004): 167–83.

TRUMP AND THE TRUMP ADMINISTRATION

Alberta, Tim. *American Carnage: On the Front Lines of the Republican Civil War and the Rise of President Trump.* New York: Harper Collins, 2019.

Amiti, Mary, Stephen Redding, and David Weinstein. "The Impact of the 2018 Trade War on US Prices and Welfare," National Bureau of Economic Research Working Paper no. 25672, March 2019.

Bossie, David, and Corey Lewandowski. *Let Trump Be Trump: The Inside Story of His Rise to the Presidency.* New York: Center Street, 2017.

Christie, Chris. *Let Me Finish.* New York: Hachette, 2019.

D'Antonio, Michael. *Never Enough: Donald Trump and the Pursuit of Success.* New York: Thomas Dunne, 2015.

Drezner, Daniel W. "Economic Statecraft in the Age of Trump." *Washington Quarterly* 42 (Fall 2019): 7–24.

Farrow, Ronan. *War on Peace: The End of Diplomacy and the Decline of American Influence.* New York: W. W. Norton, 2018.

Green, Joshua. *Devil's Bargain.* New York: Penguin, 2017.

Hennessey, Susan, and Benjamin Wittes. *Unmaking the Presidency: Donald Trump's War on the World's Most Powerful Office.* New York: Farrar, Straus Giroux, 2020.

Kurtz, Howard. *Media Madness: Donald Trump, the Press, and the War over the Truth.* New York: Regnery, 2018.

Lewis, David, Patrick Bernhard, and Emily You. "President Trump as Manager: Reflections on the First Year." *Presidential Studies Quarterly* 48 (September 2018): 480–501.

Lewis, Michael. *The Fifth Risk.* New York: W. W. Norton, 2018.

Maningault-Newman, Omarosa. *Unhinged: An Insider's Account of the Trump White House.* New York: Gallery, 2018.

Mueller, Robert S. *Report on the Investigation into Russian Interference in the 2016 Presidential Election.* New York: Scribner, 2019.

O'Brien, Tim. *TrumpNation: The Art of Being the Donald*. New York: Business Plus, 2005.

Sherman, Jake, and Anna Palmer. *The Hill to Die On*. New York: Crown Books, 2019.

Sims, Cliff. *Team of Vipers: My 500 Extraordinary Days in the Trump White House*. New York: Thomas Dunne Books, 2019.

Trump, Donald J., and Tony Schwartz. *The Art of the Deal*. New York: Random House, 1987.

Wilson, Rick. *Everything Trump Touches Dies*. New York: Free Press, 2018.

Wolfe, Alan. *The Politics of Petulance: America in an Age of Immaturity*. Chicago: University of Chicago Press, 2018.

Woodward, Bob. *Fear: Trump in the White House*. New York: Simon & Schuster, 2018.

INDEX

Made in the USA
Columbia, SC
21 April 2020